ENSURING SUCCESS FOR STUDENTS WHO TRANSFER

The Importance of Career and Professional Development

Heather N. Maietta, Ed.D.
Philip D. Gardner, Ph.D.

Editors

Cite as:

Maietta, H. N., & Gardner, P. D. (Eds.). (2023). *Ensuring success for students who transfer: The importance of career and professional development.* National Resource Center on the First-Year Experience and Students in Transition.

ISBN: 978-1-942072-66-9
ISBN (ePub): 978-1-942072-67-6
ISBN (eBrary): 978-1-942072-68-3

Published by:
National Resource Center for The First-Year Experience® and Students in Transition
University of South Carolina
1718 College Street, Columbia, SC 29208
www.sc.edu/fye

The First-Year Experience® is a service mark of the University of South Carolina. A license may be granted upon written request to use the term "The First-Year Experience." This license is not transferable without written approval of the University of South Carolina.

Production Staff for the National Resource Center:
Project Manager: Rico R. Reed, Associate Director
Reviewers: Jenna A. Seabold, Research and Grants Coordinator
                            Riley Shoemaker, Graduate Research Assistant
Design and Production: Stephanie L. McFerrin, Graphic Artist

Library of Congress Control Number: 2023920245

ABOUT THE PUBLISHER

The National Resource Center for The First-Year Experience and Students in Transition was born out of the success of University of South Carolina's first-year seminar ("University 101") and a series of annual conferences focused on the first-year experience. The momentum created by the educators and advocates attending these early conferences paved the way for the development of the National Resource Center, which was established at the University of South Carolina in 1986. As the Center broadened its focus to include other significant student transitions in higher education, it underwent several name changes, adopting the National Resource Center for The First-Year Experience and Students in Transition in 1998.

Today, the National Resource Center collaborates with institutional partners in student success, student affairs, and academic units as well as with institutions, organizations, and affiliates across the country and around the world in pursuit of its mission to advance and support efforts to improve student learning and transitions into and through higher education. The Center achieves this mission by creating opportunities for the exchange of practical and scholarly information, facilitating the discussion of trends and issues in our field, and providing thought leadership. Its primary areas of activity include:

- convening conferences and other professional development events such as webinars, workshops, and online learning opportunities

- publishing scholarly practice books, research reports, guides, a peer-reviewed journal, and an electronic newsletter

- generating, supporting, and disseminating research and scholarship

- maintaining several online channels for resource sharing and communication, including a website, listservs, and social media outlets

The National Resource Center is the trusted expert, internationally recognized leader, and clearinghouse for scholarship, policy, and best practice for all postsecondary student transitions.

INSTITUTIONAL HOME

The National Resource Center is located at the University of South Carolina's (USC) flagship campus in Columbia. Chartered in 1801, USC Columbia's mission is twofold: to establish and maintain excellence in its student population, faculty, academic programs, living and learning environment, technological infrastructure, library resources, research and scholarship, public and private support and endowment; and to enhance the industrial, economic, and cultural potential of the state. The Columbia campus offers 324 degree programs through its 15 degree-granting colleges and schools. In fiscal year 2022, faculty generated $225 million in funding for research, outreach and training programs. USC is among the top tier of universities receiving Research and Community Engagement designations from the Carnegie Foundation.

CONTENTS

TABLES & FIGURES

TABLES

FIGURES

FOREWORD

Janet L. Marling

I applaud you for picking up this book and for being curious about transfer transitions and how best to serve students engaged in this higher education journey. These individuals need your expertise, compassion, and encouragement, even if they haven't yet realized it. You are a critical piece of their student experience, and they will benefit from learning from and with you.

Your work holds a special place in my heart, as I once enjoyed a similar role. As a freshly minted master's graduate with a degree in counseling psychology, I landed my dream job in a college counseling center. It was the type of position typically reserved for doctorate-credentialed professionals, and I was thrilled to be doing exactly what I set my sights on for my first professional role. There was no better place to marry my passion for walking alongside others as they worked through things weighing heavily upon them and my fascination with the inner workings and energy of a college campus.

The philosophy at my institution supported collaboration between the counseling and career centers, with the counseling center providing career assessments for students struggling to decide on a major or a career trajectory and the career center offering practical career planning and placement support. I enjoyed helping students discover their interests and unearth how their personality attributes and personal preferences might contribute to future career choices and success. Further into my tenure at the institution, I even had an opportunity to teach a master's level career counseling course.

In retrospect, what strikes me as remarkable is that at no point during the career counseling I delivered or in the curriculum I developed did I address students who transfer as individuals or as a distinct student population, nor did I name the transfer transition. Perhaps that can be attributed to the times: Higher education was only peripherally interested in promoting transfer transitions beyond the typical community-college-to-university pathway. Furthermore, career planning and placement were focused more on students at the end of their college experience than during the transitions along the way. However, these explanations feel like rationalizations. In reality, students were moving between institutions and transferring credits all along to reach completion and career goals; they just weren't seen for their unique needs and influences.

Today there is no denying it; student mobility is a reality. Before the pandemic, nearly half of all students at most colleges had either transferred in from another institution or would move on to continue their education elsewhere (Shapiro, 2018). While the incidence of student transfer declined during the pandemic, two million individuals enrolled during the 2021–2022 academic year had college experiences that included earning credits at more than one institution (Causey et al., 2022).

Unfortunately, higher education was not designed with these students in mind. Colleges and universities are most often viewed as destinations rather than vehicles for students' degree and goal completion. Students are expected to innately understand and conform to systems, policies, and processes that were likely created for students entering directly from high school. Transfer advocates are challenging this status quo one functional area at a time, and the moment is ripe to shine the spotlight on career and professional development.

As states increase their focus on workforce development, your work takes on even more meaning, and transfer plays a vital role for students receiving an academic credential that can presumably be used to position them in the workforce. Therefore, it is important to learn how to work with these individuals, regardless of their age or stage in their college journey, to remove barriers to their momentum and to enhance their overall student experience. It is critical to understand their motivation to be at our institutions, and we must proactively design our services to catch them midstride rather than wait for them to seek us out. Students who transfer are looking for a connection to their future selves and their new institutions, and you are in the perfect role to help them connect the dots clearly.

Focusing on the transfer transition is likely well aligned with your current practices because what is good for students preparing to transition or having recently transitioned between institutions is typically good practice for all students. Supporting the transfer transition requires consideration of both where the student is coming from and where they are headed and is synergistic with your efforts to help students imagine and prepare for new careers and opportunities. Much like how career development focuses on the whole student, the transfer experience must be holistic, intentional, and inclusive.

So, what does this mean for how you conceptualize your departmental services? Are you working with students using a developmental model designed by classification? Or are you using an approach that is more needs-based and, therefore, more responsive to what the student is experiencing during various stages in their personal and collegiate lives? Is your work designed with the mindset that students' trajectories are fluid and that you have an opportunity to influence their progress?

The chapters in this volume provide an array of mechanisms for better understanding and serving students who transfer, most predominantly at four-year institutions, and there are many ways to tackle the book's content. Before jumping in, however, I encourage you to pause for a moment (something we don't always do well) and engage in personal reflection to situate your experiences, assumptions, potential biases, and motivation. Having a clear place to start absorbing the insights of this text will help elevate your transfer advocacy. Grab your favorite notebook and pen or your laptop and consider the following questions:

What is your experience with transfer?

- If you personally transferred (physically moved between institutions or transferred credit), what was your experience like? What support did you receive that propelled you toward your goals? What support do you wish you had received? Who were the people most important in your transition from or into your institutions? How were your career aspirations supported?

- If you were an interested observer while someone close to you transferred, what did you notice from their transfer journey that might influence how you view the best ways to support the needs of students who transfer?

- If your primary exposure to transfer is through work, how have students who have experienced transfer been a part of your previous or current professional activities? What have you learned from them about their experiences?

What do you know about your institution's transfer and transfer-intending students, including their motivation and outcomes?

- How did you gain this information (e.g., institutional data, working directly with students, colleagues' anecdotes)? Can you distinguish what you know by race/ethnicity or other student statuses or identity areas, such as first generation, veteran, adult learner, or income?

- How is your department currently supporting students transferring from or into your institution?

  Because you may have limited time to influence students moving out of and recently entering your institution, it is critical to know as much as you can about them categorically, although that knowledge is not a substitute for knowing them on a more meaningful personal level. For specific instruction on learning about your transfer population, I encourage you to go to the website for the National Institute for the Study of Transfer Students (www.NISTS.org) and visit the "Guides & Resources" page to locate *Using Data in Our Work with Students.*

What biases toward students who transfer and the transfer experience might you be bringing into your work? Who can help you distinguish between myths and realities associated with students who transfer? What questions do you need to answer before you can feel confident in working with your specific transfer population?

Contributing this foreword feels a bit like redemption, my opportunity to make it up to the countless students who did not get the intentional career development support they deserved from me and others who failed to consider how their needs might differ from those of other students. I am grateful to Drs. Maietta and Gardner for introducing career professionals to transfer concepts and helping to reconcile the lack of parity between the ways that students who transfer and those who do not are supported in college.

I wish you the very best in your journey to incorporate transfer-supportive practices and programs into your career development and professional readiness work. May the important voices, frameworks, and programs shared within this text create a transfer lens that informs your decisions, actions, and interactions. Never underestimate the vital impact your engagement and guidance can have on students and their transitions.

References

Causey, J., Gardner, A., Kim, H., Lee, S., Pevitz, A., Ryu, M., Scheetz, A., & Shapiro, D. (2022, September). *COVID-19 transfer, mobility, and progress: 9th in the series*. National Student Clearinghouse Research Center.

Shapiro, D. (2018). Student transfer and mobility: Pathways, scale, and outcomes for student success. In M. A. Poisel & S. Joseph (Eds.), *Building transfer student pathways for college and career success* (pp. 1–15). National Resource Center for the First-Year Experience and Students in Transition.

Janet L. Marling
Executive Director
National Institute for the Study of Transfer Students (NISTS)

Associate Professor, Education
University of North Georgia

INTRODUCTION

Redefining the Transfer Experience for Successful Career Outcomes

Heather N. Maietta and Philip D. Gardner

This book began from a failure to produce a career development chapter for a guidebook on students who transfer. It turns out that few scholars or authorities on the transfer process examined the role career development plays or could play in shaping the success of students who transfer. An exhaustive review of literature on the topic revealed that a discussion of the role of career and professional development in the transfer process is strangely absent. Even an impromptu survey of colleagues leading career service offices around the country revealed minimal direct contact with students who transfer. Most reported spending a few minutes during orientation explaining available career resources before the students merged into the general population. Others from institutions with a high percentage of students who transfer among their entering cohort provided selected resources in designated sections of their institutional home page—a passive approach, given our high-tech, high-touch 21st-century academic culture. None of our colleagues reported offering direct interventions to assist students who transfer in confirming a connection between their academic major and career pathways, career readiness, or professional development resources for postgraduate transition. This lack of reported support is concerning given that approximately 1.3 million students transferred in the 2020–2021 academic year (Bobbit et al., 2021), down from approximately 1.6 million reported in 2011 (DoE, 2020).

This feedback, and seeming lack of connection, left us with unaddressed questions. For example, how does engagement with career services influence persistence and time to graduation for a student who transfers—two key measures of student success? Do students who transfer participate in the necessary cocurricular or experiential learning activities, such as internships, in preparation for entry-level workplace demands? Do students who transfer understand the connection between their chosen academic majors and career pathways? What evidence supports any contention that engagement with career services will assist students who transfer to pursue their academic and career goals? With these questions in mind, the charge of this publication is to identify the existing career development processes that successfully support students who transfer and to explore ways in which higher education can expand these best practices.

Transfer Complexities

The process of transferring has been well examined to tackle issues surrounding articulation agreements, loss of earned credits at receiving institutions, financial concerns, academic support in adjusting to new learning environments, and socialization into the new institution. Despite policies and programs initiated by this research, many students who transfer reside at home or off-campus and continue working to offset college expenses and provide for their families. Some operate under the belief that they must finish their degree as quickly as possible, thus missing opportunities to participate in cocurricular activities or to use nonacademic support services. These beliefs and behaviors can have direct or unintended consequences on their career aspirations and, if left unattended, can jeopardize a successful transition from college to career.

Career development is a lifelong journey of continuous exploration, evolving experiences, increasing competencies, and shifting interests and priorities. This process begins well before students reach their first year of college, and each student's pre-college preparation and experiences are different. The depth and breadth of their needs for career formulation during college also vary. Many transitions happen during the undergraduate experience as students journey toward graduation, prompting the need for an individualized process of career preparation.

Some of the many challenges students face when navigating a transfer transition are unclear transfer pathways, competing programmatic choices, nonexistent support initiatives, and difficult bureaucratic navigation. Students who transfer, not unlike their traditional counterparts, also struggle with various aspects of career development and decision-making. The literature shows that all students need career support, before they become a college student and well past graduation, regardless of the length or course of study (Brand et al., 2013; Fouad et al., 2006; Gedye et al., 2004; Pascual, 2014). Retention research also indicates that commitment to education and career goals is the strongest indicator of persistence to degree completion (Bowman et al., 2019; Cambiano et al., 2000; Clayton et al., 2019; Cuseo, 2005; Hull-Blanks et al., 2005; Tudor, 2018; Wyckoff, 1999). The best career development approach, therefore, would acknowledge and accommodate a transfer process for students needing support before, during, and after this experience.

No single working definition completely captures the complexities and needs of students who transfer, and no single solution supports the postgraduate career success of this population. Our literature review on career support for students who transfer found that the concept of "transfer student" needs redefinition. Students who transfer are as heterogeneous as their career development needs and experiences. They can be traditional age, nontraditional, or returning adult students; single or married; with children, childless, caregivers, single parents, or homemakers. Students also commonly vary in economic status, full or part-time work status, and commuter or residential status. Some students who transfer attend a two-year college before transitioning, while others move from one four-year institution to another. A new form of transfer has emerged as colleges are forced to close. The forced transfer, identified as students leaving an institution because of a college closure, appears to be increasing (see Chapter 10). We argue the need to reframe the transfer as something other than a student label that some students experience during their undergraduate journey.

Reframing Transfer As an Experience

We argue that although higher education tends to label "transfer students" as an inclusive population, applying a one-size-fits-all student success solution to a widely variable population may be undeniably shortsighted. Labeling has the potential to inaccurately employ support services that may or may not be needed or prove to be successful. The result is the neglect or alienation of those students who do not fit the assumed support model. In this publication, we suggest it is time to reframe transfer as something students experience as part of their undergraduate journey—an experience rather than a student's label. Reframing the transfer as a particular kind of *transition*—versus framing transferring as an examination of a particular kind of *student*—offers a helpful reorientation that allows us to see how best to support this growing population during the career development journey. Assigning the transfer label to a student for bureaucratic purposes, such as registrar categorization or financial aid, may be necessary. However, focusing on the transfer less as an identity and rather as a transition that occurs as part of one's career lifespan opens additional support possibilities. This differentiation offers a higher degree of understanding of the unique career development needs of those students who experience transfer.

Schlossberg's (1984) transition theory provides a framework for understanding and addressing the impact of transfer on a student's career decision-making and postgraduate success (Owens et al., 2010; Wheeler, 2012). This insight can help us discern how best to address the impact of navigating a transfer experience on a student's career decision-making and postgraduate success.

Transition Theory and the Transfer Experience

Schlossberg's transition theory is a model of understanding adults in transition (Schlossberg, 1981) and is a lens to help understand and view the navigation that occurs when individuals experience events that provoke a change (Schlossberg et al., 1995). Schlossberg (1984) defined transition as an "event or nonevent resulting in change" (p. 43); this definition is uniquely applicable to students who transfer for a variety of reasons. As mentioned previously, each student experiences transfer in a different way, dictated by internal and external factors that influence the transition. These factors necessitate the type and frequency of resources needed to help the student successfully navigate the transition. For this reason, it is impossible to attach a transfer label to a student population.

All adults experience transitions, with each transition containing various stages and resulting factors (see Figure 1.1). Schlossberg and colleagues (1995) argued that all transitions result in change, whether the transition is an event or a nonevent (something that does not happen even though it is expected). As the transition unfolds, the person begins coping with the changes associated with the transition, whether it is anticipated or unanticipated. Anticipated transitions occur with a level of predictability; unanticipated transitions do not. For example, a student attending community college with plans to transfer to a four-year institution is experiencing an anticipated transition, whereas a student forced to transfer because of a college closure is experiencing an unanticipated transition. The change is the thruway for the transition and the way in which individuals experience transition over time. This experience can range from approaching the transition point to recognizing that it holds long-term implications; thus, individuals experience varying responses at different stages. These varying responses are predicated on an individual's perceptions of the transition, the context in which it occurs, and its impact on their lives. A student's situation before and after the transfer dictates the impact of the transfer experience on the student's long-term trajectory.

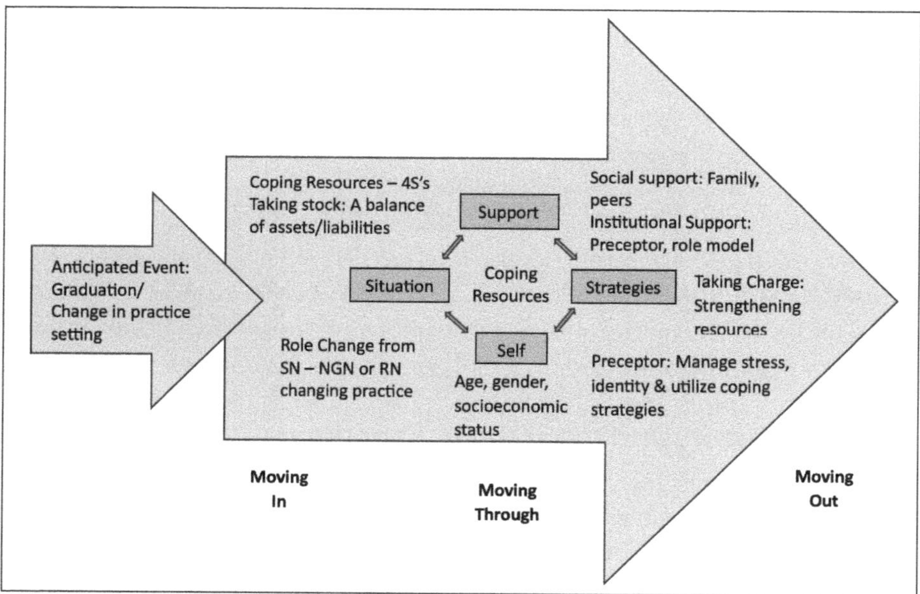

Figure 1.1. The Individual Transition

Because students approach transition differently and no two transitions are alike, the assets and liabilities associated with each transition also vary, as do the students' coping mechanisms. Anderson et al. (2012) posited, "An individual's ability to cope with transitions depends on the changing interaction and balance of his or her assets and liabilities" (p. 91). This interaction and balance of assets and liabilities can be recognized through what Schlossberg et al. (1995) called the 4 S system: situation, self, strategies, and supports. *Situation* refers to the actual event, the stimulus that triggers the transition, the individual's level of control during the transition, timing, duration, and whether the transition prompts a role change. The *self* is the feature an individual brings to a situation, such as psychological resources (self-efficacy, motivation, mindset), personal characteristics (well-being, life circumstances), and demographic characteristics (socioeconomic position, gender, age/period in life). Each is enacted differently, and many have associated power differentials.

Family, faculty, friends, community, institutions, and other individuals represent possible *supports* essential to transition (Schlossberg et al., 1995). Supports offer tangible and intangible assistance and feedback. For example, students who transfer often report a desire to acclimate to the receiving institution's campus community but find doing so challenging. The final 'S' represents the *strategies* that individuals use to cope with transitions. Stress associated with the transition will inform response and strategy deployment. For example, individuals may use hope and optimism to modify a transitional situation, reframe the situation to gain more control of the situation's meaning, and accept or reject certain aspects of the transition for more effective coping.

It is important to note that transitions have no endpoint; they are a process that occurs over time and include phases of assimilation and continuous appraisal as individuals move in, through, and out (Anderson et al., 2012). A student who is navigating a transfer *moves in* to the transition. During this phase, they are unsure and unaware of the transitional landscape. Resources and supports are often unknown, and the student negotiates their place within the transition. Their perception of the transition affects their assets and liabilities. As the student *moves through* the transition, roles and routines become more familiar. The student takes stock of their coping resources (4 S system) to navigate the transition. *Moving out* occurs when the individual approaches the end of one transition and looks toward a new one. Eventually, the transition becomes integrated, and a period of stability is re-established (Anderson et al., 2012).

Schlossberg et al.'s (1995) transition theory and its associated 4 S system provide a lens to view the phenomenon of students who experience a transfer. How change is navigated, where resources are sought, and where supports could be strengthened offer windows to understand how the transfer is navigated and how a student is affected before, during, and after the transition.

Organization of This Volume

This book refocuses the discussion on students who transfer by incorporating career development and professional readiness in achieving critical markers of student success, specifically retention, time to graduation, and transition from college to work or other desired outcomes. The chapters address ways in which institutions are creating successful career programs and pathways for students who transfer. The authors examine these practices and argue for changes in the transfer process to ensure student success. In addition, they call for more in-depth research on the role career engagement plays in the transfer transition.

The book is organized into three sections. Section 1 (Chapters 1–3) includes an in-depth review of the literature on career development in the transfer process and offers testimonials on the absence of dialogue and attention to career pathway enhancement during transfer. Section 2 (Chapters 4–8) provides specific examples of how institutions address career engagement with students who transfer, offering recommendations for college and university professionals. Section 3 (Chapters 9–12), the concluding section, presents several research efforts to expand our understanding of career engagement and its impact on students who transfer. The intention for including these chapters was to fuel the enthusiasm of others to delve into the transfer process more rigorously. In addition, the chapters provide personal insights, case studies, and research that promote best practices at higher education institutions.

The chapters in Section 1 provide a scholarly and practical introduction to the role of career development, services, and support in students' transfer experiences. To better understand the role of career development and transfer, **Heather Maietta** and **Phil Gardner** engage in an in-depth literature review in Chapter 1, focused on the challenges that students experience when navigating transfer and the ways that these challenges affect career progression. They address the challenges of academic advising, social integration, the stigma associated with career service use, professional preparation, financial challenges, and the transfer mindset. These factors have implications for the career and professional development of students who transfer. Key themes of the transfer experience are established and appear interwoven through the case studies in Section 2 (Chapters 4–8).

In Chapter 2, **Heather Adams** introduces readers to a digital community, Transfer Nation (TN), which carries the transfer discussion beyond typical transfer topics of enrollment and credit articulation. Stipulating that transfer is a journey that leads to career and entry into the workforce, she challenges educators who work with students who transfer to become informed about the college-to-work transition, gain insights on skill requirements of the workplace, and develop the programs necessary to cultivate professional readiness among students who transfer. Unfortunately, TN's conversations with transfer professionals are disconnected from those with career services professionals. TN raises a call to action for greater collaboration with career services and invites career professionals to join the TN dialogue.

In Chapter 3, **Priscilla Vallejo** shares her personal story as a student who transferred; her experience led to her professional dream of working with students who transfer to advance their career aspirations. She recognizes that early career engagement can play a vital role in a student's overall educational journey and in the value of an educational degree. Her chapter highlights the collaborative work done through the Educational Opportunity Program (EOP), a transfer career-readiness program that embeds career development tracks with personal and professional experiences. She shares her experiences working with students who transfer, like herself, and collaborating with faculty to help strengthen the support services offered to this population.

In Section 2 (Chapters 4–8), the editors cast a wide net through their networks to identify institutions that engage students who transfer in career exploration and career and professional development. Six case studies met the criteria for inclusion—intentional career engagement programs that targeted or included students who transfer and have at least preliminary assessments that point to the value-add of these programs. In Chapter 4, **Heather Butler** and **Marc Hunsaker** share how Design Your Life, an innovative course, helps students who transfer deal with two major transitions, the transition from one institution to another and the transition from college student to working professional, by promoting career exploration, career agency, and career readiness. The authors articulate the theoretical underpinnings of the course and explain how its unique approach assists students who transfer to overcome some of the challenges they face. Program data indicate that the course is an effective antidote to the anxiety felt by many students who navigate a transfer; the authors report that upon completion of the program, participants have greater career self-efficacy, hope for the future, a sense of purpose, and deeper belonging to the university. Initial results suggest that the Design Your Life course content is an effective vehicle for supporting the growth and success of students who transfer.

In Chapter 5, **Kerin Hilker-Balkissoon** and **Padmanabhan Seshaiyer** share work being done at George Mason University (GMU) to strengthen the investment and reform the community college transfer experience among STEM students who transfer. Of particular concern are the career development needs of students transferring into GMU. GMU took a proactive approach to enhance the career readiness of STEM students who transfer through a Transfer Career Capital (TCC) program. A design thinking approach identified institutional barriers and inequities in STEM career development aligned with transfer lifecycle and collaborated to make systemic transformations across the institution. The authors share GMU's early intervention outcomes and actions to leverage resources to provide comprehensive career readiness for STEM students who transfer.

At the University of Oregon's School of Journalism and Communication, the Student Service unit intentionally integrated career development modules into their course to orient students who transfer to the university, school, and profession. In Chapter 6, **Miranda**

Atkinson and **Rachel Allen** relate attempts to rectify a perceived deficit resulting from the lack of a clear connection between academic and professional success. Too often, students who transfer navigate their career journeys independently, seeking resources when capacity allows. Participation in a transfer seminar that integrated academic and career advising was associated with positive academic and career success outcomes, including reduced time to degree and more frequent use of career support resources in subsequent terms.

Not all institutions have resources to support the intensive career development preparation of students who transfer. In Chapter 7, **Aimée Eubanks Davis** shows that university–nonprofit partnerships provide a path to securing the resources and expertise to assist these students. The Braven Foundation offers a for-credit experience with concrete instruction and opportunities for professional networking and growth for young people, with the express purpose of improving economic mobility and removing significant barriers some students encounter in achieving viable employment after graduation. Davis explores Braven's course as a model for partnerships aimed at positive economic outcomes that universities can offer students, particularly students who transfer from community colleges, students from low-income backgrounds, students of color, and first-generation college students. Assessments of students who participated in the Braven program show promising results for competency development, networking, job readiness, and leadership training, all important competencies in student success.

At UCLA, students who transfer engage in professional development through campus collaboration and two key career programming initiatives, presented by **Alejandra De Alba** and **Heather Adams** in Chapter 8. The Career Ready Bootcamp (CRB) is a three-day overnight immersion program. The Early Career Engagement Certification Program (ECECP) offers a classroom approach that aims to generate a community of academic and professional support that is meaningful to students who transfer. Data collected in conjunction with CRB and ECECP show the effectiveness of transfer-specific career programming. With leadership from career counselors at the UCLA Career Center and the director of the Transfer Student Center, these programs reached capacity and improved career competencies based on NACE career competency standards.

Section 3 (Chapters 9–12) shifts focus to research-based examinations of the role of career engagement in achieving student success outcomes among students who transferred. **Tasia Cerezo**, in Chapter 9, examines challenges that influence transfer for community college students and affect their career decisions, development, and exploration. While exploring how the gaps in advising often lead to uninformed academic and career decisions, the author includes the voices of first-generation community college alums who share their barriers to persistence and their triumphs to transfer. One perspective on transfer suggests that stigmas shape expectations toward career development and create doubt in students, diminishing their self-motivation. Although research suggests students' challenges vary regarding transfer and career, professional goals and motivations play a pivotal role in their persistence and transfer. Another perspective suggests a balanced educational journey of social integration and appropriate advising will enhance a student's experience and positively affect transfer. This perspective supports the premise that a comprehensive approach should be taken to negate challenges and prepare students for careers.

In Chapter 10, **Heather Maietta** explores an emerging form of transfer stemming from the financial implications of college closure. Maietta reports a qualitative study exploring student experiences of transfer due to college closure and introduces a new subcategory of transfer, the forced transfer. Forced transfer received little attention pre-COVID, and the implications of the pandemic's financial impact on college closure are still being realized. Preliminary research on this emerging transfer experience revealed that forced transfer has implications that inform both sending and receiving institutions to better prepare students for the impact of a college closure.

Using a large institutional dataset, in Chapter 11 **Everett Weber** and **Phil Gardner** compare the students who transferred who engaged with career services and those who transferred but did not use career support resources. After merging the university student database with the Career Services engagement database, the authors employed advanced statistical analyses to investigate the use of career services resources, programs, and advising on two key student outcome measures, persistence and time to degree. Students who transferred and sought career resources were more likely to persist and graduate sooner than those who did not. The authors stress the need for further research on the role of career engagement in the transfer experience.

In Chapter 12, **Phil Gardner**, **Heather Maietta**, and **Niki Perkins** explore adult learners, a large contingent of students who transfer, focusing on their career aspirations and work expectations. Too often, adult learners avoid support services because these services fail to meet their needs; for example, career development activities are often tailored for traditional 18- to 24-year-olds with little life experience. In this chapter, attention is given to adult life experiences (family and work) and exploration of future career opportunities (desired job characteristics, career planning, and concerns about their future work). Against this backdrop, the authors appraise the implication of transferring on adult learners' career development.

The concluding chapter synthesizes and summarizes the ideas presented throughout the book with a call for career services and all campus support professionals to reimagine support for students who transfer, focusing on strengthening and deepening communities of practice, particularly in a post-pandemic world. Because a student's situation before and after the transfer dictates the transfer's impact on the student's long-term trajectory (Schlossberg et al., 1995), career exploration and planning touchpoints before and after (and, of course, during) are vital. Multiple authors (Center for Community College Student Engagement, 2018; Wang, 2020; Wyner et al., 2016) support Schlossberg's theory, concluding that support for students early and throughout the transfer allows these students to perform better and have a greater likelihood of navigating the transfer and graduating. This publication offers a primer to ensure movement in this direction.

References

Anderson, M. L., Goodman, J., & Schlossberg, N. K. (2012). *Counseling adults in transition: Linking Schlossberg's theory with practice in a diverse world* (4th ed.). Springer.

Bowman, N. A., Miller, A., Woosley, S., Maxwell, N. P., & Kolze, M. J. (2019). Understanding the link between noncognitive attributes and college retention. *Research in Higher Education, 60*(2), 135–152. https://doi.org/10.1007/s11162-018-9508-0

Brand, B., Valent, A., & Browning, A. (2013). *How career and technical education can help students be college and career ready: A primer.* College and Career Readiness and Success Center & American Institutes for Research.

Cambiano, R. L., Denny, G. S., & De Vore, J. B. (2000). College student retention at a midwestern university: A six-year study. *Journal of College Admission,* (166), 22–29. https://eric.ed.gov/?id=EJ606191

Center for Community College Student Engagement. (2018). *Show me the way: The power of advising in community colleges.* https://www.voced.edu.au/content/ngv:89620

Clayton, K., Wessel, R. D., McAtee, J., & Knight, W. E. (2019). KEY careers: Increasing retention and graduation rates with career interventions. *Journal of Career Development, 46*(4), 425–439. https://doi.org/10.1177%2F0894845318763972

Cuseo, J. (2005). "Decided," "undecided," and "in transition": Implications for academic advisement, career counseling, and student retention. In Robert S. Feldman (Ed.), *Improving the first year of college: Research and practice* (pp. 27–48). Psychology Press.

Fouad, N. A., Guillen, A., Harris-Hodge, E., Henry, C., Novakovic, A., Terry, S., & Kantamneni, N. (2006). Need, awareness, and use of career services for college students. *Journal of career assessment, 14*(4), 407–420. https://doi.org/10.1177%2F1069072706288928

Gedye, S., Fender, E., & Chalkley, B. (2004). Students' undergraduate expectations and post-graduation experiences of the value of a degree. *Journal of Geography in Higher Education, 28*(3), 381–396. https://doi.org/10.1080/0309826042000286956

Hull-Blanks, E., Kurpius, S. E. R., Befort, C., Sollenberger, S., Nicpon, M. F., & Huser, L. (2005). Career goals and retention-related factors among college freshmen. *Journal of Career Development, 32*(1), 16–30. https://doi.org/10.1177%2F0894845305277037

Owens, D., Lacey, K., Rawls, G., & Holbert-Quince, J. A. (2010). First-generation African American male college students: Implications for career counselors. *The Career Development Quarterly, 58,* 291–300. http://doi.org/10.1002/j.2161-0045.2010.tb00179.x

Pascual, N. T. (2014). Factors affecting high school students' career preference: A basis for career planning program. *International Journal of Sciences: Basic and Applied Research, 16*(1), 1–14.

Schlossberg, N. K. (1981). A model for analyzing human adaptation to transition. *Counseling Psychologist, 9*(2), 2–18. https://doi.org/10.1177%2F001100008100900202

Schlossberg, N. K. (1984). *Counseling adults in transition: Linking theory to practice.* Springer Publishing.

Schlossberg, N. K. (1989). Marginality and mattering: Key issues in building community. *New Directions for Student Services, 48,* 5–15. https://psycnet.apa.org/doi/10.1002/ss.37119894803

Schlossberg, N. K., Waters, E. B., & Goodman, J. (1995). *Counseling adults in transition: Linking practice with theory* (2nd ed.). Springer.

Tudor, T. R. (2018). Fully integrating academic advising with career coaching to increase student retention, graduation rates and future job satisfaction: An industry approach. *Industry and Higher Education, 32*(2), 73–79. https://doi.org/10.1177%2F0950422218759928

U.S. Department of Education, National Center for Educational Statistics (NCES). Postsecondary Education Data System (IPEDS). (2020). *Fall enrollment component final data (2006–2019) and provisional data (2020)* [Report]. Trend Generator. https://nces.ed.gov/ipeds/TrendGenerator/app/answer/2/4

Wang, X. (2020). *On my own: The challenge and promise of building equitable STEM transfer pathways.* Harvard Education Press.

Wheeler, H. A. (2012). Veterans' transitions to community college: A case study. *Community College Journal of Research and Practice, 36*(10), 775–792. https://doi.org/10.1080/10668926.2012.679457

Wyckoff, S. C. (1999). The academic advising process in higher education: History, research, and improvement. *Recruitment & Retention in Higher Education, 13*(1), 1–3.

Wyner, J., Deane, K. C., Jenkins, D., & Fink, J. (2016). *The transfer playbook: Essential practices for two- and four-year colleges.* Community College Research Center, Columbia University and College Excellence Program, Aspen Institute.

CHAPTER ONE

Understanding the Career Development Needs of Students Who Transfer

Heather N. Maietta and Philip D. Gardner

Career development spans a lifetime (Super et al., 1996), with college as a significant event in the development process. Career practitioners view the career development journey as beginning well before college and continuing beyond graduation. Students face other transitions during this time, such as changing living arrangements, indecision and exploration regarding a course of study, losing or acquiring a job, participating in a study-abroad experience, or transferring from one college to another. Levinson (1986) and Brown and Lent (2000) discussed transitions as *turning points* or times of tension between two periods of stability. Transitions are essential in a college student's life because they promote self-assessment, encourage a redefinition of goals, and strengthen coping strategies (Schlossberg, 1984; Schlossberg et al., 1995)—all attributes needed in today's workplace. Some transitions may be frightening or stressful, while others may bring resolution or resurgence.

Longitudinal research on transfer patterns has shown that approximately one third of first-time students transfer institutions at least once during their undergraduate experience (Hossler et al., 2012; Shapiro et al., 2017; Wang et al., 2016). The higher education literature establishes a normal baseline for the transfer process, defined as "the classic forward transfer of community college students to the university" (Gere et al., 2017, p. 335), with the community college providing students with general-education and major-preparation courses needed to transfer to a baccalaureate-granting institution (Taylor & Jain, 2017).

Poisel and Joseph (2011) and Taylor and Jain (2017) identified multiple pathways for students who elect to transfer:

> *Lateral transfer:* moving to an institution similar to the one in which the student is currently enrolled (e.g., community college to community college or four-year institution to four-year institution).

> *Vertical transfer:* moving from a two-year to a four-year institution with the intent to complete a bachelor's degree.

> *Reverse transfer:* moving from a four-year to a two-year institution.

Cross-level transfer: enrolling at two-year and four-year institutions simultaneously.

Dual credit/enrollment: taking college courses while in high school, with the courses counting toward a high school diploma and college credit.

Swirler: moving among multiple institutions without necessarily progressing toward degree completion.

Maietta (2019, 2020) identified an emerging transfer pathway: the *forced transfer,* brought about not by a student's choice but because of college closure, forcing the affected students into unanticipated transfer. Differentiating between transfer pathways may depend on the number of credits transferred, the number of previous institutions attended, the time between enrollments, and the academic and career decision-making impact resulting from the transfer (McGuire & Belchier, 2014).

How career development professionals help students manage the transfer experience depends not only on the transfer pathway the student is following but also on the transition type, context, impact, and understanding of the transition itself, as highlighted in Schlossberg's (1984) transition theory (see the Introduction to this volume). Upon transfer, students matriculate to their new institutions with ambitions to complete a credential, usually a course of study, and move toward a future career path. Their success depends on weaving together two essential strands, academic (intellectual) development and professional (work readiness) development. Often considered separately, these strands mutually support and rely on each other. In an exhaustive literature review for this chapter, we found that discussion of the role of career and professional development in the transfer process is strangely absent. The primary research focuses on the connection between academic performance (advising) and social integration to retention and degree attainment. The lack of information on the need or impact of career and professional development services before the transfer, during the transfer itself, after matriculation into the receiving institution, and finally through to graduation is troubling. At present, awareness, understanding, and discussion of the career-related needs of students who transfer are nonexistent.

Career Services: A Brief Overview

Like higher education, career services evolved alongside students' changing characteristics and needs. Historically, an increasing number of students report that their primary goal for attending college is to secure a decent job, even though "the percentage of students concerned about going to college to get a better job has declined slightly from a high of 87.9% in 2012 to 84.8% in 2016" (Eagan et al., 2017). In response to employment seeking, career service offices have significantly repurposed both brand and function to emphasize a shift to professional development and postgraduate career readiness. Experts realize that "securing a good job" is an ambiguous goal and continue to educate students on the importance of setting strength-focused, realistic objectives compatible with their values, skills, knowledge, and interests.

Equally important is how career services help all campus constituents—students, faculty, and employers—to understand how academic competencies translate to the broader world of work. Despite the ongoing evolution of career services, students' needs in two service categories have remained constant: career counseling/developmental advising (interchangeable with career coaching/career advising) and workforce/employment readiness.

Offices of Career Services serve a variety of functions for college students and alumni. These functions vary but generally fall into two categories: workforce and employment readiness services and career counseling and developmental advising.

Workforce and Employment Readiness

Internship assistance and job procurement activities are the most visible functions of the career office. In recent years, career services offices have taken an active role in shaping student employment experiences, both on campus and off, into high-impact professional practices (McClellan et al., 2018; Savoca, 2016). Activities include mock interviewing, helping with development of professional documents (e.g., resume, cover letter, ePortfolio), posting employment opportunities, hosting career fairs, helping with job search preparation, and skill assessment. These activities connect students to things they immediately need (Garver et al., 2010), but career services is often shortsightedly labeled as a placement operation. Perceived as a service but not an integral part of the learning process, students seek career resources haphazardly, as needed, and often at the last moment.

Career Counseling and Development Advising

The career counseling component embodies career education, choice, decision-making, and problem solving, and it often receives less visual attention than workforce readiness. Approaches to career counseling vary, making it hard to pinpoint, but it often involves exploring students' values, interests, strengths, and skills connected to their career-related goals. This approach requires a pyramid of information and self-exploration (Sampson et al., 1992), including communication (e.g., understanding external demands and emotions), analysis (e.g., obtaining knowledge of self and occupations), synthesis (e.g., creating alternatives), valuation (e.g., prioritizing), and execution (see Brown & Lent, 2000; Lent & Brown, 2013). With technology, including self-directed modules, e-learning can help students to complete many of these tasks. In addition, first-year and transfer seminar instructors can integrate career development tasks or learning modules into their courses.

The steps to fulfilling these actions may seem necessary, but they require a dual commitment between students and institutions. Students must reflect profoundly and act on insights from their coursework, experiential learning, and career development and coaching. In contrast, institutions need to provide qualified career specialists and staff with career development expertise who can lead students through the career discovery progression over the trajectory of the entire undergraduate experience. In most institutions, career services are responsible for assisting students in connecting their interests to a career plan or pathway but often fail to integrate their natural aptitudes. Without this integration, students become misguided in making career pathway connections.

Career services providers develop students professionally as the students grasp their academic pursuits and align their career interests and natural aptitudes. The professional phase typically begins as early as the sophomore year and continues throughout the undergraduate experience through various touchpoints and interactions. For example, professional development begins with aiding students in creating and deeply understanding the meaning and value of work-related communication materials. Students use these materials for internships, student employment, volunteer and community-based opportunities, and professional work experiences, such as full-time jobs or graduate school. Another touchpoint involves creating opportunities for students to develop professional networks with alumni, employers, and community professionals; this is an integral and ongoing element of career services. If executed together and done well, these service offerings culminate in integrated knowledge and resource base to ensure a robust postgraduate career foundation.

A career education component embeds itself in the career counseling function. Career center staff view themselves more as educators than as placement specialists, providing resources, connections, and insights to help students independently determine and pursue their professional aspirations. The methodology used by career counselors has shifted to more of a coaching model that ensures students make decisions with a forward-thinking purpose. The desired result of career coaching and of career counseling are similar: to help clients move forward in setting and meeting their career goals. However, the path to achieving these desired results differs (Maietta, 2022). The metamorphosis of the career services function gains importance as we explore how students who transfer choose and use career counseling/coaching and employment activities and resources.

Implications of the Transfer Experience on Career Development

Although career support for students who transfer is absent from the literature, various resources are geared toward and marketed to this population. However, even with increased attention to successful strategies for students who transfer, little evidence suggests that these interventions significantly affect one's transition as currently structured (Bers & Younger, 2011). A comprehensive literature review on transfer shows several areas that present challenges to students' career decision-making and development. In a close examination, we delve into academic advising, social integration, stigmas around career services, professional development, financial implications of transfer, and the transfer mindset as each relates to career development and the role of career services. Navigating transfer jeopardizes students' progress in their career decision-making.

Academic Advising

Negotiating academic decision-making hurdles on both sides of the transfer experience (matriculating from the sending to the receiving institution) is essential for an efficacious transfer. There is a long thread of research on the transfer experience focusing on academic performance and persistence to degree completion. In our investigation of the research for this publication, several issues surface regarding academic advising. First, academic advising disguised as career guidance can be an issue for some students who transfer after receiving little to no career support in high school or at their sending institution (Kuhn & Padek, 2009). These students enter a new institution without knowing about the services available. They also lack information on career pathways and transition needs related to academic and career decision-making. Depending on the time of transfer, students may also miss career activities during orientation or embedded within the first year at the receiving institution. Missed opportunities contribute to unawareness of career and professional resources and a lack of appreciation for career readiness. These deficiencies can directly affect a student's career decision-making capabilities. The deficits can be challenging to overcome for young adults with little prior career decision-making experience. Even students transferring to a new institution with firm decisions regarding their major may be at risk if their decision-making lacks guidance or is premature, unrealistic, or misinformed (Cuseo, 2001).

Second, our investigation uncovered the confusion some students experience moving from institution to institution. Commonly known in the literature as *transfer shock*, this adjustment period can cause students to experience a temporary drop in GPA (Fauria & Fuller, 2015; Hills, 1965; Thurmond, 2007). Transfer shock can also negatively affect academic engagement during the first or second terms at a student's new institution (Ghusson, 2016). Academic advising is crucial in minimizing this transfer shock disruption and increasing academic engagement (Fauria & Fuller, 2015; Glass & Harrington, 2002; Laanan, 2001; Thurmond, 2003; Tinto, 1985, 1993). Academic disconnect, such as drop in GPA, triggers student concerns about major choice, which indirectly and often directly shapes career outcomes. Historically, the academic advising process has not been intentional about weaving career conversations into academic exploration or in conjunction with academic troubleshooting, even though Tinto (1993) tied academic success to the clarity of career goals. Career indecision can affect clarity regarding academic choices, causing some students to become conflicted over their choice of their academic major—so much so that approximately 75% of students declared as undergraduates change their initial majors (Gordon, 2007; Venit, 2016). In short, academic uncertainty breeds career indecision that feeds back into academic performance.

Third, academic advisors often attempt to minimize students' angst about changing majors without engaging their colleagues in career services. Excluding career services is unfortunate as students struggle to align their academic choices and career pathway; they are reluctant to seek career professionals for additional support (Fouad et al., 2006; Bers & Younger, 2011). Moreover, academic advisors often become the patch to provide students with "helpful career information" since students seldom take advantage of campus career centers (Fadulu, 2018; Fouad et al., 2006).

Academic and career advising integration has gained momentum across university campuses as a promising approach for students' decision-making clarity. Burton et al. (2020) explained that career advising helps students clarify, specify, and create a career plan and helps students identify barriers to choosing or moving forward in a major or career path. Academic advisors and career counselors can work together to overcome the difficulties that encumber career decision-making, including lack of readiness, lack of information, and conflicting or inconsistent information in the decision-making process (Gati et al., 1996). Identifying individuals' career decision-making difficulties is among the first steps in providing them with the help they need. Students who experience a lack of readiness have low motivation to engage in career decision-making, a general indecisiveness concerning all types of decisions, and dysfunctional beliefs about career choice (Gati et al., 1996). Students who experience a lack of career decision-making knowledge do not have the self-awareness to act on their career plans, the knowledge of occupational choice, or precisely how to obtain the necessary information (Gati et al., 1996).

Additionally, students who receive conflicting or inconsistent information in the career decision-making process often gather unreliable information, wrestle with internal conflicts or contradictory preferences, or process external conflicts, which are conflicts involving the opinions of significant others. Mitigation of career decision-making difficulties can be achieved through more inclusive advising or by requiring students who transfer to engage in a continuous, integrated career services program (Amir & Gati, 2006). Through collaboration, advisors and career professionals can provide a safe space to discuss the opportunities and challenges for potential academic majors a student is considering.

Students can benefit from an integrated academic and career advising approach but cannot orchestrate this integration independently. Spearheading this integration is where institutions can be the catalyst for supporting students. Shared advising conversations, introducing new initiatives across the university targeting transfer needs, and charting success patterns are workable solutions but too-infrequently adopted. Unfortunately, participation in career-related activities is abysmal without it being mandatory or scaffolded into course requirements (Bers & Younger, 2011). Unless students are proactive in seeking career resources themselves or these resources become integrated into academic conversations, students miss essential career information, activities, and planning timelines for informed academic and workplace-related decisions.

Academic advisors who practice or partner with career advising have a better chance of providing information on the nature of the workforce and realistic preparation for career fields that students who transfer need to make sound decisions that further their goals. However, the lack of adequate training for academic advisors on principles of career decision-making, combined with the absence of career professionals during the initial stages of the transfer, often leaves students exposed to short- and long-term problems associated with their vague understanding of their chosen academic major and their career pathway requirements (e.g., required skills and competencies, expected work behaviors, and necessary professional experiences).

Social Integration

A successful transfer experience depends on the student's integration into the receiving institution's student life and culture. Social connectedness, or the feeling of belonging and creating close relationships (Allen et al., 2008; Pincus & DeCamp, 1989; Rovai, 2002), and peer support (Dennis et al., 2005) significantly shape students' transfer experiences. Students' socialization influences "how" they use available resources and their decision to persist with their studies. Conversely, the lack of social integration after transfer significantly influences whether a student chooses to remain enrolled or to leave college (Ishitani & Flood, 2018). Students who establish strong peer networks score higher on developmental constructs such as defining life purpose and on academic skills and time management (Cooper et al., 1994). Strengthening peer networks requires students to spend more time on campus or live in campus housing (De Araujo & Murray, 2010; Turley & Wodtke, 2010); in addition, students can join social groups or student professional associations (Laanan, 2007; Townsend & Wilson, 2009). Students who transfer significantly benefit from building social and cultural capital (Collier & Morgan, 2008; Terenzini et al., 1996). While cultural capital increases persistence, social capital produces robust professional networks that facilitate successful entry into the workforce. Therefore, campus involvement becomes a critical asset for short- and long-term career decisions.

Upon transfer, students' socialization challenges affect their ability to connect with other students or to participate in clubs and activities. For example, many students who transfer, primarily older students, have off-campus responsibilities (such as family obligations) that hinder their socializing ability. However, these students report high value in social engagement (Lester et al., 2013). In addition, traditional-age students with financial restrictions may need to live at home rather than in campus facilities, and many continue to work off campus, often causing them to struggle with socialization (Duggan & Pickering, 2007–2008). Predictably, students balancing multiple roles (student, employee, caregiver, parent), regardless of their enrollment status, are unlikely to take advantage of support services (Bers & Younger, 2011).

The struggle to balance work responsibilities with academic commitment frequently initiates a need for school-to-work reprioritization. When transfer forces a reduced commitment to college, it deters opportunities to build necessary social capital for professional networking, roadblocks internships, and stifles postgraduate professional support. Whether students socialize successfully or fail to make extensive campus connections during the transfer transition, they can still feel isolated by an environment that assumes everyone arrived as a first-time first-year student. Students who transfer often discover it is unlikely that faculty or classmates will validate their experiences (Whang et al., 2017). One student participant in Whang's study stressed how assumptions made by faculty could undermine academic and career aspirations as well as skew campus expectations:

> I think most resources here are centered around [a] freshman culture. I remember sitting in class and professors every now and then will talk about, "Remember you did this during your freshman year?" … and then you just feel like obviously he or she is not speaking to me because I didn't start here freshman year. I have different experiences and it would be great if these experiences are acknowledged. (p. 304)

Career Services Stigma

The 2018 Strada–Gallup Alumni Survey revealed that a mere 22% of college graduates reported accessing or using resources through their career services office often or very often. Approximately 27% of students reported never using resources or services offered by career services as an undergraduate, and 51% reported they rarely visited career services as an undergraduate (Strada Education Network, 2018). Some students are more likely to engage in career services activities merely by being on campus longer, even haphazardly. Students involved in the transfer life cycle spend less time on campus and with their peers, thereby missing fundamental career and professional development activities.

Not only do students who transfer deal with the burden of labeling, but stigma is often associated with seeking career-related support. Di Fabio and Bernaud (2008) found that high school students who valued career counseling were concerned about the negative judgment from peers about seeking these services. Additionally, university students expressed less interest in career counseling, although the stigma associated with these services was less pronounced. Male students, however, expressed greater fear of judgment from their peers in seeking career counseling services than female students did (Di Fabio & Bernaud, 2008; Rochlen et al., 1999). Rochlen et al. (1999) suggest that the devaluing of the service causes male students to feel shame in seeking support; instead, male students have fewer positive attitudes toward seeking professional help overall than female students do

(Fischer & Farina, 1995; Sanchez & Atkinson, 1983). This situation poses a particularly challenging hurdle for career service professionals to meet the needs of male students who transfer and subscribe to this stigma. Ludwikowski and colleagues (2009) found that "public stigma and personal stigma predicted self-stigma—predicted attitudes toward career counseling" (p. 412). Based on these observations, Del Mastro and Schneider (2016) suggested that stigmas lessen the value of career counseling services, making it difficult for career professionals to engage students.

While these stigmas and other transitional feelings can be present for traditional students, they may be more pronounced for students going through the transfer experience. Students who transfer to a four-year institution after the undergraduate cycle has commenced miss critical programs created specifically to ensure campus integration and an introduction to career services: first-year experience initiatives and living/learning communities. The "largest impact on stress reduction [in students who transfer] was the feeling of belonging to their learning community cohort and the university community" (Coston et al., 2013, p. 4). However, the challenge of introducing intervention that connects students who transfer with career services, even if they duplicate first-year experience initiatives or learning communities, may be necessary to reduce stress caused by the transfer and to ensure that critical programming is available during their college experience.

Di Fabio and Bernaud's (2008) study revealed that "previous positive experiences with career counseling facilitate a favorable attitude toward career counseling, which in turn may stimulate the intention to consult a career counseling center and request intervention" (p. 64). Frequent and positive exposure to career-related services and counseling supports at the sending institution—well before the transfer experience—can initiate independent connections with career-related services and supports at the receiving institution.

Professional Preparation

Available research sheds little light on the impact of the transfer experience on a student's professional preparation. Few studies directly addressed the preparation for the transition from college to the workplace, focusing on academic commitment and motivation. However, the research signals that students who transfer have professional preparation deficits. For instance, Duggan and Pickering (2007–2008) revealed that students who transferred struggled with various career issues. Confusion and lack of confidence about career or life goals ran throughout their study. However, other issues manifested differently depending on when the transfer transition occurred. Students who transferred in their first year of college reported a lack of clarity in their career path and an inability to assess their skills and traits. Students who transferred as sophomores failed to connect their classroom knowledge to their post-graduation pathways. This disconnect diminished their commitment to continue in school. Students who transitioned as juniors or seniors expressed confusion and lacked clarity about their career transition.

In their study, Dennis and her colleagues (2008) examined the retention outcomes of a group of students who transferred using a cluster analysis approach. The variables employed to drive analysis included academic self-efficacy, college commitment, support of peers, personal/career motivation for attending college, age, and first-term GPA. The students who participated had an average age of 26.7; 69% reported that they were working, 58% said that they were living at home with family members, and 42% were first-generation immigrants. The cluster analysis identified five subgroups within the population: young achievers, mature achievers, low-peer-support students, young low-achieving students, and low-confidence/ commitment students. Young achievers were students younger than the average age with high first-term GPAs and above-average scores on measures of self-efficacy and personal/ career motivation, average college commitment, and high peer support. Young low achievers expressed high peer support and above average college commitment while scoring average on measures of self-efficacy and personal/career motivation. Their poor academic performance suggested poorer college preparation, triggering some in this group to leave college. The mature achievers were above average in age; they earned above average first-term GPAs and reported above-average self-efficacy and college commitment but average scores for peer support and motivation. The low peer support cluster were of average age and reported above average first-term GPAs and college commitment but average college self-efficacy and personal/career commitment. Those students in the low confidence/commitment group were younger than the average age, earned the average first-term GPA, and reported low college self-efficacy, college commitment, and personal/career commitment and below average peer support. The authors offered strategies to engage these groups to improve their success. For mature achievers, better support systems tailored to their adult circumstances and avenues to deeper social integration in their institutions are needed. For low-confidence and low-peer-support groups, options included improved goal setting for academic performance and career decision-making; additional support from peers, faculty, and others; better social integration mechanisms; and attention to career motivation. Dennis et al.'s findings suggest that these subgroups may lack the career focus necessary to sustain their commitment to college unless addressed early in the transfer experience.

Financial Implications of Transfer

Many students who transfer matriculate to their new institution needing to work; their family and personal financial situation demand it. Evidence suggests that students who transfer devoted more hours to work and less to classes than nontransfers (Duggan & Pickering, 2007–2008). Many students who transfer are employed at the time of transfer and remain in these positions for the remainder of their time as undergraduates. Others have opportunities to work on campus to boost their career readiness. Work experiences secure a solid foundation for the post-college transition, whether employment is on campus or off campus. To ensure these experiences rise to the expectations of employers on skill development and rigor of the work assignments, career centers can assist students in reflecting on their learning and extracting examples of skills and accomplishments pertinent to postgraduate employment.

The work undertaken while enrolled in college has a downside in that it can create a false sense of postgraduate preparedness, as students who transfer assume this work will serve as a substitute for the professional experience that employers expect, such as internships (Davies & Casey, 1999; Fee et al., 2009; Hoyt & Winn, 2004). This assumption leads some students who transfer to overlook the importance of completing an internship aligned with their academic major or career pathway. When the time comes to search for full-time professional employment, this shortsightedness may undermine their job search, favoring candidates with internship experience. Furthermore, unpaid internships are challenging for low-income and working students to pursue outside of their day-to-day family and academic responsibilities, which puts them at a disadvantage in securing full-time employment with companies connected to these opportunities upon graduation. Finally, disciplinary differences may also introduce financial challenges. Employers in specific industries such as accounting, business, finance, and engineering pay their student employees and interns. Participating in unpaid assignments may not be feasible for students who need paid employment in organizations in which unpaid internships are the norm (e.g., public relations, advertising, social assistance, education, and government), which may place them at a further disadvantage.

Financial implications of transfer range from loss of resources available because students lack knowledge that resources exist and certain access to resources. Furthermore, financial implications can extend beyond resources to paid employment while in college, considering that many students participate in lucrative internships that span repeated summers and throughout the academic year. It may be necessary for students navigating transfer who also face financial hardships to hold regular employment while attending classes, prohibiting them from participating in valuable paid experiential learning. The implications of this exposure extend farther than a paid semester—internships also give students opportunities to cultivate networking relationships that open doors to employment and promotional offers post-graduation. In short, career-related financial implications of transfer extend farther than the transaction from sending to receiving institution.

Shrinking Timeline

The discussion to this point leads to important questions regarding why students who transfer choose not to avail themselves of the career services on their campuses. Because a transfer is an anticipated "event" for most students, according to Schlossberg's theory (1984), it often creates a natural pressure to "hit the ground running" with little time to explore career resources and programmatic options offered on campus (Whang et al., 2017). Does this pressure stifle motivation or commitment toward career decision-making? One participant in Whang et al.'s study revealed,

> You spend most of your time here trying to figure out how to do things, where to go, who to talk to, (but) by the time you've built your resources list, before you can really start using those resources, your time is up. (p. 305)

Discussions with our colleagues in career centers around the country confirmed this prevailing mindset of starting fast and moving quickly toward graduation among students who transferred. Career center colleagues concurred that they face challenges getting students who transferred to slow down and take time for career planning. Whang and colleagues (2017) explained that older students in their study expressed the desire to be more self-sufficient, and the research team assumed these adults had a strong handle on work readiness. Unfortunately, this assumption obscures the finding that while students who transfer may have more depth of academic experiences and exposure to employment settings, they do not know how to frame their experiences in language that reflects their resilience, acquired competencies, and career aspirations. The result is a struggle to tell their unique stories to employers, graduate programs, or others confidently and clearly. Indeed, this group often felt regret and confusion that "they should have known" about a career resource or service available after the transfer.

Transfer creates a sense of urgency, whether it is pressure to move fast or to learn a new culture, which narrows students' attention to the essential areas of campus needed to thrive post-graduation. At the forefront of those essentials are academic and financial concerns. Students who transfer view taking additional time to confirm one's career aspirations or to engage with employers as luxuries. Therefore, they are more likely to wait until the last minute to seek career direction, plan their transition strategies, and prepare recruitment materials. While this is also indicative of nontransfer, students who do not transfer are more likely to have been exposed to or participated in student success programs, such as first-year seminars and early college leadership programs, or may simply have more longevity in the four-year campus system, increasing the ease of navigating these services. Undoubtedly, career services at the receiving institutions need to be more proactive in addressing the needs of students who transfer.

Points of Contention With the Transfer Experience

Based on an exhaustive literature review, the excellent case studies chapters prepared for this publication, and the research gathered from colleagues in the field who work with and manage students who transfer, the following themes emerged.

Career Development Touchpoints

Touchpoints related to career exploration, decision-making, planning, execution, and follow-through need to be weaved throughout the entire four-year undergraduate experience for all students, not just those who experience transfer. Unfortunately, continued career development is currently absent from the transfer process because of multiple and layered barriers, such as high student-to-staff ratios, financial implications of increased support, low or no awareness of need, and disconnect between sending and receiving institutions. In addition, an overemphasis on the outgoing transfer process rather than career-related pieces is a noted barrier. Higher education professionals must understand these difficulties and implement strategies to help students accomplish these developmental milestones.

Credit-Bearing Career Development

For years, career service professionals have argued the benefits of credit-bearing career development, yet forward movement in this area has been inconsistent and slow in adaptation. Career course activity has increased since 1976 (significantly from 2015 to 2019), with approximately 36% of colleges and universities reporting that they offered for-credit career courses in 2020. However, this percentage is down from 38% in 2019 (National Association of Colleges and Employers, 2020; Reardon et al., 2021). In most cases, career development education for credit serves a vital purpose, and offering credit for career programs legitimizes the offering for students and academics. As a result, institutions that have adopted a credit-bearing model have seen a high academic return (Folsom et al., 2005), decreases in career indecision (Hung, 2002; Prescod et al., 2019), increases in career certainty (Hung, 2002; Prescod et al., 2019), decreases time to graduation (Folsom et al., 2005), and higher retention and graduation rates (Hansen et al., 2017; Reardon et al., 2015).

However, credit-bearing career programming may not be the answer for those navigating the transfer process. Although the benefits of such courses are undisputed, these students may have a challenge with earning additional credits, as students who transfer typically have a high elective count, leaving little room for credit-bearing classes beyond the required coursework. Unless career courses are designated as a graduation requirement, elective credit-bearing classes may pose a problem for students navigating transfer.

Revamping Articulation Agreements

Articulation agreements are documented pathways between sending and receiving institutions involving academic programs. They were designed to benefit three parties: the sending institution, the receiving institution, and the student. The sending institution benefits by using articulation agreements as a marketing tool, promoting ease of transfer to attract new-student enrollment. The receiving institution benefits by saving on recruiting costs and having a steady stream of college-ready students, often solving midyear retention melt. The student benefits because the agreement provides a course sequence or map to follow to degree completion.

Procedurally and legally, the process works. However, operationally, there are problems. Articulation agreements are not designed to lessen the complexity of choice, mainly because each choice affects other life choices, such as career decision-making. In all the articulation literature reviewed for this publication, no research connected or included career advising, planning or decision-making in the articulation agreement process. Simply put, students navigating the transfer journey need articulation agreements with embedded academic and career coaching to increase decision-making clarity.

Sending-to-Receiving Advising

Established levels of dialogue between academic and career services in acclimating students from sending to receiving institutions are rare. If collaborative advising happens, the partnership lasts only in the honeymoon stages of the transfer. Early identification of occupational interests and aptitudes leads to sound academic decision-making and more vital awareness of students' steps to become work-ready through their academic major. Unfortunately, uninformed students who transfer may arbitrarily decide on an academic major, holding vague career goals and lacking clarity on leveraging their degree and experiences into employment. Multiple studies have been conducted on undecided to declared and declared to major change, and while these transitions are not unique to students who experience transfer, Spight (2020) estimated that between 50% and 70% of all undergraduates change their major and future career plans during college. Students cannot successfully navigate transfer and adapt to their new environment without guidance.

Internships/Experiential Learning

Many students who transfer are nontraditional, are first generation, and have high socioeconomic needs. These demographics translate into students who work in addition to attending college. There are noted competency benefits associated with gaining work experience while in college; however, one shortcoming of needing to work while in college is missing experiential learning opportunities, especially if they are unpaid.

Many students who transfer do not take advantage of internships and other experiential learning. The timing of transfer can be an issue in the academic internship placement cycle as students miss the recruitment period for such opportunities. Other students do not think to seek short-term or unpaid internships because they need to maintain full-time employment. The result of not participating in experiential learning is that students have difficulty representing themselves through their tasks and are underprepared to discuss other essential dimensions of their experiences. Higher education and industry partners need to collaborate to reduce barriers so that more equitable opportunities and professional preparation exist for students who transfer.

Major-to-Career Pathways Understanding

Students who transfer may have a deficit in understanding career pathways or the labor market. The transition to the receiving institution does not stop once the student successfully arrives on campus—the transition continues until the student graduates. This continued transition involves connecting academic decision-making to labor market nuances, professional capital, and occupational navigation. Articulating the competencies gained across various industry-focused assignments and attitudes toward work development presented a major challenge for most students. Students understand these connections by working with professionals who can help them grasp how their experiences overlap with their academic coursework and discern the larger connection between academic competencies and work-based performance. However, for students to understand, they must be available and present to receive this support. A high percentage of students who transfer spend far less time on campus outside of attending classes, making it much more challenging to tap into this campus resource.

Conclusion

Even though researchers have established that students avoid career services resources and expertise, existing studies focus solely on individual services to understand students' help-seeking behavior regarding transfer (Del Mastro & Schneider, 2016). Further, Del Mastro and Schneider found that new-student orientation, first-year experience programs, and academic advisors are crucial in introducing and validating campus career resources and services to students. Yet students who transfer miss many of these key developmental milestones.

Career decision-making is a significant but difficult life task that bridges developmental stages (Super, 1990; Super et al., 1996). Once considered an obstacle for students in early adulthood, career decision-making is now accepted as a lifespan endeavor (Osipow, 1999). Various life transitions weaved throughout these developmental stages pose the potential for career indecision, requiring one to revisit career plans continuously. This lifelong demand increases the need to develop ways to measure and intervene in career indecision to navigate these frequent transitions successfully. However, with little research on the impact of career-related interventions on the transfer experience, understanding this population's career service needs and the most timely and effective way to provide these services is critical. Barefoot (2004) pointed to a central problem of institutional data—none of it is public. As a result, career services continually fight the misconception that their services are helpful only for finding a job or that students fail to take full advantage of what career services offer.

The entire transfer experience from orientation through graduation is orchestrated by professionals who focus primarily on academic attainment and fail to prioritize career development and professional readiness as an equal companion. Unsurprisingly, students who transfer have low awareness of career services, especially when not embedded into their required academic journey, beginning well before the transfer experience until they are fully acclimated to the receiving institution and through to graduation. The onus to engage career services should not fall solely on the shoulders of the students who transfer.

This publication focuses on reframing transfer as an experience, not a label that students are given. This publication also challenges readers to consider students' career and professional development needs as they navigate transfer—an experience that will affect them as undergraduates.

References

Allen, J., Robbins, S. B., Casillas, A., & Oh, I. S. (2008). Third-year college retention and transfer: Effects of academic performance, motivation, and social connectedness. *Research in Higher Education, 49*(7), 647–664. http://doi.org/10.1007/s11162-008-9098-3

Amir, T., & Gati, I. (2006). Facets of career decision-making difficulties. *British Journal of Guidance & Counselling, 34*(4), 483–503. http://doi.org/10.1080/03069880600942608

Barefoot, B. O. (2004). Higher education's revolving door: Confronting the problem of student drop out in U.S. colleges and universities. *Open Learning: The Journal of Open, Distance and e-Learning, 19*(1), 9–18. https://doi.org/10.1080/0268051042000177818

Bers, T., & Younger, D. (2011). The role of feeder community colleges. In M. A. Poisel & S. Joseph (Eds.), *Transfer students in higher education: Building foundations for policies, programs, and services that foster student success*. National Resource Center for The First-Year Experience and Students in Transition.

Brown, S. D., & Lent, R. W. (Eds.). (2000). *Handbook of counseling psychology* (3rd ed.). Wiley.

Burton, N. D., Martin, H. E., Alexander, R. A., & Cunningham, B. L. (2020). *Academic and career advising for undecided, exploring and major-changing students* [Pocket guide series PG13]. NACADA.

Collier, P. J., & Morgan, D. L. (2008). "Is that paper really due today?": Differences in first-generation and traditional college students' understandings of faculty expectations. *Higher Education, 55*, 425–446. http://doi.org/10.1007/s10734-007-9065-5

Cooper, D. L., Healy, M. A., & Simpson, J. (1994). Student development through involvement: Specific changes over time. *Journal of College Student Development, 35*, 98–102.

Coston, C., Lord, V., & Monell, J. (2013). Improving the success of transfer students: Responding to risk factors. *Learning Communities Research and Practice, 1*(1), Article 11. https://files.eric.ed.gov/fulltext/EJ1112866.pdf

Cuseo, J. (2001, November). *The transfer transition* [Preconference workshop]. Students in Transition Eighth National Conference, Oakbrook, IL, United States.

Davies, T. G., & Casey, K. (1999). Transfer student experiences: Comparing their academic and social lives at the community college and university. *College Student Journal, 33*, 60–71.

De Araujo, P., & Murray, J. (2010). Channels for improved performance from living on campus. *American Journal of Business Education, 3*(12), 57–64. http://doi.org/10.19030/ajbe.v3i12.965

Del Mastro, L. N., & Schneider, N. M. (2016). *The use of academic student services and help-seeking behaviors among undergraduate college students* [Student project]. University of Illinois at Urbana-Champaign, IDEALS. http://hdl.handle.net/2142/90190.

Dennis, J. M., Calvillo, E., & Gonzalez, A. (2008). The role of psychosocial variables in understanding the achievement and retention of transfer students at an ethnically diverse urban university. *Journal of College Student Development, 49*(6), 535–550. https://doi.org/10.1353/csd.0.0037

Dennis, J. M., Phinney, J. S., & Chuateco, L. I. (2005). The role of motivation, parental support, and peer support in the academic success of ethnic minority first-generation college students. *Journal of College Student Development, 46*(3), 223–236. http://doi.org/10.1353/csd.2005.0023

Di Fabio, A., & Bernaud, J. L. (2008). The help-seeking in career counseling. *Journal of Vocational Behavior, 72*(1), 60–66. https://doi.org/10.1016/j.jvb.2007.10.006

Duggan, M. H., & Pickering, J. W. (2007–2008). Barriers to transfer student academic success and retention. *Journal of College Student Retention: Research, Theory & Practice, 9*(4), 437–459. https://doi.org/10.2190/CS.9.4.c

Eagan, M. K., Stolzenberg, E. B., Zimmerman, H. B., Aragon, M. C., Whang Sayson, H., & Rios-Aguilar, C. (2017). *The American freshman: National norms Fall 2016*. Higher Education Research Institute, UCLA.

Fauria, R. M., & Fuller, M. B. (2015). Transfer student success: Educationally purposeful activities predictive of undergraduate GPA. *Research and Practice in Assessment, 10,* 39–52.

Fee, J. F., Prolman, S., & Thomas, J. (2009). Making the most of a small midwestern university: The case of transfer students. *College Student Journal, 43*(4) 1204-1216.

Fischer, E. H., & Farina, A. (1995). Attitudes toward seeking professional psychological help: A shortened form and considerations for research. *Journal of College Student Development, 36,* 368–373.

Folsom, B., Peterson, G. W., Reardon, R. C., & Mann, B. A. (2005). Impact of a career planning course on academic performance and graduation rate. *Journal of College Student Retention: Research, Theory & Practice, 6*(4), 461–473. https://doi.org/10.2190/4WJ2-CJL1-V9DP-HBMF

Fouad, N. A., Guillen, A., Harris-Hodge, E., Henry, C., Novakovic, A., Terry, S., & Kantamneni, N. (2006). Need, awareness, and use of career services for college students. *Journal of Career Assessment, 14*(4), 407–420. https://doi.org/10.1177/1069072706288928

Garver, M. S., Spralls III, S. A., & Divine, R. L. (2010). Need-based segmentation analysis of university career services: Implications for increasing student participation. *Research in Higher Education Journal, 3*(1) 99-123.

Gati, I., Krausz, M. & Osipow, S. H. (1996). A taxonomy of difficulties in career decision making. *Journal of Counseling Psychology, 43,* 510–526. http://doi.org/10.1037/0022-0167.43.4.510

Gere, A. R., Hutton, L., Keating, B., Knutson, A. V., Silver, N., & Toth, C. (2017). Mutual adjustments: Learning from and responding to transfer student writers. *College English, 79*(4), 333–357. https://library.ncte.org/journals/CE/issues/v79-4/28970

Ghusson, M. (2016). *Understanding the engagement of transfer students in four-year institutions: A national study* (UMI No. 10109010) [Doctoral dissertation, Seton Hall University]. ProQuest Dissertations and Theses database.

Glass, J., C., Jr., & Harrington, A. R. (2002). Academic performance of community college transfer students and "native" students at a large state university. *Community College Journal of Research and Practice, 26*(5), 415–430. https://doi.org/10.1080/02776770290041774

Gordon, V. N. (2007). *The undecided college students: An academic and career advising challenge* (3rd ed.). Charles C. Thomas.

Hansen, J. M., Jackson, A. P., & Pedersen, T. R. (2017). Career Development courses and educational outcomes: Do career courses make a difference? *Journal of Career Development, 44*(3), 209–223. https://doi.org/10.1177/0894845316644984

Hills, J. R. (1965). Transfer shock: The academic performance of the junior college transfer. *The Journal of Experimental Education, 33*(3), 201–215. https://doi.org/10.1080/0022 0973.1965.11010875

Hossler, D., Shapiro, D., Dundar, A., Ziskin, M., Chen, J., Zerquera, D., & Torres, V. (2012, February). *Transfer and mobility: A national view of pre-degree student movement in postsecondary institutions* (Signature Report No. 2). National Student Clearinghouse Research Center.

Hoyt, J. E., & Winn, B. A. (2004). Understanding retention and college student bodies: Differences between drop-outs, stop-outs, opt-outs, and transfer-outs. *NASPA Journal, 41*(3), 395–417. https://doi.org/10.2202/1949-6605.1351

Hung, D. (2002). A career development course for academic credit: An outcome analysis. *Canadian Journal of Career Development, 1*(1), 22–26. https://cjcd-rcdc.ceric.ca/index. php/cjcd/article/view/317

Ishitani, T. T., & Flood, L. D. (2018). Student transfer-out behavior at 4-year institutions. *Research in Higher Education, 59*(7), 825–846. http://doi.org/10.1007/s11162-017-9489-4

Kuhn, T., & Padek, G. (2009). From the co-editors: Reflecting on 30 years of growth and the future. *NACADA Journal, 29*(1), 3–4. https://doi.org/10.12930/0271-9517-29.1.3

Laanan, F. S. (2001). Transfer student adjustment. *New Directions for Community Colleges, 2001*(114), 5–13. https://doi.org/10.1002/cc.16

Laanan, F. (2007). Studying transfer students: Part II: Dimensions of transfer students' adjustment. *Community College Journal of Research and Practice, 31*(1), 37–59. http://doi.org/10.1080/10668920600859947

Lent, R. W., & Brown, S. D. (2013). Understanding and facilitating career development in the 21st century. In S. D. Brown & R. W. Lent (Eds.), *Career development and counseling: Putting theory and research to work* (2nd ed.). Wiley.

Lester, J., Leonard, J. B., & Mathias, D. (2013). Transfer student engagement: Blurring of social and academic engagement. *Community College Review, 41*(3), 202–222. http://doi.org/10.1177/0091552113496141

Levinson, D. J. (1986). A conception of adult development. *American Psychologist, 41*, 3–13. https://doi.org/10.1037/0003-066X.41.1.3

Ludwikowski, W. M. A., Vogel, D., & Armstrong, P. I. (2009). Attitudes toward career counseling: The role of public and self-stigma. *Journal of Counseling Psychology, 56*(3), 408–416. https://doi.org/10.1037/a0016180

Maietta, H. N. (2019). *The forced transfer experience: Implications for career services* [Paper presentation]. National Career Development Association Annual Conference, Houston, TX.

Maietta, H. N. (October 14, 2020). *College closure and the forced transfer student experience* [Paper presentation]. National Conference on Students in Transition 27th Annual Virtual Meeting.

McClellan, G. S., Creager, K. L., & Savoca, M. (2018). *A good job: Campus employment as a high-impact practice.* Stylus Publishing, LLC.

McGuire, S. P., & Belchier, M. (2014). Transfer student characteristics matter. *Journal of College Student Retention, 15*(1), 37–48. https://doi.org/10.2190/CS.15.1.c

National Association of Colleges and Employers. (2020). *2019–20 career services benchmarks survey report.*

Osipow, S. (1999). Assessing career indecision. *Journal of Vocational Behavior, 55,* 147–154. https://psycnet.apa.org/doi/10.1006/jvbe.1999.1704

Pincus, F. L., & DeCamp, S. (1989). Minority community college students who transfer to four-year colleges: A study of a matched sample of B.A. recipients and non-recipients. *Community Junior College Research Quarterly of Research and Practice, 13*(3–4), 191–219. https://doi.org/10.1080/0361697890130306

Poisel, M. A., & Joseph, S. (Eds). (2011). *Transfer students in higher education, building foundations for policies, programs, and services that foster student success.* National Resource Center for The First-Year Experience and Students in Transition.

Prescod, D., Gilfillan, B., Belser, C., Orndorff, R., & Ishler, M. (2019). Career decision-making for undergraduates enrolled in career planning courses. *College Quarterly, 22*(2). https://files.eric.ed.gov/fulltext/EJ1221402.pdf

Reardon, R. C., Melvin, B., McClain, M.-C., Peterson, G. W., & Bowman, W. J. (2015). The career course as a factor in college graduation. *Journal of College Student Retention: Research, Theory & Practice, 17*(3), 336–350. https://doi.org/10.1177/1521025115575913

Reardon, R. C., Peace, C. S., & Burbrink, I. E. (2021). College career courses and instructional research from 1976 through 2019. *Scholarship of Teaching and Learning in Psychology.* Advance online publication. https://doi.org/10.1037/stl0000254

Rochlen, A. B., Mohr, J. J., & Hargrove, B. K. (1999). Development of the attitudes toward career counseling scale. *Journal of Counseling Psychology, 46,* 196–206.

Rovai, A. (2002). Building sense of community at a distance. *International Review of Research in Open and Distributed Learning, 3*(1), 1–16. https://doi.org/10.19173/irrodl.v3i1.79

Sampson, J. P., Jr., Peterson, G. W., Lenz, J. G., & Reardon, R. C. (1992). A cognitive approach to career services: Translating concepts into practice. *The Career Development Quarterly, 41*(1), 67–74. https://doi.org/10.1002/j.2161-0045.1992.tb00360.x

Sanchez, A. R., & Atkinson, D. R. (1983). Mexican American cultural commitment, preference for counselor ethnicity and willingness to use counseling. *Journal of Counseling Psychology, 30,* 215–220.

Savoca, M. (2016). *Campus employment as a high impact practice: Relationship to academic success and persistence of first-generation college students* [Doctoral dissertation, Colorado State University]. Mountain Scholar Home. http://hdl.handle.net/10217/173353

Schlossberg, N. K. (1984). *Counseling adults in transition: Linking theory to practice.* Springer Publishing.

Schlossberg, N. K., Waters, E. B., & Goodman, J. (1995). *Counseling adults in transition: Linking practice with theory* (2nd ed.). Springer Publishing.

Shapiro, D., Dundar, A., Huie, F., Wakhungu, P.K., Yuan, X., Nathan, A. & Hwang, Y. (2017, September). *Tracking transfer: Measures of effectiveness in helping community college students to complete bachelor's degrees* (Signature Report No. 13). National Student Clearinghouse Research Center.

Spight, D. B. (2020). Early declaration of a college major and its relationship to persistence. *NACADA Journal, 40*(1), 94–109. https://doi.org/10.12930/NACADA-18-37

Strada–Gallup. (2018). *2018 Strada–Gallup alumni survey: Mentoring college students to success.* Gallup Inc. and Strada Education Network. https://news.gallup.com/reports/244058/2018-strada-gallup-alumni-survey.aspx

Super, D. E. (1990). A life-span, life-space approach to career development. In D. Brown & L. Brooks (Eds.), *Career choice and development: Applying contemporary theories to practice* (2nd ed., pp. 197–261). Jossey-Bass.

Super, D. E., Savickas, M. L., and Super, C. M. (1996). The lifespan, life-space approach to careers. In D. Brown, L. Brooks, & Associates (Eds.), *Career choice and development* (3rd ed., pp. 121–178). Jossey-Bass.

Taylor, J. L., & Jain, D. (2017). The multiple dimensions of transfer: Examining the transfer function in higher education. *Community College Review, 45*(4), 273–293. https://doi.org/10.1177/0091552117725177

Terenzini, P., Springer, L., Yaeger, P., Pascarella, E., & Nora, A. (1996). First-generation college students: Characteristics, experiences, and cognitive development. *Research in Higher Education, 37*(1), 1–22. http://www.jstor.org/stable/40196208

Thurmond, K. (2003). Communicating among 4-year institutions. In T. Grites, T. Kerr, & M. King (Eds.), *Advising transfer students.* (pp. 25-28). National Academic Advising Association.

Thurmond, K. C. (2007). *Transfer shock: Why is a term forty years old still relevant.* NACADA Clearinghouse of Academic Advising Resources.

Tinto, V. (1985). Dropping out and other forms of withdrawal from college. In U. Delworth & G. Hanson (Eds.), *Increasing student retention* (pp. 28–43). Jossey-Bass.

Tinto, V. (1993). *Leaving college: Rethinking the causes and cures of student attrition* (2nd ed.). University of Chicago Press.

Tinto, V. (2012). *Leaving college: Rethinking the causes and cures of student attrition* (3rd ed.). University of Chicago Press.

Tovar, E., & Simon, M. (2006). Academic probation as a dangerous opportunity: Factors influencing diverse college students' success. *Community College Journal of Research & Practice, 30*(7), 547–564.

Townsend, B. K., & Wilson, K. B. (2009). The academic and social integration of persisting community college transfer students. *Journal of College Student Retention: Research, Theory & Practice, 10*(4), 405–423. https://doi.org/10.2190/CS.10.4.a

Trombley, C. M. (2000). Evaluating students on academic probation and determining intervention strategies: A comparison of probation and good standing students. *Journal of College Student Retention, 2*(3), 239–251.

Trowler, P. (2002). Introduction: Higher education policy, institutional change. In P. Trowler (Ed.), *Higher education policy and institutional change: Intentions and outcomes in turbulent environments* (pp. 1–24). SRHE and Open University Press.

Turley, R. N. L., & Wodtke, G. (2010). College residence and academic performance: Who benefits from living on campus? *Urban Education, 45*(4), 506–532. http://doi.org/10.1177/0042085910372351

University of Alaska – Fairbanks. (2020). *Academic standards.* https://catalog.uaf.edu/academics-regulations/academic-standards/

University of South Carolina (n.d.). *Academic probation notice sent to first-year students.* Columbia, SC: University of South Carolina

Venit, E. (2016). *How late is too late?: Myths and facts about the consequences of switching college majors*. EAB Student Success Collaborative. https://www.luminafoundation.org/resource/consequences-of-switching-college-majors/

Versalle, G. L. (2018). *Understanding the experiences of students re-admitted after academic suspension as part of a university-initiated process: a qualitative study* [Doctoral dissertation, Western Michigan University]. ScholarWorks. https://scholarworks.wmich.edu/dissertations/3357

Waltenbury, M., Brady, S., Gallo, M., Redmond, N., Draper, S. & Fricker, T. (2018). *Academic probation: Evaluating the impact of academic standing notification letters on students*. Higher Education Quality Council of Ontario.

Wang, X., Wickersham, K., & Sun, N. (2016). The evolving landscape of transfer research: Reconciling what we know in preparation for a new era of heightened promise and complexity. *New Directions for Institutional Research, 170*, 115–121). https://doi.org/10.1002/ir.20189

Whang, L., Tawatao, C., Danneker, J., Belanger, J., Edward Weber, S., Garcia, L., & Klaus, A. (2017). Understanding the transfer student experience using design thinking. *Reference Services Review, 45*(2), 298–313. http://hdl.handle.net/1773/40336

Yeager, D. S., & Dweck, C. S. (2012). Mindsets that promote resilience: When students believe that personal characteristics can be developed. *Educational Psychologist, 47*(4), 302–314. https://doi.org/10.1080/00461520.2012.722805

Yosso, T. J. (2005). Whose culture has capital? A critical race theory discussion of community cultural wealth. *Race Ethnicity and Education, 8*, 69–91.

CHAPTER TWO

Transfer Nation:
A Digital Community in Support of Transfer

Heather Adams

Evidence suggests that individuals without bachelor's degrees will be hardest hit post-COVID-19 pandemic, while those with bachelor's degrees will rebound sooner (Carnevale, 2020; Georgetown University Center on Education and the Workforce [CEW], 2021; Lund et al., 2021; Merisotis, 2020). The community college transfer pathway has long offered a gateway to a bachelor's degree and the promise of economic mobility for millions of students. Undergraduate student communities include disproportionately large numbers of students of color and students from low-income households (American Association of Community Colleges, 2021; Belfield & Bailey, 2011; Cahalan et al., 2021; Carnevale et al., 2018; Century Foundation, 2019; CEW, 2021; Minaya & Scott-Clayton, 2020; National Center for Education Statistics, 2011). Almost half of the students earning bachelor's degrees have enrolled at a community college at some point in their college careers, and one in five master's degree holders and 1 in 10 doctoral-research degree earners began their postsecondary education at a community college (National Student Clearinghouse Research Center [NSC], 2017b). However, while four in five students entering community college aspire to earn a bachelor's degree, just 15% attain the credential after six years (Community College Research Center [CCRC], 2021; NSC, 2017a, 2021a). White students were twice as likely as Black and Latino peers of this cohort to receive a degree (CCRC, 2021; Cahalan et al., 2021; Shapiro et al., 2017). These inequitable outcomes have increased since the 2019 pandemic (Jenkins & Fink, 2016; NSC, 2021a, 2021b). For transfer professionals, much work remains.

The COVID-19 pandemic and subsequent enrollment trends highlight higher education challenges, with extraordinary numbers of students changing direction and re-evaluating their higher education options (Goebel et al., 2020; NSC, 2021b). As more students collect college credits and careen between colleges and the workforce, more students may consider transferring as an affordable option (Goebel et al., 2020; NSC, 2017a, 2021). The increases expected in student mobility and transfer warrant re-evaluating transfer policies and practices and additional knowledgeable staff to serve this population.

Research shows that students who are supported throughout the transfer process perform better academically, are more likely to navigate the transfer experience successfully, and are more likely to graduate (Center for Community College Student Engagement [CCCSE], 2018; Wang, 2020; Wyner et al., 2016). However, the onus often rests on the student to pilot the higher education system, sift through confusing institutional websites and student resources (not necessarily tailored to their needs), and know what questions to ask college and university officials (Schudde et al., 2020, 2021; Wang, 2020). Beyond degree completion, the focus and support surrounding career and workforce preparation are often overlooked or left out of the conversation entirely.

The plethora of research on the transfer process outlines essential strategies educational leaders can take to develop effective practices, policies, and partnerships to support equitable transfer success (CCCSE, 2018; Handel & Strempel, 2016, 2017; Ishitani, 2008; Ishitani & McKitrick, 2010; Jain et al., 2020; Laanan et al., 2010; Wang, 2020; Wyner et al., 2016). Many chapters in this book identify ways to support students' career success post-graduation. This support comes in many forms—a critical one being the assurance that those who work with students who transfer receive adequate training, are supported by accessible professional development resources, and have access to career and labor market information. Professionals who work with students can also benefit from mentorship, peer consultancy, coaching, and a network of professionals to learn from and to brainstorm ideas and insights. *Transfer Nation*, a community, aims to provide these benefits to professionals supporting students in transition.

Transfer Nation: A Community Focused on Transfer Success

Developed as a pilot in 2018 and launched more broadly in April 2019 as a public Facebook group, Transfer Nation (TN) is a community that provides a collaborative space for professionals who celebrate and advocate for all-things transfer. TN was initially developed as a way to connect with other educators and transfer advocates, who can often feel alone in their work on transfer issues and with students who transfer. From the immediate interest and surge in membership in the early months, it became clear that many professionals wanted to connect on the topic of transfer.

As TN grew, communication pathways were developed to gauge and capture interest in contributing, hosting events, and creating content for the community. Many people volunteered, and TN has continued to be supported by a collection of volunteers—all former students who transferred and/or higher education staff, faculty, and administrators passionate about the transfer experience and process. A team of 22 volunteers meets weekly to oversee the open-access platforms. Volunteers work together on social content and initiatives, collecting feedback from the membership regarding what content and materials they want and need.

Membership in TN is open to anyone interested in joining. Members are encouraged to post transfer and transfer-related questions, articles, and other insights. There are no restrictions on who can post on the TN platforms other than universal group norms and requests to be courteous of others, refrain from posting spam or ads that are not related to transfer, and respect the privacy of other members. Members who do not abide by the guidelines are contacted and are subject to being blocked from the platform by an admin.

The community offers seasoned and new professionals a think tank to explore ideas, learn, and grow in our collective knowledge on the topic. At the time of this publication, the TN Facebook group had over 1,900 members from 10 different countries and has expanded to other platforms like Twitter, Instagram, TikTok, and LinkedIn. Members have a broad range of roles both in and outside of higher education, including faculty, transfer center directors, advisors, admission reps, staff from both community colleges and four-year institutions, graduate students, researchers, nonprofit advocates, education-technology experts, and others. The group also welcomes current students who have or are contemplating a transfer to join the group so that members can learn from their representative voices.

However, there is a significant problem: A notable absence of career service professionals in TN conversations and member collaboration leaves a big hole in understanding students who transfer and their processes. Whether career professionals do not seek opportunities to engage or are not actively and effectively invited to participate in transfer-specific collaborations is unknown. Excluding their essential voice in conversations related to the transfer experience is troubling. Career support is a large part of the transfer success puzzle, and career professionals need to be involved in solving this puzzle. Where is the disconnect?

Lessons Learned: What the Feed Has Not Told Us

When a keyword search for the word "career" on the TN Facebook page is performed, other than the plethora of transfer job opportunities (only a few of which had "career" in the title or the job description; the majority focused on admissions, evaluation, enrollment management, and academic advising), only three significant discussions emerged related to transfer and career. One post centered on the value of pursuing a degree from a religious school and the potential bias attached to listing faith-based institutions on a resume. This post sparked a sideline discussion on the realities of transfer and community college bias in hiring practices. The second correspondence that was related to transfer and career discussed factors that might influence employers to place more value on the associate degree and to require associate degrees for certain positions (as opposed to a bachelor's degree). The third post mentioning transfer and career was specific to a University of Houston, Downtown (UHD) campus program offering transition and career development for UHD students in the Accelerated Transfer Academy. This post didn't receive any comments or engagement from TN members despite its promising collaboration model that included transfer and career professionals in serving students who transfer. Moreover, during a 2021 outreach campaign to increase membership, TN had one career professional sign up out of 1,700 members reached. So, the question is, why?

TN wants to address this question by inviting career service professionals to join the conversation on transfer. In this chapter, I call for career professionals from community colleges and four-year institutions to bring their expertise to the table and work collaboratively with others in the field. I hope this call will strengthen the connection between career development professionals and those supporting transfer students. As the authors of several chapters in this book point out, educators who practice in career services or partner with career professionals have a better chance of providing students with the vital information and experiences needed to prepare for their chosen career pathways. We must expand the career presence on TN and in the transfer conversation. Many opportunities exist for collective action and knowledge sharing on transfer as a workforce issue; TN is a terrific place to start. As one member shared, "TN is a space for anyone within higher ed or higher ed related organizations to learn and grow and to engage in the form of self-study of all-things transfer—become 'students of transfer students'—together" (personal communication, October 24, 2020). How incredible would it be if career professionals added their expertise by engaging in the conversation?

Live From the TN Newsfeed

TN provides a platform for those interested in learning from others in the field—a sounding board for advice. Forum subscribers rely on shared information to keep updated on the latest trends, advance advising practices, and learn how institutions can improve policy. For this chapter, I performed a 2022 keyword search on the TN newsfeed, which revealed three central themes: transfer-specific services; professional development; and mentoring, community building, and moral support.

Transfer-Specific Services

This theme centers on the vital need for information on setting up transfer-specific services (academic, professional, and social) that meet the needs of students who transfer and guide institutional practice/policy to ensure success throughout the process. Members expressed a desire for more direct access and clear answers on the "how-to" of the transfer process to serve students more successfully. Relevant topics aligned in conversations with the community college and the four-year college members. Topics most frequently cited include

- Understanding policies and practices regarding transfer advising,

- Guiding career pathways for students who transfer, from pre-transfer to life after graduation,

- Engaging faculty more actively in the transfer academics-to-career conversation,

- Building cross-campus and cross-sector advocacy and collaboration,

- Designing early advising and building first-year preparation courses for students who transfer, and

- Establishing transfer-specific communication outlets such as social media platforms and websites.

Professional Development

TN members expressed a strong need for professional development related to transfer practices. This feedback appeared in weekly questions, social-hour discussions, and other networking events as well as through direct messages and emails. For example, some members are looking for growth opportunities to help supplement and deepen their training at conferences; others are interested in advising on niche majors and career paths such as pre-med or art; others are simply looking to find job opportunities.

TN provides an outlet for many of these professional development needs. In addition, engagement opportunities with other professionals in the field, either through TN events or simply in the news feed and comment discussions, provide coaching opportunities for new and established professionals. Career professionals have a unique and deep knowledge of career development and labor market trends. For example, transition theory addresses how students often lose some of their support systems through the transfer process, including friends, family, mentors, academic and career advisors, and available institutional structures (Goodman et al., 2006; Schlossberg, 1984). Career professionals understand how to use goal setting and action-planning strategies to rebuild some of these supports. Career professionals can advance the care of students who transfer by sharing their expertise with other higher education professionals through the TN platform. The opposite is also true—career professionals can learn more about the complex transfer journey and identity with transfer experts to support their work and development through the TN platform.

Mentoring, Community Building, and Moral Support

One of TN's main goals is to continue the conversation, community building, and the momentum gained at transfer-specific conferences. To provide professionals a central hub where they can mentor, be mentored, and grow their knowledge and support system on all-things transfer—anywhere, any time. Members often express that the ability to immediately connect with a diverse community of people committed to transfer keeps them returning to TN. This aspect of TN provides members with an ecosystem of professionals they can reach out to when facing student situations and circumstances beyond their expertise. It also provides a supportive environment to ask questions, check assumptions, and discover how other aspects of the field may address a particular transfer situation. Monthly practitioner panels and Transfer Think Tank sessions help members build their knowledge on transfer best practices and develop relationships with others in the field, areas in which career professionals could play critical roles in advancing TN's mission.

One aspect often missing from transfer-specific conferences and community building in transfer is insight from all areas of higher education. It would be an immense boon for transfer professionals to have the support and knowledge that career professionals bring to the table. Examples of the mentoring and support possible through TN include cross-training, trading information, or instigating collaborative efforts across field areas.

TN misses a valuable opportunity to cross-train with career colleagues when career professionals do not engage in mentoring and networking conversations. How wonderful would it be for the transfer field to have career professionals mentoring transfer professionals to better understand the need for career exploration as part of the transfer process? Moving forward, TN's goal is to engage a substantial number of career professionals to support the missing link between transfer and career. The themes in the next section highlight opportunities for collaboration.

Future Action and Advocacy

Shifting mindsets to regenerate a higher education system that comprehensively and systematically guides students through transfer events that connect educational transitions to career development requires multiple constituents from sending and receiving institutions. Threading career development throughout the educational process is crucial, particularly when transferring from one institution to another and one career to another is common. Transfer professionals knowledgeable in career development and decision-making can help students plan and execute sound career pathways, provide tools for students to build their transferable skills, and coach them to articulate the transferability of these skills from college to career. Alternatively, career professionals can help students who transfer navigate the procedural steps that comprise the transfer transition. However, the challenge is that transfer professionals are not professional career coaches, and career coaches are not professional transfer counselors. Both sets of professionals need each other to support students who transfer fully.

Transfer is not just about enrollment and articulation of credits. Transfer takes on a different meaning for each student, shaped by the type of transfer, the student's circumstances at the time of transfer, and the impact of the transfer on the student (see Chapter 1). For this reason, higher education professionals must advocate for transfer beyond the concept of the hand-off from one institution to another; rather, they must view transfer as a shared responsibility between and across institutions and sectors, a relationship-rich journey that leads to career and success after degree completion. Professionals who work in the transfer space should remain informed, gain the required skills, and develop the necessary programs to cultivate professional readiness among students who transfer. Forging collaborative relationships across campus and beyond is essential, and a partnership with career services is ever required.

Based on the evidence from the TN feed (and the forthcoming chapters), many opportunities exist to collaborate, learn from, and learn with career services professionals. That is why TN plans to commit to three career-centric advocacy actions:

1. To integrate further and expand the voice of career services professionals in the transfer conversation,

2. To foster networking and mentoring between transfer and career professionals, and

3. To increase education and professional development cross-training opportunities between transfer and career professionals.

We will achieve these outcomes through the three actions discussed in the next sections.

Include Career-Centric Voice in Transfer Nation Outreach

TN collaborates with the National Institute for the Study of Transfer Students and many transfer experts to host a knowledge-sharing podcast series. The TN podcast series provides transfer-specific practices, policies, and evidence-based research from higher education professionals worldwide. TN will host career professionals to share expertise in various areas beneficial to the transfer journey. Discussing the transfer career journey through a career services lens will educate professionals on the importance of these conversations outside of career services. In addition, interviewing career professionals will highlight professionals doing excellent work on transfer-related career initiatives and will help to gather perspectives on the ways in which career exploration could benefit the transfer community.

TN will also offer panels, transfer think tanks, and a series of 15-minute webinars for higher education professionals on specific topics, such as building transfer-receptive culture, creating transfer peer-mentor programs, and, vital to the focus of this book, career exploration for students who transfer. These opportunities allow members to participate in self-study and research to build agency and collect knowledge of transfer in real time. In addition, TN would like to support at least three career services-focused events a year in partnership with career-related associations or experts in the field.

It is simple: Everyone, including career professionals, must be in the conversation. TN plans to work with organizations such as the National Association of Colleges and Employers (NACE), the National Career Development Association (NCDA), and the National Society for Experiential Education (NSEE), among others, to identify guests for the podcast. In addition, TN will explore future opportunities to attend and present at career-related conferences for further outreach and engagement. The exposure created by attending conferences could spark career service professionals' much-needed participation in TN newsfeeds and discussion boards.

Organize Networking and Mentoring Around Transfer and Career

The organically cultivated TN community shows that building a more robust transfer network of professionals and advocates is possible. TN is committed to developing a framework for more formal networking events and a mentorship platform to effectively connect transfer advocates across interests, divisions, and institutions. TN wants career professionals to be an active part of this effort.

The goal is to grow and evolve this community of practice in its scope and vision. A formal mentoring structure that pairs professionals new to transfer with seasoned transfer experts promotes a focused professional network for those early in their careers or new to the transfer community. Mentorship will provide the one-to-one encouragement needed to foster professional growth in a complex field that requires individuals to have multiple skill sets to be effective. Networking and mentorship are reciprocal. Career experts will have opportunities to connect with new and experienced transfer professionals to strengthen their awareness of milestones in the transfer journey while fostering more collaboration and outreach between those in the transfer fields.

Celebrate and Amplify Transfer Career Success Globally

TN celebrates students who transfer, including successes, services, and transfer champions—students and professionals who transform culture across the nation. An example is the #TransferTuesday initiative, which allows institutions and individuals to tell their stories or nominate students, alums, or colleges to share their stories. The #TransferTuesday initiative also provides an educational opportunity, spreading the message of transfer and promoting community college as an excellent pathway to success. TN has yet to spotlight a career center, career services personnel, or a career program doing solid work for transfer success. This book opens the door to emphasize transfer and career.

Spotlights like #TransferTuesday, #EndCCStigma (Jaschik, 2019), #CCMonth (Association of Community College Trustees, 2021), and others promote transfer awareness, endorse transfer as a pathway of success, highlight resources available, uphold the facts surrounding the transfer, and aim to help shift the national narrative on community college transfer. These initiatives also provide real-life examples of the ways in which the community college pathway offers millions of students access to higher education and economic mobility. It is an incredible opportunity for career services to elevate their work in the field, supporting success outcomes for internships, career engagement, and post-college success of students who transfer.

Conclusion

The TN community has been a lifeline of professional development as transfer momentum continues to grow. Higher education professionals charged with supporting students who navigate the transfer transition seek advice from one another in this space. We rely on the information shared to help keep us up to date, understand where our institutions can do better, and recognize where we can do better. We continue building a support network that serves students and the educators who offer them support. However, we cannot effectively support students navigating the academic and career journey without constant professional development and knowledge growth. With the workforce under continual pressure to change, student affairs and other educational professionals must remain aware of the system's changes to advise students in all phases of the career journey effectively. We need open-access platforms and instant updates on best practices and innovations in the field to move beyond entrenched mindsets and pivot to support students. We cannot do this work alone, and everyone plays a critical role in improving student outcomes.

An Invitation to Contribute to the Transfer Nation Community

If you want to contribute to the TN learning community and connect with others dedicated to improving the transfer journey, consider these options:

- **Be a guest speaker on the TN podcast and videocast.** Showcase best practices, career development, and more. To be considered for an episode, email a brief description of your topic idea to WeAreTransferNation@gmail.com. Access previous podcast episodes on Spotify, Apple podcasts, Amazon Music, or the TN YouTube channel.

- **Join the transfer conversation.** Bring the career services voice and expand career presence on the TN discussion board. This group focuses primarily on knowledge sharing, engaging in conversation, and learning. Join the discussion on the TN Facebook page.

- **Host an event for or with other TN members.** TN hosts monthly events such as panels, think tanks, happy hours and other social events, networking opportunities, and live webinars. If you have an idea for an event, email TN at WeAreTransferNation@gmail.com.

- **Nominate a terrific transfer program, event, student, or champion.** TN celebrates all aspects of the transfer journey. If you have a transfer-centric story, program, or staff member to highlight, visit the TN Facebook page and fill out the #TransferTuesday form.

- **Browse transfer-related content.** Join any TN social media sites for self-paced learning, engagement, and insights on the transfer experience, resources, and topics of interest. To learn more, visit TransferNation.com.

References

American Association of Community Colleges. (2021). *Fast facts 2021*. https://www.aacc.nche.edu/research-trends/fast-facts/

Association of Community College Trustees. (2021). *April is community college month!* https://www.acct.org/ccmonth

Belfield, C., & Bailey, T. (2011, January 16). The benefits of attending community college: A review of the evidence. *Community College Review, 39*(1), 46–68. https://doi.org/10.1177/0091552110395575?rss=1

Cahalan, M. W., Addison, M., Brunt, N., Patel, P. R., & Perna, L. W. (2021). *Indicators of higher education equity in the United States: 2021 Historical trend report*. The Pell Institute for the Study of Opportunity in Higher Education, Council for Opportunity in Education (COE), and Alliance for Higher Education and Democracy of the University of Pennsylvania (PennAHEAD). http://pellinstitute.org/downloads/publications-Indicators_of_Higher_Education_Equity_in_the_US_2021_Historical_Trend_Report.pdf

Carnevale, A. (2020, May 19). *Education, race, and jobs in the COVID-19 crisis*. Georgetown University CEW. https://medium.com/georgetown-cew/education-race-and-jobs-in-the-covid-19-crisis-c927be2c2487

Carnevale, A., Strohl, J., Rideley, N., & Gulish, A. (2018). *Three educational pathways to good jobs: High school, middle skills, and bachelor's degree*. Georgetown University Center on Education and the Workforce. https://cew.georgetown.edu/wp-content/uploads/3ways-FR.pdf

Center for Community College Student Engagement. (2018). *Show me the way: The power of advising in community colleges*. https://www.voced.edu.au/content/ngv:89620

Century Foundation. (2019, April 25). *Recommendations for providing community colleges with the resources they need*. https://tcf.org/content/report/recommendations-providing-community-colleges-resources-need/

Community College Research Center. (2021). *Community college FAQs*. https://ccrc.tc.columbia.edu/Community-College-FAQs.html

Georgetown University Center on Education and the Workforce. (2021). *COVID-19's impact on education and the workforce.* https://cew.georgetown.edu/cew-reports/covid-research/

Goebel, C., Strauss, D., & Hesel, R. (2020, April). *Looking ahead to fall 2020: How COVID-19 continues to influence the choice of college-going students* [Special Edition, 2020]. Art and Science Group, LLC. https://www.artsci.com/studentpoll-covid-19-edition-2

Goodman, J., Schlossberg, N. K., & Anderson, M. L. (2006). *Counseling adults in transition* (3rd ed.). Springer Publishing Company, Inc.

Handel, S. J., & Strempel, E. (Eds.). (2016). *Transition and transformation: Fostering transfer student success.* National Institute for the Study of Transfer Students.

Handel, S.J., & Strempel, E. (Eds.). (2017). *Transition and transformation: Vol. 2. New research fostering transfer student success.* National Institute for the Study of Transfer Students.

Ishitani, T. T. (2008). How do transfers survive after "transfer shock"? A longitudinal study of transfer student departure at a four-year institution. *Research in Higher Education, 49*(5), 403–419. http://www.jstor.org/stable/25704572

Ishitani, T. T., & McKitrick, S. A. (2010). After transfer: The engagement of community college students at a four-year collegiate institution. *Community College Journal of Research and Practice, 34*(7), 576–594. https://doi.org/10.1080/10668920701831522

Jain, D., Bernal Melendez, N. S., & Herrera, A. R. (2020). *Power to the transfer: Critical race theory and a transfer receptive culture.* Michigan State University Press.

Jaschik, S. (2019, February 18). *Fighting the stigma about community college.* Inside Higher Ed. https://www.insidehighered.com/admissions/article/2019/02/18/community-college-presidents-campaign-against-stigma-about-two-year

Jenkins, D., & Fink, J. (2016, January). *Tracking transfer: New measures of institutional and state effectiveness in helping community college students attain bachelor's degrees.* CCRC Publications, Teachers College, Columbia University. https://ccrc.tc.columbia.edu/publications/tracking-transfer-institutional-state-effectiveness.html

Laanan, F. S., Starobin, S. S., & Eggleston, L. E. (2010). Adjustment of community college students at a four-year university: Role and relevance of transfer student capital for student retention. *Journal of College Student Retention: Research, Theory & Practice, 12*(2). 191-197. https://doi.org/10.2190/CS.12.2.d

Lund, S., Madgavkar, A., Manyika, J., Smit, S., Ellingrud, K., Meaney, M., & Robinson, O. (2021, February 18). *The future of work after COVID-19.* McKinsey & Company.

Merisotis, J. (2020). *Human work in the age of smart machines.* Rosetta Books.

Minaya, V., & Scott-Clayton, J. (2020, August 1). Labor market trajectories for community college graduates: How returns to certificates and associate's degrees evolve over time. *Education Finance and Policy, 17,* 53–80. https://doi.org/10.1162/edfp_a_00325

National Center for Education Statistics. (2011, November). *Community college student outcomes: 1994–2009* (NCES 2012–253) [Web tables report]. U.S. Department of Education. https://nces.ed.gov/pubs2012/2012253.pdf

National Student Clearinghouse Research Center. (2017a, Spring). *Contribution of two-year public institutions to bachelor's completions at four-year institutions* [Snapshot report]. https://nscresearchcenter.org/snapshotreport-twoyearcontributionfouryearcomplet ions26/

National Student Clearinghouse Research Center. (2017b, November 1). *From community college to graduate and professional degrees* [Snapshot report]. https://nscresearchcenter. org/snapshotreport-from-community-college-to-graduate-and-professional-degrees30/

National Student Clearinghouse Research Center. (2021a, September 23). *Tracking transfer measures of effectiveness in helping community college students to complete bachelor's degrees.* https://nscresearchcenter.org/tracking-transfer/

National Student Clearinghouse Research Center. (2021b, November 18). *Stay informed with the latest enrollment information: COVID-19.* https://nscresearchcenter.org/stay-informed/

Schlossberg, N. K. (1984). *Counseling adults in transition: Linking theory to practice* (1st ed.). Springer Publishing.

Schudde, L., Bradley, D., & Absher, C. (2020). Navigating vertical transfer online: Access to and usefulness of transfer information on community college websites. *Community College Review, 48*(1), 3–30. https://doi.org/10.1177/0091552119874500

Schudde, L., Jabbar, H., & Hartman, C. (2021). How political and ecological contexts shape community college transfer. *Sociology of Education, 94*(1), 65–83. https://doi. org/10.1177/0038040720954817

Shapiro, D., Dundar, A., Huie, F., Wakhungu, P., Yuan, X., Nathan, A., & Hwang, Y. A. (2017, April). *Completing college: A national view of student attainment rates by race and ethnicity—Fall 2010 cohort* (Signature Report No. 12b). National Student Clearinghouse Research Center. http://pas.indiana.edu/pdf/SignatureReport12b_ Race&EthnicitySuppCohort2010.pdf

Wang, X. (2020, April). *On my own: The challenge and promise of building equitable STEM transfer pathways.* Harvard Education Press.

Wyner, J., Deane, K. C., Jenkins, D., & Fink, J. (2016). *The transfer playbook: Essential practices for two- and four-year colleges.* Community College Research Center, Columbia University & College Excellence Program, Aspen Institute. https://eric.ed.gov/?id=ED565894

CHAPTER THREE

Navigating Unfamiliar Spaces: My Voice As a Student Who Transferred and a Professional Advisor of Transfers

Priscilla Vallejo

The vignette presented in this chapter offers the personal journey of one community college student who later transferred as an undergraduate to a four-year selective university, then worked professionally to support students' transfer experience and career and professional growth.

This chapter shares my personal and professional journey as a student who transferred and later became a career services practitioner at a community college and a four-year university. I share the personal journey through my lens, coupled with recommendations to inform career centers and practitioners on best practices to serve students who transfer and to address their career development needs. Postsecondary education was not a typical conversation at the dinner table for a first-generation student from a low-income background. However, I knew pursuing a college degree would open more career possibilities, and because of this, I decided to attend a local community college after high school.

My time and energy as a community college student focused on identifying an academic goal and completing the required coursework in two or three years. Conversations about career planning and applying classroom learning to the workforce were uncommon, as the priority was placed on doing well academically and completing my degree. Discussions about connecting my major to potential career pathways rarely occurred in the classroom or with advisors. I was learning success skills both in and out of the classroom (e.g., written and verbal communication, teamwork, critical thinking) but never received formal coaching on integrating these skills into work or academic experiences, especially when telling my story in an interview. As a result, I was not prepared to interview successfully, navigate a job search, or even articulate a chosen career path. The assistance provided by the career center and the resources available across campus to help me connect the classroom to career were unknown to me. As a result, I missed opportunities to explore different academic majors that I was curious about, develop my career, and improve my interviewing skills when searching for work. I did not know where to look, whom to seek out for support, or what questions to ask.

During conversations with my community college counselor, I serendipitously discovered the career path I wanted to pursue—I wanted to do what they were doing, helping students like me. This position matched my interest in helping others, especially those from underserved backgrounds. Unknowingly, I conducted an informational interview with my counselor, initiated career planning, and created action steps toward my goal. Until this point, I received no formal instructions on career planning. My journey would have been more straightforward and less complicated with assistance from career staff and professors.

Once I was aware of the academic preparation needed to pursue these career goals, I applied for a transfer to a four-year university in California to study human services. The program of study combined strong academic standards infused with experiential learning, something that spoke to me as a hands-on learner. The program required students to complete 120 hours of fieldwork in three internship rotations. Fieldwork creates a solid foundation that prepares students for success in the workplace and lifelong career management (National Association of Colleges and Employers, [NACE] 2021), which is precisely what the internship rotation did for me. For example, reflective journaling helped me to synthesize my internship experiences. By completing reflective journal entries, I shared the skills I learned during internship rotations and made connections between the world of work and my academic studies.

As a new student who transferred, I had class visits from the career center staff to share information about resume writing, graduate school, and other unfamiliar career development topics. After transfer, career planning became deeply planted in my thinking. Through this exposure, I learned how to communicate academic and professional experiences on paper and during interviews and slowly began to create an action plan to achieve my goals. Little by little, I felt more prepared and confident applying for jobs and, eventually, graduate school. These actions stemmed from the conversations with faculty and staff, people taking the time to help me navigate my career decision-making and graduate school planning.

Fast forward five years. My role as a professional in career services began at California State University, Monterey Bay, and the experience has been instrumental in supporting students, especially transfer students, with their career endeavors. In addition, my personal and professional experiences have provided a better understanding of the transfer experience and the need for increased engagement in career planning. This chapter highlights ways to increase career engagement through professional experiences.

Transfer Indicators

In recent years, enrollment at community colleges has grown significantly, with students moving on to pursue a baccalaureate degree (Berger & Malaney, 2003; Goebel et al., 2020). According to the National Student Clearinghouse Research Center (2022), transfer enrollment demonstrated more stability in Fall 2021, with a drop of less than 1%

compared to a 9.2% decline in Fall 2020. As mentioned in Chapter 1, longitudinal research on transfer indicates that approximately one third of first-time students transfer institutions at least once as undergraduates (Hossler et al., 2012; Shapiro et al., 2017; Wang et al., 2016). However, research about community college transfer focuses on academic achievement as an indicator of how well students have adjusted at new four-year institutions (Berger & Malaney, 2003) and provides little to no research on career development and career success for this population (see Chapter 1). Addressing several factors can help us to understand and improve the transfer experience, including individual student characteristics, community college experience, and university experiences (Berger & Malaney, 2003). Based on my experiences and professional observations and on feedback from the students whom I have coached as a transfer coordinator, several key indicators differentiate a student who transfers from students who do not, as discussed in the following sections

Timeline

Students who transfer tend to complete many of their lower division courses at the community college, which shortens the time spent at the receiving institution. As a result, students have less time to connect with career-related campus resources, network with peers and professionals, acclimate to clubs and organizations, and involve themselves in alumni-sponsored events—all of which contribute to postgraduate career planning. In addition, the truncated timeline can leave students overwhelmed and missing practical experiences essential for work acclimating. Taking advantage of the plethora of resources and opportunities is essential; however, new transfer students may not always know where to start, so delivering clear roadmaps that lead to these resources is key.

Major Declaration

Many students who transfer know what academic path they want to pursue upon acceptance to their receiving institution. Therefore, they enter the receiving institution with a clear understanding of their academic focus. However, this does not mean that students who transfer understand how their chosen academic path translates to the world of work. Students who transfer enter the receiving institution with varied levels of career guidance—some students understand the potential career pathways, while others are less aware and lack the support or resources to gain insights into various career options. For example, depending on the time of transfer, students may have missed major declaration fairs or "What to do with a major in?" fairs that help students discern career options for chosen majors. Missing these connection events can put students who transfer at a disadvantage if they do not enter their receiving institutions with this information and do not make the connection or are not offered support after transferring. Therefore, ongoing academic-to-career-pathway advising is essential for students who transfer.

Transition From Sending to Receiving Institution

Students who transfer typically move from smaller community colleges (sending institutions) to larger four-year institutions (receiving institutions). Others move from public school environments to private ones. Transferring from a familiar experience to an unfamiliar one, regardless of size, scope, or location, causes all students, and especially students who transfer, to feel intimidated by the unfamiliar environment. These students are unaware of where to seek support and who can help them navigate this unfamiliar, complex system; the experience can be confusing and overwhelming. In addition, career centers do not always have access to students transferring into their university because the priority from the receiving institution is helping students get oriented to the college itself and, more specifically, within the academic major. Some institutions do not have the resource capacity to support high student caseloads. Others do not have systems or programs designed to connect with students who transfer—a population less inclined to seek direct, individual support without being prompted.

Students who transfer are highly motivated to achieve the goal of obtaining a bachelor's degree. However, engagement related to their career endeavors may come too late in the transfer experience, causing a lack of awareness, support, and preparation. Partnerships among the career center, admissions office, new-student programs, and students and families can serve as a comprehensive approach that engages students who transfer successfully from sending to receiving institutions and beyond.

Transfer Insights

Community colleges serve as the gateway to a four-year degree for many students who transfer (Maliszewski Lukszo & Hayes, 2019). While the reasons for transferring vary among students (e.g., selecting the college setting that best fits their interests, academic ability, and educational and career aspirations), students look at what each college offers. In addition, affordable education and being a "good fit" with the campus are important to many students, regardless of the transfer pattern (see the Introduction to this book).

An analysis by the National Student Clearinghouse indicated that 45% of students who transferred from community colleges completed bachelor's degrees at the end of the 2010–2011 academic year (Handel, 2013). Additionally, in 2015–2016, 49% of students who completed a bachelor's degree attended a community college at least once within the previous 10 years (Maliszewski Lukszo & Hayes, 2019). The number of students reporting as having transferred is significant for receiving institutions because the figure suggests the possible gap between these students' academic planning and career preparation.

The transfer literature focuses on strategies to ease transitions from two-year to four-year colleges, completion rates of students who transfer to the receiving institution, academic performance, and understanding of the experience surrounding a student who transfers.

However, little research touches on what institutions currently do to support students who transfer concerning their career development needs at the sending and receiving institutions. Nor does the literature provide details and insights on best practices, programming, or how to support the needs related to this transition. Career centers facilitate career awareness, preparation, and planning—activities currently missing from the integration process for students who transfer.

Collaborative Relationships

California State University, Monterey Bay (CSUMB) is a four-year public university that is part of the California State University (CSU) system. As a growing campus, CSUMB's priorities focus on student success, inclusive excellence, stewardship, global engagement, and organizational learning. These priorities guide CSUMB's processes and decision-making to accomplish their strategic plans for their students and community. They annually host approximately 7,500 students from diverse backgrounds who pursue an educational experience through personal attention in small classes in more than 25 undergraduate and 9 graduate majors (California State University, Monterey Bay, n.d.). Between 900 and 1,083 of these 7,500 students have transferred from Monterey County and other counties in California.

Establishing Partnerships: Career Center and the Educational Opportunity Program

The Career Center at CSUMB is an opt-in service that acts as a resource for students to help with their professional development and engagement with employers. As an opt-in option, students are not required to engage with the career center. As a result, many students do not realize the benefits of career preparation.

The Career Center has established long-lasting partnerships with campus stakeholders to overcome this lack of awareness of services and programs that support students' career readiness. Partnerships range from classroom visits in psychology classes to first-year and second-year seminar course collaborations. For many students, classroom interactions are the first opportunities to hear about the Career Center. All touchpoints allow the Career Center to educate students about services and support related to career readiness and ways that the staff can help them prepare for their futures. Career Center interactions are intentionally designed to help students visualize their futures by facilitating conversations and activities related to making informed decisions about their major and career, understanding and identifying skills learned in an out of the classroom, and translating those skills and experience into tangible workplace examples during interviews with employers.

Throughout the campus community, the Career Center advocates the importance of career decision-making during a student's educational journey. While this effort can sometimes be uncoordinated, the CSUMB Career Center has successfully established pockets of career champions who are faculty, staff, and special programming departments. One partnership is with the Educational Opportunity Program (EOP), which serves a population of students from underserved backgrounds. EOP is a federal outreach and student-services initiative, one of eight programs under TRIO. These programs identify and provide services for individuals from disadvantaged backgrounds, such as low-income individuals, first-generation college students, and individuals with disabilities, to support their progress through the academic pipeline from middle school to postbaccalaureate completion (U.S. Department of Education, 2022).

At CSUMB, the EOP program serves as an upward mobility vehicle for students who are newly admitted or transferred into the CSU system. The program includes efforts to increase access, retention, and academic success for California's historically minoritized student populations. The program is open to first-year and community college students who transfer and welcomes a new cohort every fall term. Each student admitted into EOP attends an orientation to gain more in-depth knowledge about the program and expectations. The student contract outlines the program requirements and responsibilities, including course completion, participation in EOP and campus activities, academic and career workshops, meeting with an EOP counselor each semester, and attending the required summer Transfer Bridge program for transfer admits. In addition, accepted students receive details about the services offered to help facilitate a smooth transition from sending to receiving institution.

Access, advocacy, support services, and EOP grants are the program's cornerstones, which are aimed at helping students succeed throughout their college experience (CSUMB, 2021). By providing access to enrich student engagement, the program is a vehicle for increasing student success. According to Kuh (2008), to enhance students' engagement and increase student success, an institution must make it possible for them to participate in high-impact programs during their undergraduate program. Transfer students in the EOP program are offered various ways to engage in high-impact programs, including partnership between EOP and the Career Center, service-learning engagements, and interacting with employers at career services events.

In addition, the program offers academic advising, one-on-one peer mentoring, skill development, and enrichment programs like Summer Bridge and Transfer Bridge. Transfer Bridge is a high-impact practice (HIP) summer program available for incoming students who transfer. HIP programs are widely tested teaching and learning practices that are proven beneficial for college students from diverse backgrounds, especially underserved students. Research shows that students who engage in HIPs have a higher chance of retaining at an institution than students who do not engage in this type of programming (American Association of College and Universities, 2022).

Students who transfer receive an introduction to the university and its resources, which helps create a successful transition to their new campus. Transfer Bridge connects students to campus stakeholders such as faculty, staff, and various departments to encourage early interaction. In addition, the Career Center has been a frequent guest, as the EOP counselor and the Career Center promote early career engagement. Evaluation of the program is ongoing through qualitative assessments such as focus groups, individual interviews, and post-program reviews. If the program leaders notice a decrease in student engagement, adjustments to program content can be made that are better tailored to student needs related to graduate school planning, study skills, and other academic and career development topics. For example, a noticeable drop in program engagement with upper level students led the EOP to redesign offerings, such as adding workshops on life after graduation and graduate school preparation. The EOP counselor decided to implement these components into contracts for students who transfer, including participation in three academic and/or career development activities during their junior and senior years. Similar to early transfers, upper-division transfers sign a student contract that outlines program requirements and requires selecting a career path, including career events in which they will participate. These pathways help students to think about their career development the moment they step on campus and begin their career planning rather than to wait until the semester before graduation. In addition, the Career Center has worked with EOP to facilitate career development workshops, employer events, and one-on-one career counselors for their students.

Students who transfer, especially those in EOP, may have experienced very few conversations about career planning. The EOP program that I participated in as a community college student concentrated solely on academic performance and preparing for transfer from sending to receiving institution. This lack of focus on career planning is one of the reasons I was underprepared for my transfer. As a career counselor, I notice common challenges for students who transfer, including (a) adapting to the new university setting, (b) understanding the academic expectations of faculty, (c) managing personal and work responsibilities outside of the classroom, (d) creating a sense of belonging and engagement on campus, (e) understanding campus resources, and (f) learning how to prepare for their career and professional aspirations. Grites (2013) shared that academic standards and faculty expectations influence students who transfer and experience a shock from transitioning from one university to another. Students who transfer may face different classroom experiences with class sizes often significantly larger, which requires students to be proactive learners. In addition, classes are often taught or assisted by graduate students who present new classroom structures to navigate. This brief list of experiences can be intimidating and overwhelming. As Grites stated, students attempt to negotiate and acclimate to many differences.

EOP fosters collaborative learning that creates space for students to connect and learn with other peers who are in the same stages of transition. Specifically, students who transfer can engage during the summer before the fall semester through Transfer Bridge. This program is a one-day, nonresidential event to ease the transition from sending to receiving institutions. Students connect to other campus services such as tutoring, undergraduate research, academic advising, and study abroad. Additionally, they gain insight into their academic workload, the academic expectations of their new institution, and postgraduate goal setting and career planning.

During Transfer Bridge, the Career Center facilitates the "Blueprint to Graduation" workshop, which introduces students to early career engagement by helping them connect their academic and career goals. First, students complete a roadmap exercise in which they envision life post-graduation. Next, students conceptualize the steps needed to reach their postgraduate career goals and map out specific engagement opportunities that could take place throughout their junior and senior years, and students brainstorm plans to pursue these opportunities. For example, a student interested in continuing their academic studies in social work may investigate a "day in the life" of a social worker by interviewing a professional or job shadowing someone in the field of social work or family services. Next, the student might learn the different career paths a social worker might take and what it takes to prepare for these pathways, including graduate school planning workshops, clinical practice how-to's, and job fairs.

The Career Center at CSUMB hosts and participates in small and large-scale employer connection events at which students meet with employers and university representatives to learn about career and graduate school opportunities. These events include graduate school information sessions, CSUMB's Graduate and Professional School Fair, and the California Forum for Diversity in Graduate Education, a large graduate school fair that connects students to more than 100 graduate programs across the country. Before students attend these events, the Career Center helps them prepare questions for university representatives to maximize their time at the events and feel less intimidated.

Additionally, all transfer EOP students must meet with the EOP counselor within the first month of the fall semester to build rapport, review the EOP contract, and further discuss the program requirements. This meeting allows the EOP counselor to cultivate a relationship with the student, learn about their academic and career interests, and create a customized career development plan. For example, students transferring as juniors explore their career options and establish career readiness so that by the time senior year arrives, they have the necessary tools, knowledge, and resources to act on their career goals. Career engagement includes resume and cover letter building, job and internship strategies, mock interviewing, and graduate school preparation if these elements are part of their customized career development plan.

The Career Center staff creates space for EOP students who transfer to engage in intentional programming beyond simply checking all the boxes. The program attempts to make lasting connections with faculty and professional staff.

From personal experience as a student who transferred, I know the benefits of career planning can make a significant difference in career growth. My goal as a career counselor is always to help students confidently make connections between their academics and the world of work. Whether students are preparing for the workforce, graduate school, or a slightly less defined future, the career center facilitates a growth mindset and curiosity and provides a safe space for conversations and reflection. Students create a game plan with the action steps and select from career advising tools that foster successful career development, including access to one-on-one coaching sessions, career assessments, workshops, events, and opportunities to engage with employers from various industries. Learning is assessed through post-reflective surveys by asking students to share their experiences. These reflections help the Career Center better understand students' awareness from the learner's perspective (see Hine, 2008). In the most recent reflections (2020–2021), students said they were satisfied with their interactions with the career center and throughout the presentation. However, more formal research efforts are warranted to fully evaluate students' learning, satisfaction, and eventual career success.

Career Education at Ohlone College

Ohlone College is a two-year community college that enrolls over 10,000 students annually at its three campuses: Fremont, Newark, and online (Ohlone College, n.d.). The college offers 189 associate degrees and certificates, including 27 associate degrees for transfer. In 2019, 996 Ohlone students transferred to baccalaureate colleges and universities, including 577 to CSU campuses and 261 to University of California campuses.

In 2019, I transitioned from career advising at CSUMB and started a new endeavor as Transfer Center Coordinator and Career Specialist at Ohlone College. Given my background in career development and experience going through a transfer transition, I was uniquely positioned to support the Transfer Center personally and professionally. Many students seeking transfer inquire about the process—where and how to prepare for transfer, identify transfer paths for majors at specific four-year institutions, or seek guidance exploring transfer programs. As a result, conversations about career planning rarely, if ever, surface. The absence of career conversations reminded me of my experience as a community college student.

Being both a student who transferred and a career center professional, I knew the importance of early career engagement to foster a mindset among students (especially first-generation and low-income students) and that academic decisions connect to career decisions in many ways. From Day One in this new role, I formed connections, built relationships with multiple campus stakeholders, and found ways to interact with students in and out of the classroom. Whenever the Transfer Center was invited into classrooms to present about our transfer services and programs, it was important to spend time discussing career planning. I intended to help students understand that every decision had options and that major declaration was only one piece of the puzzle. Discussions centered on "beginning with the end in mind" (Covey, 2013) by helping students visualize what they want to do in life while at the community college rather than waiting until after they leave to think about or plan for these decisions.

During classroom presentations, students were encouraged to consider ways to prepare for internship opportunities once they transfered to four-year institutions. Discussions included brainstorming how their time at the community college was spent building and sharpening their soft skills and identifying how they gained project management and experience working in teams. In addition, presentations helped educate students about resources and topics with which they were unfamiliar, exposing them to the Career Center and Transfer Center staff. These little connections helped students understand the necessity of early career planning.

In addition to creating relationships with multiple campus partners, the Transfer Center offered drop-in advising, traditional career development workshops related to resumes, cover letter writing, interviewing, networking, creating LinkedIn profiles, and using LinkedIn for job searching and networking. As more students sought services, the need arose to increase access to career engagement and tools. Thus, I proposed to the Career Center a *What Can I Do With This Major* software program. The new resource increased exploration support during one-on-one student meetings, supplementing meaningful connections between major and career pathways.

Lessons Learned and Moving Forward

My experiences as a student who transferred and then became a transfer coordinator have allowed me to engage with students following this same path in myriad ways. Many students who transfer from community college to a four-year institution, like me, have already chosen a major and have a career path in mind but are unaware of where to start their career planning and have little knowledge of operationalizing that career. Prior to the transfer, students focus heavily on completing core courses, and while career and life planning classes are often available, few students take advantage of them. Furthermore, many students who transfer have small networks to rely on to help them navigate the college-to-career transition, something that career professionals know is extremely important for postgraduate and professional success. Finally, students who transfer face a shortened and different completion timeline than more traditional students, heightening their need for career support at the onset of transfer and a readied pace until graduation. Given these lessons learned from my experiences as a student and professional, below are four recommendations to increase transfer support.

Building Buy-In With Institutional Stakeholders

Career support cannot be successful if delivered by the career center in isolation—it must be a concerted effort across campus involving multiple constituents. Buy-in from administrators, faculty, staff, alums, employers, and peers across various levels can lead to tremendous strides in ensuring students who transfer receive support from all areas of campus. From sending to receiving institution, students who transfer need to be connected with continuous support touchpoints. Career champions heighten the importance of career development and raise awareness of career engagement across campus from Day One and throughout the transfer experience.

Early Relationship Building With Students

Career centers can work with the admissions department and new-student programs to identify incoming transfers for early outreach efforts. For example, receiving institutions can design career planning programs, activities, and communication through the lens of students who transfer, keeping in mind that their timeframes, priorities, and career engagement needs may differ from students who did not transfer. Ideas for such programming may include (a) bridge programs, (b) summer boot camps, and (c) major-to-career exploratory programs. In addition, institutions might consider assigning one or two career staff to work directly with this population on a micro and a macro level. Finally, with university support, career services can create partnerships to increase the exposure, experimental learning opportunities, and participation of students who transfer in career engagement, planning, and preparation at entry and during early onboarding.

Identify Campus Programs That Target Transfers

Government-sponsored programs like TRIO or campus-specific programs such as CSUMB's EOP are designed for populations often needing additional services and support to meet graduation requirements. These programs can also support students who transfer, even if they are not designed for or do not target this population. While career development may not be an initial focal point of these programs, career centers have an opportunity to build and establish intentional partnerships that can lead to long-term integration of career services (i.e., CSUMB's Career Center partnership with EOP). A long-term partnership must identify program champions (e.g., directors, counselors, student leaders) and create a strategy around need-based support.

Structured support programs like TRIO are often cohort based, so students have a group of like-minded peers to lean on for support. The discussions are topical and tailored to the populations' needs, often addressing socioeconomic and other inequities that may arise as students navigate the college experience (e.g., professional network, education about student loan repayment, the value of experiential learning). Students participating in structured support programs can gain a wider lens to consider how their career development weaves into their journey before, during, and after college and can close some of the equity gaps in the process.

Collect Data To Tell a Story

With limited research on transfer and career engagement, Career Centers should consider holding focus groups to better understand the career-related experience and needs of students who transfer. Start small by identifying campus programs or groups that work directly with transfers. Then, build partnerships with these enterprises to identify students who transfer and offer incentives to help secure participation. Collecting qualitative and quantitative data on career engagement will help colleges understand the needs of students who transfer and understand whether they are prepared for the jobs they land following graduation.

In addition, collecting surveys from career development workshops helps measure career readiness. Questions may include "What does career support look like for students who transfer?" "Where are students in their career development and planning journey at the time of transfer?" "How have students who transfer engaged in career exploration in and out of the classroom?", and "How does the student feel prepared for the world of work?" Collecting data will inform the university of the ways in which the campus is creating a platform for holistic development and engagement of students who transfer and, more important, where there is room for growth.

Final Thoughts on Career Engagement

Career engagement is essential to the holistic development of college students, especially those transferring from one college to another. Now, more than ever, universities are instrumental in elevating career conversations as part of students' educational journey and championing a workforce with career-ready students. It is important to hone in on the transfer student capital as it is critical to building students' self-efficacy, a lens for understanding the sources of capital that students use to navigate a transfer experience (Maliszewski Lukszo & Hayes, 2019). Understanding transfer student capital can provide a framework for community colleges and four-year institutions to support transfer while incorporating career conversations and engagement across the campus experience.

To increase the career development experiences of students who transfer, career centers may benefit by identifying their campus partners and programs to track and measure engagement. Creating partnerships and tracking touchpoints will help practitioners identify where students who transfer are in their career journey and where engagement touchpoints need to increase. For example, becoming familiar with the National Association of Colleges and Employers (NACE), which employs various resources and collects data to highlight trends and best practices, can help integrate career readiness in and out of the classroom. Colleges can explore and incorporate NACE's (2021) eight career readiness competencies that serve as a foundation to prepare college students for success in the workplace and beyond. Including these in dialogue about academics with faculty can help encourage the institution to move to a place that enriches its overall educational journey with a career-readiness lens.

Community colleges, as sending institutions, have an excellent opportunity to plant the seed of the importance of career development for students who plan on transferring to a receiving institution. Furthermore, while that is always hope and not a victory, we can still create a vision and celebrate the wins for our students and those who champion career engagement early, often, and after a student's time in college.

Conclusion

To fully integrate career development into a student's educational journey, it is important to acknowledge areas that the university can improve to ensure that the needs of students who transfer are met. Engaging with students who transfer early and often, developing cross-campus partnerships, and educating campus stakeholders about the career center's offerings and resources is a solid first step. Helping students and campus partners understand the benefits of engaging with career services can build a culture that includes "career" naturally and seamlessly into academic discussions and planning. Teaching students how to articulate the skills and experiences they gain from the classroom, extracurricular activities, and work experiences leads them one step closer to entering the workforce confidently.

References

American Association of Colleges and Universities. (2022). *High-Impact practices.* https://www.aacu.org/trending-topics/high-impact

Berger, J. B., & Malaney, G. D. (2003). Assessing the transition of transfer students from community colleges to a university. *NASPA Journal, 40*(4), 3–10. https://doi.org/10.2202/0027-6014.1277

California State University, Monterey Bay (CSUMB). (n.d.). (2021). *Educational Opportunity Program.* https://csumb.edu/eop

California State University, Monterey Bay. (2022). *About CSUMB | California State University, Monterey Bay.* Retrieved February 21, 2022, from https://csumb.edu/about/

California State University, Monterey Bay. (n.d.). *Mission and strategic plan | California State University, Monterey Bay.* Retrieved November 2, 2022, from https://csumb.edu/about/mission-strategic-plan/

Convey, S. R. (2013). Habit 2: Begin with the end in mind: Principles of personal leadership. *The 7 habits of highly effective people: Powerful lessons in personal changes* (25th anniversary ed., pp. 116–126). Simon & Schuster.

Goebel, C., Strauss, D., & Hesel, R. (2020, April). *Looking ahead to Fall 2020: How COVID-19 continues to influence the choice of college-going students* [Special edition]. Art and Science Group, LLC. https://www.artsci.com/studentpoll-covid-19-edition-2

Grites, T. J. (2013). Successful transition from two-year to four-year institutions. In J. L. Marling (Ed.), *Collegiate transfer: Navigating the new normal* (pp. 61–68). Jossey-Bass. https://doi.org/10.1002/he.20057

Handel, S. J. (2013). The transfer moment: The pivotal partnership between community college and four-year institutions in securing the nation's college completion agenda. In J. L. Marling (Ed.), *Collegiate transfer: Navigating the new normal* (pp. 5–15). Jossey-Bass. https://doi.org/10.1002/he.20052

Hine, A. (2008). *Mirroring effective education through mentoring, metacognition and self-reflection* [Paper presentation]. Annual Conference of the AARE, Sydney, Australia. https://www.aare.edu.au/data/publications/2000/hin00017.pdf

Hossler, D., Shapiro, D., Dundar, A., Ziskin, M., Chen, J., Zerquera, D., & Torres, V. (2012, February). *Transfer and mobility: A national view of pre-degree student movement in postsecondary institutions* (Signature Report No. 2). National Student Clearinghouse Research Center.

Kuh, G. D. (2008). Excerpt from high-impact educational practices: What they are, who has access to them, and why they matter. *Association of American Colleges and Universities, 14*(3), 28–29.

Maliszewski Lukszo, C., & Hayes, S. (2019). Facilitating transfer student success: Exploring sources of transfer student capital. *Community College Review, 48*(1), 31–54. https://doi.org/10.1177/0091552119876017

National Association of Colleges and Employers (NACE). (2021, January 3). *Competencies for a career-ready workforce.* https://www.naceweb.org/career-readiness/competencies/career-readiness-defined/

National Association of Colleges and Employers. (2022). *What is career readiness?* Retrieved January 2, 2022, from https://www.naceweb.org/career-readiness/competencies/career-readiness-defined/

Ohlone College. (n.d.). *Quick facts.* https://www.ohlone.edu/quick-facts

Shapiro, D., Dundar, A., Huie, F., Wakhungu, P.K., Yuan, X., Nathan, A., & Hwang, Y. (2017, September). *Tracking transfer: Measures of effectiveness in helping community college students to complete bachelor's degrees* (Signature Report No. 13). National Student Clearinghouse Research Center. https://files.eric.ed.gov/fulltext/ED580214.pdf

U.S. Department of Education. (2022). *Federal TRIO programs.* Office of Postsecondary Education. https://www2.ed.gov/about/offices/list/ope/trio/index.html

Wang, X., Wickersham, K., & Sun, N. (2016). The evolving landscape of transfer research: Reconciling what we know in preparation for a new era of heightened promise and complexity. *New Directions for Institutional Research, 170,* 115–121. https://doi.org/10.1002/ir.20189

CHAPTER FOUR

A Case for Life Design:
An Innovative Seminar To Foster Success for Students Who Transfer Through Career Exploration, Agency, and Readiness

Heather A. Butler and Marc C. Hunsaker

> "This was the perfect class for me because I actually figured out what I wanted to do."
>
> – Ivett

> "This class motivated me to achieve my goals … before this class, I was pretty depressed."
>
> – Anthony

Career exploration and development are critical parts of emerging adulthood. The term "emerging adulthood" describes a time in modern societies during which young adults explore potential roles they want to fulfill, careers they want to embark on, and lifestyles they want to lead (Arnett, 2000). This transition is difficult, no matter the size of the transition, how long the transition takes, or how consequential the changes to one's life. Transitioning from college into a first professional job is especially difficult for college students. Many college students report anxiety and depression about the future (Rottinghaus et al., 2009) as they wrestle with the questions *What do I want to do for the rest of my life?* and *Will I be able to get a job after graduation?*

This chapter presents a case for an innovative course, Design Your Life (DYL), which helps students through the transfer transition by promoting career exploration, career agency, and career readiness. The course is impressive in terms of both its pedagogy and its outcomes. We argue that this DYL course would provide students navigating a transfer with a suite of valuable skills, mindsets, and supports that would enable them to succeed and overcome some of the unique challenges they will face as they transfer into their new institutions.

Students Who Transfer: Contexts and Outcomes

In 2015, just over half of all students who started college finished with degrees (Shapiro et al., 2015). Such findings made student success, particularly retention and persistence, an area of concern for higher education administrators and researchers. Recent research suggests that this focus on student success is beginning to pay off as college graduation rates slowly improve (Causey et al., 2022). Another less commonly known statistic is that over a third of students (37.2%) completing bachelor's degrees at four-year institutions are students who have transferred from one institution to another (Shapiro et al., 2015). A growing body of research indicates that transferring between higher education institutions has become relatively commonplace; the data have led scholars to encourage colleges and universities to accept that nontraditional pathways are becoming the new normal.

Unique Challenges Faced by Students Who Transfer

Students who transfer face many unique challenges in higher education. Unfortunately, most university policies and programs overly focus on the involvement and outcomes of native students, often at the expense of students who transfer (Manning et al., 2013). The pervasiveness of this "native student paradigm," which ignores the needs of students who transfer (Lanaan et al., 2011), likely contributes to academic "transfer shock" (Hills, 1965) and a range of other systemic challenges prompted by the transfer as students attempt to be successful in their new institutions. Studies have demonstrated the lack of institutional services and support that are provided to students who transfer (Tobolowsky & Cox, 2012) and have shown that these students are often unaware of available supports (Quaye et al., 2020), including career development resources and opportunities. Many students who transfer have reported experiencing academically oriented challenges that complicate their degree completion, including poor academic advising and difficulty transferring credits (Laanan et al., 2010). Unfortunately, many institutions lack awareness about the challenges and outcomes resulting from the transfer experience, and many receiving institutions fail to identify or to consistently monitor students after matriculation (Jenkins & Fink, 2016). This lack of resource awareness and institutional support can cause students who transfer to struggle to adjust to the culture of their new college environments. In turn, maladjustment can lead to lower levels of campus engagement and unsatisfactory academic performance (Townsend & Wilson, 2006).

Lack of campus support and engagement correlates with less-than-desirable outcomes among students who experience a transfer. For example, while 69% of students who initiate their studies at four-year public institutions will earn bachelor's degrees within 6 years, only 42% of students who vertically transfer to a four-year institution will accomplish the same (Causey et al., 2022). Additionally, on average, students vertically transferring from a two-year college will lose approximately eight credits (~ 20%) at their new institution

(Simone, 2014). Challenges like this also negatively affect college outcomes. For example, students who vertically transfer and obtain a bachelor's degree have an average time to degree of 5.4 years, an entire year longer than those who did not transfer (Li, 2010).

A deeper look into retention data trends on the transfer experience reveals deep inequities within an already shocking problem. Research on the socio-demographics of students who transfer indicates that the systemic challenges may disproportionately affect students of color (Crisp & Nuñez, 2014). The vertical transfer process represents a viable pathway to a bachelor's degree for many students, particularly for students from underrepresented and historically marginalized groups. National research data has shown that many minority students are likely to begin postsecondary education at community colleges (Chronicle of Higher Education, 2021; Nuñez & Elizondo, 2013). In California, the state with the nation's largest postsecondary system (and the site of the research data presented in this chapter), these numbers are even more striking: approximately 69% of Latino students and 65% of Black students begin their postsecondary education at community colleges, compared to 60% of White students and 42% of Asian students (Gandara et al., 2012). Findings like this have revealed a "racial transfer gap" among students who transfer and complete a degree and/or transfer to a four-year college (Martinez-Wenzl & Marquez, 2012, p. 6). For example, one national data set shows that, among first-generation students, 49% of White students and 61% of Asian students successfully earned a degree or certificate and/or transferred to a four-year institution within six years, while only 40% of Black students and 35% of Latino students accomplished similar outcomes (U.S. Department of Education, 2012). It is evident that this racial transfer gap is present in California as well—30% of White students and 41% of Asian students engaged in vertical transfer, but only 17% of Latino students and 19% of Black students transferred to four-year institutions after enrolling in a community college (Sengupta & Jepsen, 2006).

The downward trends and underlying inequities in transfer outcomes and experiences in college will likely negatively affect post-college outcomes. Research has shown that completing a bachelor's degree correlates with many positive post-college benefits, especially those associated with career success. For example, research suggests that bachelor's degree holders have broader career options and more job security (Ma et al., 2019), higher levels of income (Carnevale et al., 2015; Torpey, 2021), and more satisfaction with their work (Pew Research Center, 2016) than people without degrees. The evidence is clear: Success in college is deeply linked to career success after college. Therefore, sending and receiving institutions must intentionally navigate students through a successful transfer transition. Doing so will require higher education leaders to develop greater awareness of the challenges faced by students who transfer and to employ support strategies designed to help them overcome these challenges.

Success Strategies From Students Who Transfer

Researchers have sought to understand the factors that effectively support students who transfer and contribute to their success. For example, Laanan (1998, 2004) created the Laanan-Transfer Students' Questionnaire (L-TSQ) to explore the social, psychological, and institutional factors that helped community college students successfully transfer to their four-year institutions. Laanan (2007) developed his "transfer student capital" (TSC) construct to describe the essential skills and knowledge students need to experience success as they transfer from two-year to four-year institutions. To effectively gain TSC, transfer students must build cultural and social capital through robust engagement with their new campuses and the various ecological and organizational influences that shape the campus culture of the receiving institutions (Laanan et al., 2010).

While most of the research and programming on the transfer process has focused primarily on students' actions in acquiring the skills and knowledge to navigate their transfer successfully, we have chosen to focus on organizational influences and the oft-neglected role of the receiving institution in supporting transfer success. Based on the findings outlined here, we argue that colleges and universities have an ethical obligation to create institutional policies and targeted programming designed to facilitate the development of TSC for the nonnative students they are welcoming (and recruiting) into their schools (Townsend & Wilson, 2008–2009). This ethical obligation to support students who transfer more intentionally and effectively comes into sharper focus when considering the high numbers of underrepresented minority community college students who have expressed the desire to transfer to a four-year institution and who see a bachelor's degree as an opportunity to further their own life and career success.

For the remainder of this chapter, we argue that colleges and universities should draw upon an increasingly popular methodology called "life design" (Burnett & Evans, 2016) to support students and equip them to achieve successful outcomes during the transfer. We describe how the life design approach is uniquely suited to promote student capital and career development agency while helping to mitigate some common challenges associated with transfer shock.

Life Design for Students Who Transfer

Some institutions have sought to improve transfer success through a high-impact practice (HIP) known as the first-year experience or through transfer seminar courses (Kuh, 2008). Such courses help new students develop cultural and organizational knowledge and a more profound sense of social belonging at their new institution. Based on our experiences teaching DYL courses and assessment data collected by the primary author, we contend that a life design focus would be an excellent way for colleges and universities to make transfer seminars even more impactful.

The Importance of Career Agency Development

According to Bandura (1989), human agency is "the capacity to exercise control over one's thought processes, motivation, and action," through which "people can effect change in themselves and their situations through their efforts" (p. 1175). Bandura investigated the mechanisms that explain how we develop agency, including self-efficacy beliefs, goal representations, and anticipated outcomes. Self-efficacy, the belief that one's ability to exert control and affect one's life outcomes, is the most important contributor to agency.

Possessing career development agency means having the ability to exercise control over thoughts, motivation, and actions relating to pursuing one's vocation. People who expect their efforts will be successful are, in fact, more successful. A study on male college graduates in Germany who had high expectations of success received more job offers (Oettingen & Mayer, 2002). It is important to note that positive self-talk alone is insufficient for agency development. True self-efficacy builds through mastery experiences. When students perform actions and receive formative feedback about their performance, they have space to improve. Self-efficacy is also encouraged through vicarious mastery experiences, such as hearing inspirational stories of others in the domain or learning from a professional mentor.

Self-efficacy develops from four sources: mastery experiences, vicarious learning experiences, social support, and physiological and emotional states (Bandura, 1989). For students to truly believe in themselves, they need evidence that they can perform, which comes from prior performance or the support of people they trust. Scott and Ciani (2008) assessed whether an undergraduate course to enhance the four sources of self-efficacy increased students' career self-efficacy. Students who took the course participated in a variety of career development activities. For instance, they participated in career-readiness workshops, consulted with the university's career center, listened to professionals on a career panel talk about their experiences, had discussions with instructors and classmates, and learned about anxiety management. The results indicated that students who took the course had higher self-efficacy upon completion than when they began. The impact was especially strong for women. These findings were corroborated by research on the DYL courses in which students' career-related self-efficacy was improved by participating (Bono et al., 2018; Butler, 2019; Butler & Bono, 2018; Butler et al., 2018, 2020).

Design Thinking: A Framework for Success Among Students Who Transfer

To understand the life design methodology, one must understand the framework that undergirds it: design thinking. Design thinking is a unique approach to solving problems; designers follow a methodology to develop innovative new products, such as the latest smart gadget or a more ergonomic chair. The design thinking process consists of six steps (accept, empathize, define, ideate, prototype, and test) and a set of important mindsets (reframing, radical collaboration, curiosity, mindfulness of process, and a bias toward action; Burnett & Evans, 2016). The steps need not be linear (see Figure 4.1); instead, designers are encouraged to revisit earlier steps when the outcome is not innovative, delightful, efficient, or effective enough.

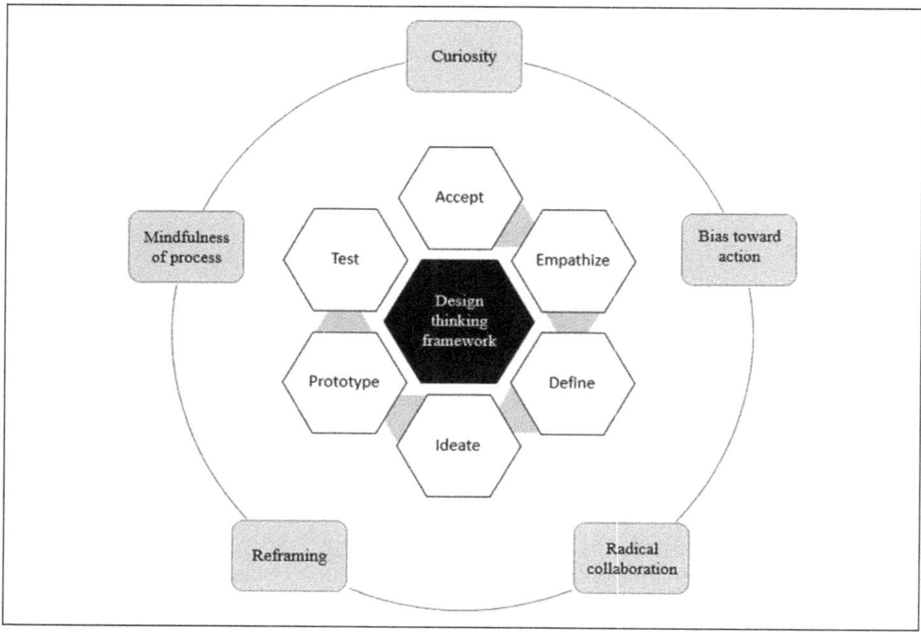

Figure 4.1. The Design Thinking Framework and Mindsets (Adapted From Burnett & Evans, 2016)

The first step in the design thinking process is *acceptance*, which involves identifying and accepting the unchangeable variables and constraints that frame the problem. In the DYL course, instructors spend time asking students to identify a series of common college and career myths, assumptions about college and life after college that many students have uncritically inherited and unconsciously hold (e.g., my major determines or defines career options, my first job will be my forever job, I should have it all figured out by now). Many of these myths do not align with reality and, as such, act as dysfunctional beliefs that keep students feeling stuck, anxious, and fearful about the future. For example, many students put off researching possible careers out of fear that they will make the wrong decision (Haghbin et al., 2012). When students who transfer are helped to identify and correct these college and career myths, they are better positioned to accept the reality of an unknowable future and to accept any true constraints (i.e., "gravity problems") they might have as they consider what their lives in and after college might look like (e.g., having children, needing to financially support themselves or others while in college). The purpose of this initial phase is to help students accept the things they cannot change, question their assumptions about what those factors are, and cultivate curiosity about the pathways and choices they might take as they journey through and from college.

The second step is *empathy*. In this step, students practice empathizing with themselves, each other, and their employers through a series of challenging exercises. Students explore the unique challenges of first-generation college students, women, and underrepresented minorities in school and the workplace. Through this exploration, students practice active listening and critical thinking as they share and consider the perspective of others (Halpern, 2014). They consider what employers are looking for in a potential employee and explore research on the topic, including career readiness competencies (National Association of Colleges and Employers, 2021). Students are then asked to compare their career preparedness to the ideal applicant and incorporate the missing elements into their college and career action plans. Through activities such as "good time journaling" (Burnett & Evans, 2016), students learn to empathize with themselves and pay close attention to the activities and environments that give (or take) their energy, prompt deep engagement (or lack thereof), and identify when and where they find themselves in a state of flow (Csikszentmihalyi, 1990). Once students have identified their primary energy-giving (and draining) activities, they are asked to visualize their energy and engagement patterns on a timeline, reflect on patterns, and make changes to maximize their energy and engagement. These empathy activities would be valuable for helping mitigate the academic 'transfer shock' many students experience as they transfer into their new institutions. By empathizing with themselves, students are encouraged to reflect, identify, and address some of the academic challenges they may face in their new environments (e.g., organizing time, study habits, course difficulty).

The third step is *defining* a point of view. In this step, students define their worldview (e.g., What is my purpose? Why are we on this earth?) and their work view (Why do I work? What is worth doing?). Researchers have found that a person's worldview commitments are often central in forming the meaning-making frameworks that shape the fundamental ways they see their work and themselves as workers (Park, 2012). Research has also shown that people are likely to find greater meaning in their work when they perceive coherence between their core commitments (e.g., beliefs, values, orientations) and their life and career goals (Dik et al., 2013). The DYL curriculum asks students to reflect on their worldviews and work views to identify points of synergy between them. In doing so, students construct a personal inner compass that provides a sense of direction and a set of meaningful criteria to identify some of the personal and professional goals that are important to them. This activity helps students develop career agency by asking them before they transfer to clearly define (or redefine) what a successful and joyful life, career, and college experience would look like, thus offering a sense of clarity as they transition through this journey.

The fourth step is *ideation*, during which students learn to brainstorm effectively and to generate ideas for multiple career pathways or possible futures. It is easy to gravitate toward judgment during brainstorming sessions when practicality or financial constraints appear too early in the process. Judgment hinders the formation of new, creative solutions. Osborne (1953) said, "It's easier to tame down a wild idea than it is to invigorate a weak one" (p. 320). Accordingly, designers celebrate wild ideas and extract new insights about potential solutions to their problems. In DYL courses, students engage in ideation and consider their wild ideas through activities like Odyssey Planning (Burnett & Evans, 2016), in which they imagine three lives they could lead beyond college that would be exciting and meaningful to them. The Odyssey Planning tools ask students to articulate a series of major milestones they want to experience/achieve across a five-year timeline for each plan. The timeline necessarily involves their college years and helps students who transfer to intentionally and creatively think about their desired goals for their college experience and to consider how their time in college might connect to and prepare them for their desired life and career goals after college. The Odyssey Planning tools also could become artifacts that students who transfer could share with others (e.g., faculty, advisors) to discuss how best to use their time in college to reach their goals.

The fifth step is *prototyping*. In product design, prototyping means building a cheap and quick product model to be viewed by various stakeholders for feedback and further reiteration. Prototyping typically involves conversations or informational interviews, volunteer experiences, shadowing professionals, and student internships. In DYL classes, prototype ideation is the subject of group brainstorming, which helps students become aware of the wide range of opportunities and possibilities at their institutions. Group prototyping activities include ways to crowdsource ideas (from faculty, staff, and peers) about how students can leverage their college experience to explore, refine, and prepare for their life and career goals. As described previously, group prototyping activities could help students who transfer better understand how to engage in the campus culture effectively and to leverage campus resources and opportunities to explore and progress toward their goals. Understanding includes connecting what students learn in their courses and how it might benefit their lives after college. Used thoughtfully, this activity could help students establish transfer capital and help them see that their college experience should be viewed as a suite of available resources and opportunities instead of a series of requirements to be checked off.

The final step is *testing*. Students put their prototypes into action during testing, reflect on the experience, and use that information to move forward or redesign their plan. This stage of the design thinking process is critical because it provides feedback to the student that is quickly gathered and inexpensive. For example, students might do an internship, job shadow, or conduct a company site visit. Through these activities, students obtain information that grounds their goals or challenges them to rethink their plans while still in school. Testing out their life and career choices soon after transferring to their receiving institutions could give students greater confidence in their goals and could reinforce engagement with many career development resources that colleges offer.

Both of us (the authors of this chapter) have seen students bounce into our classrooms, excited to share their prototype experiences. In other instances, students have returned to the previous stages in the design thinking process after discovering their desired work environment was no longer a good fit. For example, students interested in providing mental health services to incarcerated populations are encouraged to visit early for this exact reason. Some come away confident in their choice and well-prepared for the challenge, while others realize that they would be miserable working in that environment in the long term. Either way, the testing process allows students to learn more about various careers that may or may not work for them.

Mindsets for the Success of Students Who Transfer

The design thinking process also emphasizes five important mindsets: reframing, radical collaboration, curiosity, process mindfulness, and a bias toward action (Burnett & Evans, 2016). Each of these mindsets, and the design experiences that regularly promote their development, would be tremendously valuable for fostering the success of students who transfer both in and after college.

The first mindset, *reframing*, involves rethinking the parameters of the problem. In psychology, the "problem space" (Newell & Simon, 1972) is the metaphorical box created when the problem is considered with boundaries and parameters set by situational constraints such as budget, ethics, history, and feasibility. Reframing involves rethinking the problem space or how you have defined the problem. This mindset is especially helpful when solutions to problems are too limited or not innovative enough to be good solutions. A classic example is a simple math problem suggested by Seelig (2012) in her book about creativity, *InGenius*, and her talk to Google employees (Seelig, 2012). She asks the reader, "What is 5 + 5?" When framed this way, this problem has only one solution. When reframed as "What two numbers add up to 10?" the problem space changes, and the number of possible solutions to the problem changes as well. Reframing is one way that designers get unstuck. They examine the parameters of the problem and the problem space and think of new ways to frame the problem. For example, in the DYL classes, students regularly engage in critical thinking by reframing common assumptions about college and life after college. This exercise helps them begin to identify dysfunctional beliefs that keep them stuck. Reframing can be especially beneficial for students who transfer, helping them to critically examine the purpose of college and to consider questions such as "How could college help me reach my goals?" instead of "What do I need to graduate?".

As described previously, the DYL course identifies and reframes a series of common college and career myths and replaces them with marketplace realities. Reframing college and career-related dysfunctional beliefs is arguably one of the most beneficial parts of the course. Instructors continually reinforce some of the most memorable takeaways (e.g., major does not equal career, your first job is not your forever job, you don't have to have it all figured out right now, there is no perfect career). By regularly reframing these kinds of college and career myths throughout the DYL course, both instructors have observed students exhibiting greater clarity, confidence, and curiosity about their futures and more appreciation for how their college experience affords them opportunities to explore and make progress toward their life and career goals.

Radical collaboration involves appreciating diverse perspectives in problem solving. Designers frequently pull together teams from different backgrounds (e.g., engineers, psychologists, artists) and encourage these teams to take different perspectives in finding solutions to problems. For example, you may have thought of several solutions when the math problem was framed in terms of what two numbers add up to 10, such as 1 and 9 or 2 and 8. Did you consider negative numbers that could be added together to equal 10? Perhaps someone from a different background or perspective would have, and by doing so, they would have increased the number of solutions to your problem. Radical collaboration is an antidote to groupthink (Janis, 1971), a concept in psychology used to explain how a group of people can be so invested in group harmony, conformity, or consensus that they do not think critically about the problem. When groupthink occurs, negative or dysfunctional outcomes are likely to follow. Radical collaboration occurs when diversity of perspective is valued and encouraged and when the group leader invites critical evaluation for the sake of innovation. Collaborative classroom activities to facilitate this mindset can be extremely valuable for students who transfer, in particular activities that require students to work with and alongside their classmates regularly. Collaborative classroom activities build relationships with peers and create intentionally structured opportunities for new students to develop engagement habits, social capital, and critical networks as they transfer into their new environments and throughout their college experience.

The *curiosity* mindset asks students to approach problems with inquisitiveness. Most educational systems ask students to spend an enormous amount of time practicing convergent thinking, narrowing down options, and selecting the most well-established answer (Guilford, 1988). Students spend ample time practicing this skill and less time practicing its opposite: divergent thinking. Creative thinking is divergent thinking (Halpern, 2014). Students use their curiosity about their future profession and life in DYL courses by exploring their options. This career and life exploration involves two critical thinking skills, questioning assumptions and examining source credibility. They question assumptions about their professional choices and examine where they obtained information about these choices and the credibility of the sources. Students have many dysfunctional career beliefs perpetuated by society, friends and family members, and television depictions of certain professions. For example, a student once mentioned she dreamed of being a criminal profiler and going to crime scenes to collect forensic evidence. She was shocked when she learned that criminal profilers do not go to active crime scenes or collect forensic evidence. After researching career options and obtaining accurate information from reliable sources, she identified her new "dream" profession as a forensic psychologist. After that, she took steps toward pursuing the graduate degree needed to achieve her goal. These discoveries provide students who transfer opportunities to seek and receive guidance and/or retraining while in school, and by doing so, they become aware of the institutional resources available.

Being mindful refers to "the skill of paying close attention to what is happening in the present moment in the mind, body and external environment, nonjudgmentally and with an attitude of curiosity and openness" (Newman, 2016, p. xi). In design thinking, being mindful of the process means you are consciously aware of the stage of the design thinking process you are in, your goals, and where you want to go. The design thinking process can be laborious and frustrating at times. Students taking the DYL course are encouraged to empathize with themselves and with their place in the process and are asked to adopt a beginner mindset to remain curious and open. Helping students who transfer develop mindfulness skills could help them be more aware of and patient with this part of the college process, giving themselves grace and responding strategically when specific challenges arise.

The final mindset is a *bias toward action*. Put simply, designers do. They build prototypes, learn from them, and then build new prototypes. Frequently we get stuck in our thoughts in what is referred to as "analysis paralysis" (Zuckerberg, 2008). We invest time thinking about the decisions and researching possible options but never act. The more important the decision, the more likely we get stuck because the decision has consequences. Paradoxically, the more options we have, the less likely we will decide at all. In an elegant test of this theory, Iyengar and Lepper (2000) presented grocery store shoppers with either 24 or 6 different flavors of jam. They recorded how many shoppers stopped to try a sample and how many bought one of the jams. One might think that with 24 jam possibilities, more shoppers would have found a jam they liked, resulting in more purchases. However, paradoxically, the opposite occurred. Though more shoppers stopped to sample the 24 jams, fewer made a purchase. It seems that decision-making is more difficult when too many choices are provided because each option often has a feature that we like, and entertaining and choosing one option means losing the feature of the option we did not choose. Accordingly, if my choice is between strawberry or grape jam, the decision is easy (*strawberry!*), but if the number of options increases, my choice becomes more difficult because although I may love the refreshing taste of strawberry jam, apple-pie cinnamon jam sounds delightful and warm, and jalapeno cranberry sounds exciting and could be used on more than toast. Making the choice from 24 options is more difficult than making it from 6 because a choice requires giving up the features of the other jams, so I might walk away to avoid deciding at all.

In the DYL course, students learn about analysis paralysis, why it happens, and the conditions under which it is likely to occur. Throughout the term, they are asked to act toward building their future, and they do. They take a step (or two or three), reflect on what they have experienced and learned, then prototype and test it again. This cycle is often referred to as giving students "failure immunity" by helping them learn to fail forward and learn from their mistakes and misfortunes. This generative reframing of "failure" could help ease the transfer shock that students often experience as they struggle to adjust to new academic standards, experience lower grades, and possibly discover that some portion of their previous credits (20% on average) will not be accepted by the four-year school (Simone, 2014). Reframing transfer shock as a natural part of the transfer process could encourage and empower students to be actively learning and growing through all the challenges they will face on the way.

The Effectiveness of the DYL Course

Thus far in this chapter, we have argued that design thinking is an effective framework through which some of the unique challenges of students who transfer could be addressed. In the next section, we share the origins of life design and research on the effectiveness of the *DYL* course. The life design program and DYL course were founded in the Design School at Stanford University to help students design lives with purpose and meaning (Burnett & Evans, 2016). In 2008, the first course offered to (a) help students explore their career options, (b) debunk dysfunctional career-related beliefs that might hinder their progress, (c) practice skills that will help them on the job market, and (d) become career ready. The course uses active learning techniques and liberation pedagogies and frequently serves as a HIP (e.g., a first-year experience/transfer seminar).

The Stanford Life Design program has trained hundreds of faculty, staff, and administrators worldwide who return to their campuses with plans for how to incorporate life design at their universities (Stanford Life Design Lab, 2022). We, the authors of this chapter, are but two graduates of the program who return to Stanford each year to share what we are doing at our universities and how we measure the program's impact on students.

One of us, Dr. Butler, has been working with colleagues to measure the effectiveness of our DYL course over five years (2016–2021). The course is a transfer seminar course at a large public state university in southern California that is both a minority-majority campus and a transfer-majority campus. Survey responses from 429 students were included in this analysis, with 59% who took the DYL course and 41% in the control group, consisting of students who transferred but had yet to take the DYL course. Most of the students in the courses were from underrepresented minority groups (76%), were first-generation college students (75%), and were female (81%). Those who took the DYL course shared similar demographic characteristics (i.e., age, gender, ethnicity, and first-generation college student status) with the control group. All students completed the pre-course and post-course assessments anonymously. The assessment measured career self-efficacy (Kaminsky & Behrend, 2015), career motivation and search knowledge (Noe et al., 1990), wellness (Rashid et al., 2017), career anxiety (Rochlen et al., 2004), hope for the future (Snyder et al., 1991), sense of belonging (Yorke, 2016), and a sense of purpose (Bronk et al., 2018).

The results indicate the course is highly effective (see Figures 4.1–4.3; see also Bono et al., 2018; Butler, 2019; Butler & Bono, 2018; Butler et al., 2018, 2020). Compared to the control group, students who took the DYL course reported less career anxiety, greater career self-efficacy, more search knowledge, and more career resilience (see Figure 4.2; cf. Butler, 2019; Butler et al., 2020). In addition, by the end of the course, students had more hope for the future, a greater sense of purpose, higher wellness scores (measured using the P.E.R.M.A. approach to wellness; see Figure 4.2), and a greater sense of belonging to campus than those in the control group (see Figure 4.3; Butler et al., 2020; Hall & Butler, 2019). Very few group differences were found. Most notably, the Black students began the course with lower overall wellness scores. As such, over the semester, they saw greater improvement in wellness than students from the other ethnic groups. Additionally, the first-generation college students' gained more confidence that they could effectively search for a job and more career identity resilience than students who were not first-generation college students did.

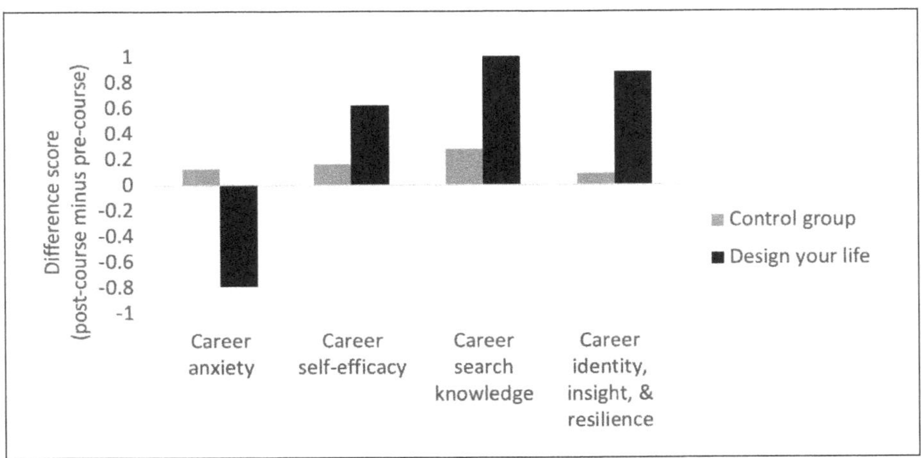

Figure 4.2. Mean Differences (Pre-Course to Post-Course) in Career Anxiety, Career Self-Efficacy, Career Search Knowledge, and Career Identity Resilience

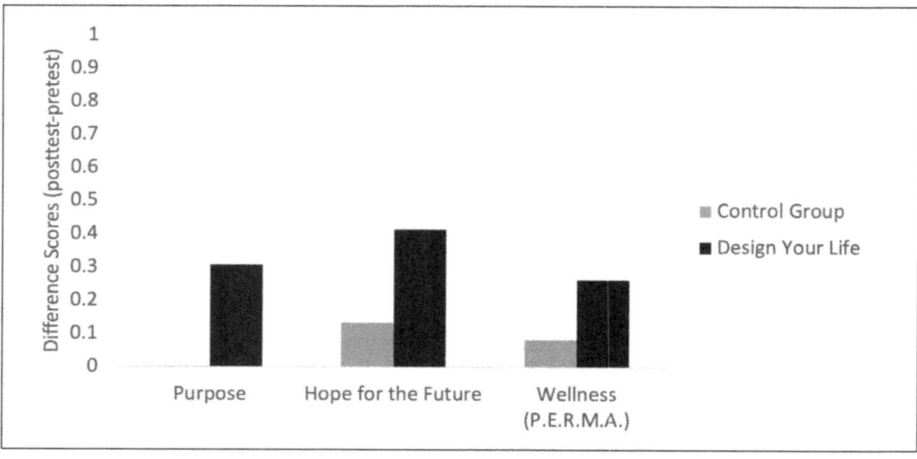

Figure 4.3. Mean Differences (Pre-Course to Post-Course) in Sense of Purpose, Hope for the Future, and Wellness

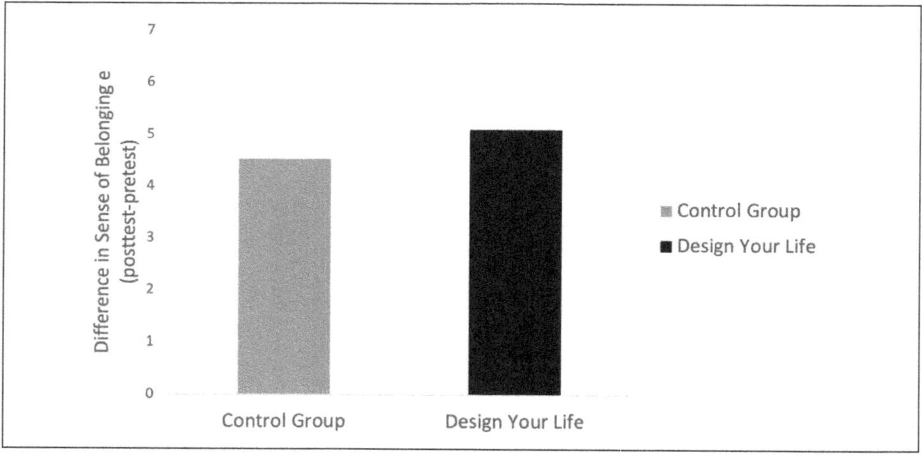

Figure 4.4. Mean Difference (Pre-Course to Post-Course) in Sense of Belonging to the University

Discussion of Findings

Overall, this research suggests that the design thinking framework helped students who had transferred to feel connected to the receiving university, improve their career development agency and career self-efficacy, develop career-readiness skills, and improve their confidence to use those skills. These findings are particularly important when we reconsider the three challenges students who transfer face: lack of institutional, academic, and financial support (Hills, 1965; Laanan et al., 2010; Quaye & Harper, 2015). Students who transfer often struggle as they transition into a new campus climate. Participating in the DYL supports them by increasing their sense of belonging to the campus. The exact mechanism was not directly tested, but one hypothesis is that the course pedagogy (e.g., active learning, role play, active listening) and content (i.e., the students' lives) allow for more and deeper interaction between the students and the instructor about a topic that is meaningful to the students (i.e., their future). In addition to imparting knowledge, the instructor becomes an advisor and mentor who creates a safe, judgment-free space for the students to explore and refine the impact they want to have on the world. Students are also put into small groups and taught active listening skills and to feel heard by their classmates, fostering a sense of community. Altogether, the messages received by students who transfer are that this institution values me and cares about my success, this professor who is helping me articulate my goals and strengths believes in me, and my classmates are colleagues who affirm my aspirations and are valuable resources.

Additionally, several students reported that identifying a career goal allowed them to approach their academic studies differently. Instead of seeing their courses as a requirement to check off, they started to see their coursework as preparation for their future career. As one student explained, "I will eat, breathe, and live statistics now" because that knowledge was important to her future career goal. Articulating the connection between what they are learning in the classroom and how that knowledge or skill has prepared them for their future is necessary for students who transfer who may not have received career preparation at their sending institution and who will soon be entering the job market.

As with all research, this study had methodological limitations. We could not randomly assign students to conditions (i.e., to take the DYL class or not). This limitation means that a self-selection bias cannot be ruled out. It is possible that the students who chose to enroll in the course were systematically different from those who did not. It should also be noted that these results are not generalizable outside of public universities, universities in southern California, or ethnically diverse institutions. That said, the findings have been remarkably consistent over time, and the students who enrolled in the course the first time it was offered selected a "special topic" course but were not privy to what the topic was until the first day of class. These factors do not allow us to rule out selection bias entirely but might lessen some concerns about the results being driven by the type of student who enrolls in a career course. Future research could address these limitations.

Additionally, future research needs to follow up with students to ascertain the program's long-term impacts after a significant period has passed. Did students who transferred pursue the careers they planned? Did they use the design thinking framework to prototype and plan additional aspects of their life or a different career if the career they pursued was not a good fit? Did students who took the course finish college more quickly or with higher GPAs than students who didn't? We hypothesized that the course might indirectly help students with their financial challenges (a known barrier to the success of students who transfer) because the course empowers students to manage their lives by encouraging a sense of agency, but we did not measure this variable. Future research would do well to explore this and other indirect benefits of the course.

In sum, we argue that the DYL curriculum offers a fresh and effective approach for supporting career development and success for students who transfer. Five years of program data indicate that the course is effective in helping students develop career agency and to identify postgraduate career and life goals. We contend that this course would be especially beneficial for students who transfer because it would address some unique challenges accompanying this transition. By regularly reframing how their new college context could help them pursue their emerging lives and career goals more effectively, we believe this course would also support transfer success and persistence in college. Since first-year experiences, including transfer seminars, have been empirically identified as HIPs (Kuh, 2008), we recommend that colleges and universities adopt DYL as a core framework for their transfer seminar course curriculum.

Finally, in the spirit of design thinking, we encourage you, the reader, to prototype a small life design seminar (or at least a workshop) for your students navigating transfer. Not only will you learn more about how to better support students in transition, but in doing so, the institution will also move closer to being the kind of institution that all students who transfer so desperately need: one that intentionally promotes their success both in college and beyond.

References

Arnett, J. J. (2000). Emerging adulthood: A theory of development from the late teens through the twenties. *American Psychologist, 55*(5), 469–480. https://doi.org/10.1037/0003-066X.55.5.469

Bandura, A. (1989). Human agency in social cognitive theory. *American Psychologist, 44*(9), 1175–1184. https://doi.org/10.1037/0003-066X.44.9.1175

Bono, G., Butler, H., & Jaquez, R. (2018, April). *Design your life: Helping underrepresented students transition from college into their first career* [Poster presentation]. Annual meeting of the Western Psychological Association, Portland, OR, United States.

Bronk, K. C., Riches, B. R., & Mangan, S. A. (2018). Claremont purpose scale: A measure that assesses the three dimensions of purpose among adolescents. *Research in Human Development, 15*(2), 101–117. http://doi.org/10.1080/15427609.2018.1441577

Burnett, B., & Evans, D. (2016). *Design your life: How to build a well-lived joyful life.* Knopf.

Butler, H. A. (2019, January). *Design your life: An innovative career-readiness program* [Paper presentation]. American Association of State Colleges and Universities Winter Meeting, Amelia Island, FL, United States.

Butler, H. A., & Bono, G. (2018, February). *Design your life: Helping underrepresented college students transition from college to career* [Paper presentation]. Alliance of Hispanic-Serving Institutions Educators Conference, Chicago, IL, United States.

Butler, H. A., Bono, G., & Mendez, B. (2018, March). *Design your life: A framework to improve career readiness and students' transition from college to career* [Paper presentation]. High Impact Practices (HIPs) State Conference, Carson, CA, United States.

Butler, H. A., Villanueva-Russell, Y., Manke, B., & Mendez, B. (2020, March). *Inspiring career exploration and development among first-generation students at minority-majority campuses in the United States* [Paper presentation]. HIPS State Conference, College Station, TX, United States.

Carnevale, A. P., Strohl, J. & Melton, M. (2015). *What's it worth? The economic value of college majors.* Georgetown Center on Education and the Workforce. https://cew.Georgetown.edu/wp-content/uploads/2014/11/whatsitworth-complete.pdf

Causey, J., Pevitz, A., Ryu, M., Scheetz, A., & Shapiro, D. (2022, February). *Completing college: National and state report on six-year completion rates for Fall 2015 beginning cohort* (Signature Report 20). National Student Clearinghouse Research Center. https://nscresearchcenter.org/wp-content/uploads/Completions_Report_2021.pdf

Chronicle of Higher Education. (2021). *Almanac of higher education: 2021–2022.* https://www.chronicle.com/package/almanac-2021-22

Crisp, G., & Nuñez, A. (2014). Understanding the racial transfer gap: Modeling underrepresented minority and nonminority students' pathways from two- to four-year institutions. *The Review of Higher Education 37*(3), 291–320. https://doi.org/10.1353/rhe.2014.0017.

Csikszentmihalyi, M. (1990). *Flow: The psychology of optimal experience* (1st ed.). Harper & Row.

Dik, B. J., Byrne, Z. S., & Steger, M. F. (Eds.). (2013). *Purpose and meaning in the workplace.* American Psychological Association.

Gandara, P., Alvarado, E., Driscoll, A., & Orfield, G. (2012). *Building pathways to transfer: Community colleges that break the chain of failure for students of color* [Full report]. The Civil Rights Project.

Guilford, J. P. (1988). Some changes in the structure of intellect model. *Educational and Psychological Measurement, 48*, 1–4. https://doi.org/10.1177/001316448804800102

Haghbin, M., McCaffrey, A., & Pychyl, T. A. (2012). The complexity of the relation between fear of failure and procrastination. *Journal of Rational-Emotive & Cognitive-Behavior Therapy, 30*, 249–263. http://doi.org/10.1007/s10942-012-0153-9

Hall, R., & Butler, H. A. (2019). *The effect of a career readiness course and first-generation status on college sense of belongingness* [Poster presentation]. Annual meeting of the Western Psychological Association, Pasadena, CA, United States.

Halpern, D. F. (2014). *Thought and knowledge: An introduction to critical thinking* (5th ed.). Psychology Press.

Hills, J. (1965). Transfer shock: The academic performance of the junior college transfer. *Journal of Experimental Education, 33*, 201–216. https://doi.org/10.1080/00220973.1 965.11010875

Iyengar, S. S., & Lepper, M. R. (2000). When choice is demotivating: Can one desire too much of a good thing? *Journal of Personality and Social Psychology, 79*(6), 995–1006. https://doi.org/10.1037/0022-3514.79.6.995

Janis, I. L. (1971, November). Groupthink. *Psychology Today, 5*(6), 84–90. https://web. archive.org/web/20100401033524/http:/apps.olin.wustl.edu/faculty/macdonald/ GroupThink.pdf

Jenkins, D., & Fink, J. (2016). *Tracking transfer: New measures of institutional and state effectiveness in helping community college students attain bachelor's degrees.* Community College Research Center, Teachers College, Columbia University.

Kaminsky, S. E., & Behrend, T. S. (2015). *Career self-efficacy scale* [Database record]. PsyTESTS. http://doi.org/10.1037/t44167-000

Kuh, G. D. (2008). *High-impact educational practices: What they are, who has access to them, and why they matter.* Association of American Colleges and Universities.

Laanan, F. S. (1998). *Beyond transfer shock: A study of students' college experiences and adjustment processes at UCLA* [Unpublished doctoral dissertation]. Graduate School of Education and Information Studies, University of California, Los Angeles.

Laanan, F. S. (2004). Studying transfer students: Part I: Instrument design and implications. *Community College Journal of Research and Practice, 28*, 331–351.

Laanan, F. S. (2007). Studying transfer students: Part II: Dimensions of transfer students' adjustment. *Community College Journal of Research and Practice, 31*(1), 37–59. https:// doi.org/10.1080/10668920600859947

Laanan, F. S., Starobin, S. S., & Eggleston, L. E. (2010). Adjustment of community college students at a four-year university: Role and relevance of transfer student capital for student retention. *Journal of College Student Retention: Research, Theory & Practice, 12*(2), 175–209. https://doi.org/10.2190/CS.12.2.d

Li, D. (2010). They need help: Transfer students from four-year to four-year institutions. *Review of Higher Education, 33*(2), 207–238. http://doi.org.10.1353/rhe.0.0131

Ma, J., Pender, M., & Welch, M. (2019). *Education pays 2019: The benefits of higher education for individuals and society,* College Board. https://eric.ed.gov/?id=ED572548

Manning, K., Kinzie, J., & Schuh, J. (2013). *One size does not fit all: Traditional and innovative models of student affairs practice* (2nd ed.). Routledge. https://doi.org/10.4324/9781315885353

Martinez-Wenzl, M., & Marquez, R. (2012). *Unrealized promises: Unequal access, affordability, and excellence at community colleges in Southern California.* The Civil Rights Project.

National Association of Colleges and Employers. (2021). *Career readiness: Competencies for a career-ready workforce.* https://www.naceweb.org/career-readiness/competencies/career-readiness-defined/

Newell, A., & Simon, H. A. (1972). *Human problem solving.* Prentice-Hall, Inc.

Newman, M. (2016). *The mindfulness book: Practical ways to lead a more mindful life* (concise advice). LID Publishing.

Noe, R. A., Noe, A. W., & Bachhuber, J. A. (1990). An investigation of the correlates of career motivation. *Journal of Vocational Behavior, 37*(3), 340–356. https://psycnet.apa.org/doi/10.1016/0001-8791(90)90049-8

Nuñez, A.-M., & Elizondo, D. (2013). Closing the Latino/a transfer gap: Creating pathways to the baccalaureate. *Perspectivas Issues in Higher Education Policy and Practice, Spring 2013*(2), 1–15. https://eric.ed.gov/?id=ED571016

Oettingen, G., & Mayer, D. (2002). The motivating function of thinking about the future: Expectations versus fantasies. *Journal of Personality and Social Psychology, 83*(5), 1198–1212. https://doi.org/10.1037/0022-3514.83.5.1198

Osborn, A. F. (1953). *Applied imagination: Principles and procedures of creative thinking.* Charles Scribner's Sons.

Park, C. L. (2012). Religious and spiritual aspect of meaning in the context of work life. In P. Hill & B. J. Dik (Eds.), *Psychology of religion and workplace spirituality* (pp. 223–238). Information Age.

Pew Research Center. (2016, October). *The state of American jobs: How the shifting economic landscape is reshaping work and society and affecting the way people think about the skills and training they need to get ahead.* https://www.pewresearch.org/social-trends/wp-content/uploads/sites/3/2016/10/ST_2016.10.06_Future-of-Work_FINAL4.pdf

Quaye, S. J., Harper, S. R., & Pendakur, S. L. (Eds.). (2020). *Student engagement in higher education: theoretical perspectives and practical approaches for diverse populations* (3rd ed.). Routledge.

Rashid, T., Louden, R., Wright, L., Chu, R., Maharaj, A., Hakim, I., Uy, D., & Kidd, B. (2017). Flourish: A strengths-based approach to building student resilience. In C. Proctor (Ed.), *Positive psychology interventions in practice* (pp. 29–45). Springer International Publishing AG. https://doi.org/10.1007/978-3-319-51787-2_3

Rochlen, A. B., Milburn, L., & Hill, C. E. (2004). *Career Anxiety Measure* [Database record]. APA PsyTESTS. http://doi.org/10.1037/t40394-000

Rottinghaus, P. J., Jenkins, N., & Jantzer, A. M. (2009). Relation of depression and affectivity to career decision status and self-efficacy in college students. *Journal of Career Assessment, 17*(3), 271–285. https://doi.org/10.1177/1069072708330463

Scott, A. B., & Ciani, K. D. (2008). Effects of an undergraduate career class on men's and women's career decision-making self-efficacy and vocational identity. *Journal of Career Development, 34*(3), 263–285. https://doi.org/10.1177/0894845307311248

Seelig, L. (2012). *InGenius: A crash course on creativity.* HarperOne.

Sengupta, R., & C. Jepsen (2006). *California's community college students.* Public Policy Institute of California. https://www.ppic.org/publication/californias-community-college-students/

Shapiro, D., Dundar, A., Wakhungu, P.K, Yuan, X., & Harrell, A. (2015, July). *Transfer and mobility: A national view of student movement in postsecondary institutions, Fall 2008 cohort* (Signature Report No. 9). National Student Clearinghouse Research Center.

Simone, S. A. (2014). *Transferability of postsecondary credit following student transfer or coenrollment* (NCES 2014-163). U.S. Department of Education, National Center for Education Statistics. https://nces.ed.gov/pubs2014/2014163.pdf

Snyder, C. R., Harris, C., Anderson, J. R., Holleran, S. A., Irving, L. M., Sigmon, S. T., Yoshinobu, L., Gibb, J., Langelle, C., & Harney, P. (1991). The will and the ways: Development and validation of an individual-differences measure of hope. *Journal of Personality and Social Psychology, 60*(4), 570–585. https://doi.org/10.1037/0022-3514.60.4.570

Stanford Life Design Lab. (2022, April 6). *A movement of life design in the academy.* http://lifedesignlab.stanford.edu/

Tobolowsky, B. F., & Cox, B. E. (2012). Rationalizing neglect: An institutional response to transfer students. *Journal of Higher Education, 83,* 389–410. https://doi.org/10.1080/00221546.2012.11777249

Torpey, E. (2021). *Education pays, 2020.* U.S. Bureau of Labor Statistics.

Townsend, B. K., & Wilson, K. (2006). "A hand hold for a little bit": Factors facilitating the success of community college transfer students to a large research university. *Journal of College Student Development, 47*(4), 439–456. https://doi.org/10.1353/csd.2006.0052

Townsend, B. K., & Wilson, K. B. (2008–2009). The academic and social integration of persisting community college transfer students. *Journal of College Student Retention: Research, Theory and Practice, 10,* 405–423. https://doi.org/10.2190/CS.10.4.a

U.S. Department of Education. (2012). *Community college student outcomes: 1994–2009* (Technical report, NCES 2012–253). National Center for Education Statistics.

Wood, J. L., & Moore, C. S. (2015) Engaging Community College Transfer Students. In S. J. Quaye & S. R. Harper (Eds.), *Student Engagement in Higher Education* (271-287). New York, NY: Routledge.

Yorke, M. (2016). Student belongingness, engagement and self-confidence survey [Database record]. APA PsycTESTS. https://doi.org/10.1037/t48020-000

Zuckerberg, B. (2008). Overcoming 'analysis paralysis.' *Frontiers in Ecology and the Environment, 6*(9), 505–506.

CHAPTER FIVE

Career Pathways by Design:
An Innovative Framework to Enhance Professional Preparation for STEM Students Who Transfer

Kerin Hilker-Balkissoon and Padmanabhan Seshaiyer

Natalia is a first-generation Latina who excelled academically, graduating in two years from a community college, with honors, and then transferring to George Mason University, where she earned a biology degree, also with honors. Natalia next received a master's degree in biology from an elite university. A dedicated student, she balanced college with a part-time retail job while fast-tracking toward STEM career success. However, a few months after completing her master's, Natalia reached out to her community college counselor and shared her struggles finding a job. Natalia labored to find full-time employment despite her impressive academic credentials and well-publicized STEM industry efforts to increase diversity in the STEM workforce.

Despite strengthened investment in supporting community college transfers, experiences like Natalia's happen all too frequently. This chapter highlights one institution's replicable efforts to enhance the career readiness of STEM students who transfer. This investigation dives deep into data, employing a design thinking approach to uncover barriers and inequities in the transfer process and leveraging findings to design and implement a transfer-focused, STEM career pathways intervention framework.

Exploring Systemic Barriers to Career Readiness for STEM Students Who Transfer

George Mason University (GMU) champions success for students who transfer. Two decades of partnership with Northern Virginia Community College (NOVA) has yielded collaborative, systemic transfer pathways, including the award-winning NOVA/GMU ADVANCE initiative. GMU centers the transfer experience in broad diversity, equity, and inclusion (DEI) work, supporting strategic investments to improve the transfer experiences. This commitment extends to GMUs College of Science (COS), where 36% of the undergraduates are students who transfer.

To better support students like Natalia, COS launched our design thinking challenge with an investigative phase, framed by three guiding questions to identify barriers to professional readiness for STEM students who transfer. Although a body of research on STEM career readiness focuses on student populations that intersect with community college matriculants, including first-generation students (Maietta, 2016) and minoritized populations (García & McNaughtan, 2019; Rios, 2019), and some research disaggregates by gender (Hu & Ortagus, 2019), limited research addressed both career readiness and attainment among transfers pursuing STEM credentials.

Recent attention on transfer reform focuses on curricular pathways and advising innovation. Cross-institutional guided pathways provide relatively seamless academic pipelines, simultaneously addressing planning complexity and reducing excess credits (Wyner et al., 2016). In addition, incorporating meta-majors within guided pathways aligns similar curricula, further easing transfer planning (Jenkins et al., 2017). While these efforts have shown promise (Wyner et al., 2016), their postbaccalaureate career attainment impacts remain unclear.

DT Guiding Question 1: Do Advisors Providing Academic and Career Advising to Community College STEM Students Possess Current Knowledge of 21st Century STEM Career Pathways?

Many community colleges employ generalist advisors to support first-year students (King, 2002). These advisors guide students in academic, career, and transfer planning but are unlikely to possess knowledge in technical sectors such as STEM (Packard & Jeffers, 2013). Packard et al. (2012) noted that inadequate advising contributes to delayed transfer among community college STEM students. Limited access to sector-specific career development readily available at research universities widens this advising gap. At COS, first- and second-year university matriculants have immediate access to mentoring and advising by research faculty and near-peers in their disciplines, along with career-focused student organizations and curricular flexibility to incorporate experiential learning into their degree plans.

DT Guiding Question 2: What Do Community College Students Who Transfer Know About Today's STEM Career Pathways and How To Prepare For Them, and How Are They Getting Their Information?

Multiple studies have found that community college students are more likely to have limited social and cultural capital (Laanan et al., 2010; Starobin et al., 2016). Laanan et al. (2010) collectively framed this concept as *transfer student capital* (TSC), with limited capital strongly correlated to pre-and post-transfer success barriers (Maliszewski Lukszo & Hayes,

2019). Data suggest that, without access to professional networks, students often rely on friends and family or inaccurate representations of careers in media to support decision-making (Kazi & Akhlaq, 2017; Whitehead, 2018). Lack of access is particularly problematic in STEM, in which media depictions of professionals are often inaccurate (Steinke & Tavarez, 2018).

While TSC refers primarily to academic and navigational readiness, limited social capital extends to career attainment. We reframe this concept as *transfer career capital* (TCC). The impacts of limited TCC not only encompass initial job placement but span the entire career lifecycle. Graduates with limited TCC do not possess robust professional networks that facilitate entry-level employment, increasing the likelihood of delayed career entry. Negative career impacts of limited TCC can extend to low starting salaries, downcycle salary compression, and low job security due to limited access to career-advancement opportunities (Eismann, 2016; NACE, 2020).

DT Guiding Question 3: What Institutions Are Currently Best Positioned To Design and Implement Sector-Based Career Readiness Across the Transfer Lifecycle?

The emerging best practices of guided pathways, meta-majors, and enhanced first-year advising have addressed many academic challenges in the transfer process but place the burden of reform on already under-resourced community colleges (Goldrick-Rab, 2010). We argue that these models are promising but represent an incomplete solution, as they do not address the sector-based career development needs of students who transfer.

Musoba and Nicholas (2020) stated it best: "For too long, universities have seen transfer as a community college issue; instead, universities must own and improve the post-transfer experience" (p. 3). Universities are best positioned to leverage their robust, sector-specific resources to provide STEM career development to community college students pre- and post-transfer. The intersectionality of minoritized and undergraduate transfer populations further justifies investment in students who transfer as a key target group in university DEI efforts.

STEM Transfer Career Capital: Cross-Institutional Needs Assessment

Substantive data indicate high attrition among community college STEM students (Bettinger, 2010; Labov, 2012). Recognizing that students who transfer arrive on campus with limited TCC and fail to develop it, we developed a comprehensive needs assessment of the COS transfer community.

Evaluation began with reviewing existing institutional reports, observing admissions and transfer onboarding processes, and exploring the first-year university experience for students who transfer into GMU COS. The inability of GMU to disaggregate some institutional data by transfer/nontransfer status complicated the evaluation. The authors collected quantitative data to address the following questions and to provide validity and guidance for qualitative study:

1. Do COS undergraduate students who transfer participate in internal experiential learning programs at a rate equivalent to their percentage in the undergraduate student population?

2. Do COS undergraduate students who transfer complete minor programs of study at a rate equivalent to nontransfer university students?

A human-centered design thinking (DT) research methodology was selected to guide the assessment of issues affecting career readiness for the COS undergraduate transfer population. DT is an iterative process employing design-based techniques to gain insight and yield innovative solutions to real-world challenges (Ward, 2020). DT consists of five decisive steps: empathy, define, ideate, prototype, and test; it is a powerful model to guide data collection within the context of this design challenge—to evaluate and address barriers to developing TCC.

The DT empathy framework was employed to explore the needs of COS students who transfer, focusing on pre-transfer, onboarding, and first-year university experiences. Launched in the summer of 2018, the assessment included individual and group sessions with 125 diverse stakeholders, including 26 GMU faculty and professional advisors, 36 community college STEM faculty and professional advisors, 39 COS university-matriculated transfer students, and 35 prospective students seeking to transfer. Stakeholders were engaged in the order noted, with prepared questions. Responses collected from earlier stakeholder groups informed the design of questions for later stakeholder sessions.

Group 1: COS faculty and professional advisors
1. How would you describe the issues that affect the success of COS undergraduate students who transfer?

2. What are some of the challenges these students experience upon matriculating?

3. How would you describe the participation in academic, career, and experiential learning opportunities of first-year COS undergraduate students who transfer?

4. What is your perspective on engaging students who transfer in STEM undergraduate research and experiential learning opportunities? (Faculty only)

Group 2: Community college STEM faculty and professional advisors
1. How would you describe the primary questions and concerns that STEM students have about transferring?

2. What are some of the common issues that frequently arise in the transfer process or after a STEM student transfers?

3. How would you describe the level of importance of the undergraduate internship to a STEM student's overall career readiness?

4. How would you describe the level of importance of undergraduate research to a STEM student's overall career readiness?

5. In your advising role, do you specialize in supporting STEM students or do you support a general population?

Group 3: Actively enrolled COS university students who transferred

1. What are some of the issues that have affected your success as an undergraduate student who transferred? (If identified) Could you tell me about any specific barriers you experienced/more about the specific barrier you shared?

2. What has your experience been with accessing GMU's academic, career, and experiential learning opportunities? (If challenges arose) Could you tell me more about those challenges? (If no/limited access) Are there any specific factors that affected your ability to access these opportunities?

3. What is something you wish you had known before you transferred to GMU's COS?

4. How have you engaged with the university community as a first-year GMU student? (If no/limited engagement) Are there any specific factors that affected your ability to engage on campus?

Group 4: Prospective and matriculating students who transfer

1. What is/are your biggest question(s) or concern(s) about transferring to GMU as a STEM scholar?

2. How familiar are you with GMU's science lab policies and protocols?

3. How familiar are you with GMU's science lab report formatting?

4. How familiar are you with academic, career, and experiential learning opportunities either within GMU or outside GMU relevant to your major?

5. How important is an undergraduate internship to your overall career readiness?

6. How important is undergraduate research to your overall career readiness?

7. How do you plan to engage with the university community as a GMU student?

Feedback and responses from the DT empathy phase defined our problem statements, which further clarified the needs of students who transfer. Affinity mapping techniques framed and prioritized the issues, followed by a root-cause analysis exercise. From this second phase of DT assessment, two specific problems emerged:

Defined Problem 1: Knowledge and Awareness Barriers

- Students and community college advisors had limited awareness of emerging, interdisciplinary STEM career pathways.

- Fewer than one third of prospective and actively matriculating transfers identified undergraduate research as a priority.

- Fewer than half of actively matriculating GMU STEM transfers reported an intention to complete a career-related undergraduate research experience in their first year.

- More than half of GMU-matriculated transfers reported they first became aware of the importance of undergraduate research in their third GMU semester.

- Orientation and onboarding programming included limited career information.

Defined Problem 2: Access, Equity, and Inclusion Barriers

- University faculty reported their primary means of filling non-work-study undergraduate research positions was through networking or direct offers to students they knew well.

- A few university faculty openly expressed concerns about community college transfer students' academic preparation and their readiness to engage in experiential learning pending the completion of several semesters at GMU.

- University-matriculated students who transferred reported struggles in obtaining research experiences.

- Thirty-six percent of COS undergraduates are students who transferred, but participation in internal undergraduate research programs varied from 0% to 18%.

- COS transfers completed minor programs of study at a rate of 19.2%, compared with 31.1% for nontransfer COS students.

- More than two thirds of continuing university transfers reported that existing experiential learning opportunities were inaccessible or particularly challenging to access.

Holistic Design: A Novel STEM Career Pathways Framework

Upon defining individual and systemic barriers for students who transfer, DT ideation guided the review of data and definitions to brainstorm holistic solutions. The authors identified and explored the journey of STEM students who transfer. Student lifecycle models are regularly applied to postsecondary student success interventions (Roberts, 2018; Thomas et al., 2002), leading to the articulation of a STEM transfer lifecycle (see Figure 5.1) and further exploration of student needs and institutional barriers to TCC within lifecycle stages.

Bates and Hayes (2017) cited the importance of embedding career development content across the postsecondary experience. This data-driven STEM career pathways framework assumes prospective and current transfer students possess limited TCC. Leveraging the STEM transfer lifecycle (see Figure 5.1), we identified specific stages and juncture transitions in which STEM-sector-based interventions could be applied to enhance TCC. This approach informs students about how and when career information is delivered, ensuring that content is specific, relevant, and actionable at their current lifecycle stage while preparing them for the next stage.

Additionally, DT ideation clarified a five-pillar model of student-directed intervention to enhance TCC, grounded by cross-institutional collaboration and systems change. These pillars—college and career navigation, mentorship and community building, experiential learning and research, STEM identity & professional development, and cross-disciplinary curricula and global fluency—align with best practices for supporting underserved and minoritized students. Figure 5.2 reflects a replicable intervention design framework to enhance TCC, integrating STEM transfer lifecycle, pillars of service, and systemic barrier mitigation.

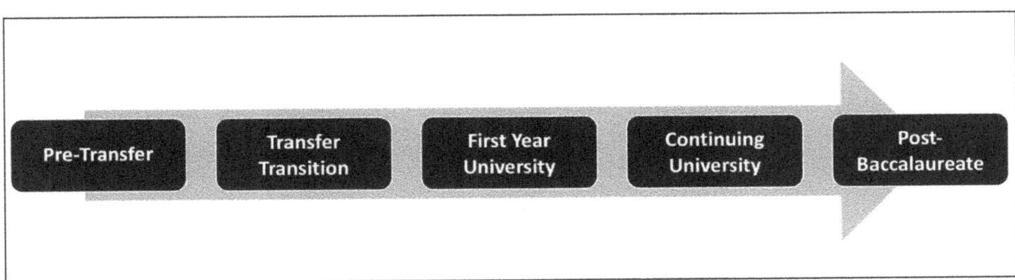

Figure 5.1. Five-Stage STEM Transfer Lifecycle

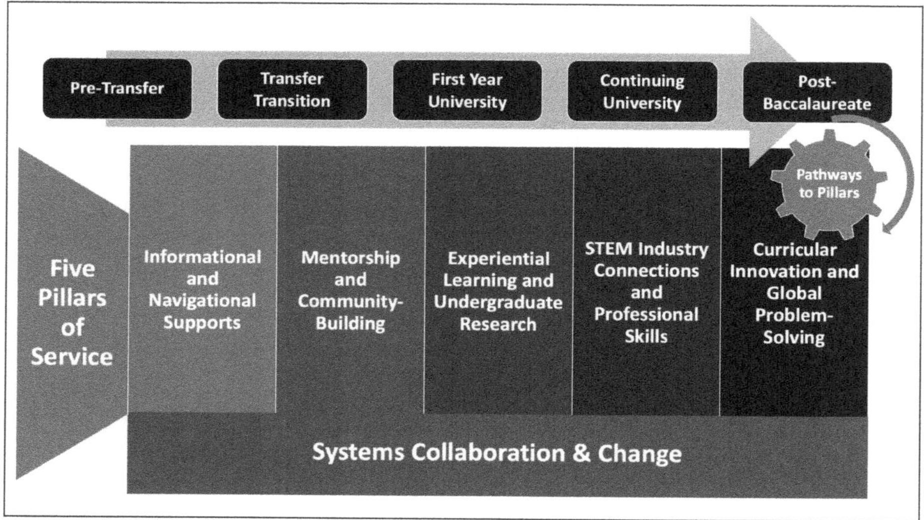

Figure 5.2. TCC Intervention Design Framework

Implementation: Interventions to Enhance Transfer Career Capital

The TCC intervention design framework provides structure for the penultimate DT stage, the prototype of COS interventions to enhance TCC. The framework ensures that all interventions are tailored to address barriers specific to the GMU COS transfer pipeline, supplementing existing institutional resources and cross-institutional partnerships. Leveraging existing resources reduces service duplication while enhancing efficiency and student access to career-formative experiences.

Systems Collaboration and Change

Improving the quality of STEM career information and advising delivered to students who pre-transfer is a cornerstone intervention. To accomplish this objective, COS directly engages students who pre-transfer through cross-institutional collaboration. Several times annually, COS faculty facilitate STEM career pathways training for community college advisors. This training highlights emerging, high-growth STEM careers, STEM-sector career competencies, formative career experiences open to students desiring to transfer, and graduate school admissions requirements. Empowering community college advisors with accurate career information and updated STEM pathway resources strengthens and enhances the TCC of students' pre-transfer.

Another systemic intervention is collaborative STEM transfer advising. Engaging the COS faculty liaison to join community college advising sessions enhances the quality of academic and career information and cross-institutional knowledge, proactively identifying systemic informational and resource gaps that negatively affect student success. Sessions are offered both on campus and virtually, maximizing access for students.

COS also addresses intra-institutional barriers to TCC by integrating students who transfer into COS DEI efforts, addressing implicit and explicit biases affecting STEM career development. STEM faculty transfer champions within academic departments disseminate to their peers data and information that dispel misconceptions about students who transferred from community colleges, especially the myth of underpreparation. Champions also raise awareness of the challenges in accessing resources and experiential learning. Their efforts shift faculty mindset, supporting department and lab-level access for COS students who transferred.

College and Career Navigation

Conley (2007) demonstrated that students are more likely to struggle in college because they have gaps in knowledge and challenges navigating unfamiliar, complex institutional systems. Our interviews revealed that many students who transferred felt overwhelmed by the quantity of information and resources presented through the COS transfer process. COS carefully chunks career information into relevant and actionable bits across each stage of the transfer lifecycle.

Students with limited TCC are unlikely to demonstrate broad knowledge of STEM professions or emerging, high-demand STEM fields. Therefore, early exposure to STEM career pathways and professions is a core TCC intervention. Students who transfer are afforded opportunities to meet STEM faculty and employers and receive early information on sector competencies and supplemental requirements, such as security clearances.

Additionally, all stakeholders interviewed in the DT needs assessment cited gaps in accessibility of transfer-focused STEM pathways information. In response, content of transfer and STEM career pathways are integrated into high school and community-centered COS outreach activities. Coupled with engagement events for current community college students, COS promotes a transfer-receptive environment while building awareness of STEM career pathways.

Student navigational support of institutional, career, and community resources is also addressed. For example, needs assessment revealed that first-semester COS transfers at GMU often struggle in lab courses because of cross-institutional differences in lab rules and reporting. STEM-focused bridge and welcome sessions embed navigational tools to guide students who transfer through a "hidden curriculum" that nontransfers have long since mastered, from COS lab expectations to scheduling appointments with advisors and registering for classes. Students who transfer also learn to access and verify the accuracy of their transfer credit evaluations, proactively addressing missing or misapplied credit to degree requirements that could affect timely baccalaureate completion.

Mentorship and Community Building

Kuh's (2008) high-impact educational practices (HIEP) extol student engagement and community involvement, from robust first-year experiences to undergraduate learning communities. However, HIEP programs are frequently delivered as opt-in, extracurricular experiences. Engagement is simply not enough to support the development of TCC. Universities must engineer STEM HIEP, community building, and mentorship across the transfer lifecycle.

Community building begins pre-transfer by modeling collaborative student–faculty relationships. COS provides a dedicated faculty contact for prospective students who transfer; this contact coordinates virtual and on-site transfer programming. Research faculty and COS transfer ambassadors visit local colleges and host virtual events, sharing their stories and research—these cross-institutional connections model early transfer engagement in experiential learning. Peer community building begins in earnest during the transfer transition stage, including STEM Transfer Bridge and COS Transfer Welcome events hosted each semester.

COS's signature intervention is the Scientific Community of Transfer Researchers (S-CTR), a learning community for students who recently transferred with a shared affinity for STEM research. Onboarding in fall and spring semesters to maximize access, S-CTR facilitates rapid development of TCC through mentor–mentee relationships while creating a transfer shock safety net. Expectations for S-CTR participation are explicitly outlined and agreed upon via an online application form, as are incentives for active engagement. All eligible applicants are invited to join the program.

S-CTR incorporates faculty, industry, and peer mentoring with monthly seminars and learning community courses. Seminars are safe spaces where participants and mentors share transfer-focused navigational and career content while highlighting resources and engagement opportunities. Self-advocacy is modeled through student-led discussions and Blackboard interactions. Engaging students who transferred as experts in addressing near-peers' navigational needs empowers collaborative problem solving and builds TSC.

A developmental networking, multi-mentoring approach further enhances the development of TCC (Dobrow et al., 2012; Nicholson et al., 2017). S-CTR participants are guided in the intentional design of personalized support networks that include research faculty, advisors, peers, undergraduate and graduate assistants, and service through student and community organizations. Early and ongoing engagement is encouraged with STEM industry mentors through networking events and formal industry mentor–mentee pairings. Students who meet S-CTR engagement expectations receive a $250 micro-scholarship award.

Experiential Learning and Research

Multiple studies highlight experiential learning as a HIEP that supports postbaccalaureate career attainment (Coker et al., 2017; Kuh, 2008). However, students who transfer are less likely to engage in experiential learning because they may have excess credit upon transferring, limited financial resources, or nonacademic responsibilities (Wang, 2021). Navigating experiential learning options, including internships, research, shadowing, study abroad, and service learning, can be challenging for students with limited TCC.

Observers acknowledge that undergraduate research is the preferred experiential learning format within the STEM sector. Assignments may include research assistantship under a faculty or industry supervisor; team-based research experiences on collaborative, faculty-led projects; or original research projects supervised by a faculty mentor.

The rationale for prioritizing undergraduate research over other STEM experiential options originates from several factors:

1. The American Association of Medical Colleges (n.d.) cites undergraduate research as a core medical admission qualification.

2. Holistic graduate admissions frameworks disseminated at the National Science Foundation-funded East Coast Holistic Review Institute include multiple semesters of undergraduate research in admissions screening criteria (Posselt & Miller, personal communication, December 11, 2018).

3. Many entry-level STEM positions (e.g., data analysis, project design) fall under research and development, design, and practitioner fields, as classified by the Bureau of Labor and Statistics (SOC Policy Committee, 2019).

As a Carnegie Research 1 institution, research is central to GMU's mission. Needs-assessment data confirmed that COS students who recently transferred are uninformed that undergraduate research is key to STEM career readiness and later struggle to access undergraduate research and other experiential learning. Interventions were designed across the transfer student lifecycle to enhance experiential learning awareness and participation.

STEM Identity and Professional Development

Rodriguez et al. (2019) noted that the development of STEM identity through immersive experiences across industry, academic, and near-peer engagement influences retention and success. Enhancing STEM identity requires early and ongoing effort to dispel feelings of inadequacy and lack of belonging across academic, research, and professional communities for students who transfer, popularly referred to as "impostor syndrome," or the *impostor phenomenon* (Chakraverty, 2019; Lee et al., 2020). COS needs-assessment findings aligned with Chakraverty (2019) in that COS students self-identified their impostor phenomenon early in high school. The majority of university-matriculated COS students who transferred reported experiencing impostor phenomenon throughout their transfer lifecycle. This student experience amplified systemic challenges in obtaining faculty mentors and experiential placements.

To support STEM identity development, COS leverages multiple career-readiness models. Growth across the NACE Career Competencies (Griffin et al., 2012) are assessed pre- and post-intervention. Critical thinking, creativity, collaboration, and communication; along with key skills identified by the STEM industry including diversity, leadership, and entrepreneurship (Jang, 2016), are embedded across lifecycle interventions. Additionally, asset-based models that center resilience and the development of professional identity (Garoutte & McCarthy-Gilmore, 2014), such as *CliftonStrength*, are leveraged to combat the impostor phenomenon.

Cross-Disciplinary Curricula and Global Fluency

Experiential programming alone is not sufficient to support TCC. Academic and career success requires a comprehensive approach, leveraging multiple HIEPs. The COS intervention model centers on the undergraduate learning community (Kuh, 2008). As needs-assessment data confirmed that existing course offerings did not meet COS students' STEM career development needs, COS embarked on an ambitious curricular design process with the following goals:

- Address career-readiness gaps as identified by STEM employers

- Integrate professional skills into the STEM curriculum

- Develop interdisciplinary curricula to address evolving global industry priorities

The result was an innovative curricular solution tailored to enhance TCC. The S-CTR learning community requires enrollment in two undergraduate courses: COS 300, Professional Preparation for STEM Disciplines, and COS 400, Problem-Solving and Leadership in STEAM (Science, Technology, Engineering, Arts, and Mathematics). These courses provide hands-on learning that supplements extracurricular programming to accelerate STEM career readiness. They further provide a guided introduction to STEM experiential learning and global fluency. More than half of the undergraduates who enroll are first-year GMU students who transferred.

COS 300 and 400 further serve as the scientific literacy core for an 18-credit minor in scientific leadership and practice. This interdisciplinary curriculum develops academic and professional skills most desired by today's STEM employers. The minor also includes a capstone internship or experiential learning course, ensuring students receiving financial aid can access credential-required experiential learning.

Early Outcomes, Lessons Learned, and Next Steps

The last step of the design thinking approach is to test interventions. COS is actively in the testing phase, a formal research design that directs a rigorous evaluation of novel interventions. COS intends to collect additional data through focused interviews, surveys, and formative and summative feedback. These data will support a quasi-experimental research design that compares students who transferred and engaged in COS interventions with students who transferred but opted not to engage in these interventions.

Outcomes to date suggest that the TCC intervention framework supports effective intervention design that enhances sector-specific TCC. Benefits of this framework include

- Integration of existing and novel interventions: Mapping existing programming informs service gap identification, facilitating requests for new resources and programming to build sector-specific career readiness.

- Staggered implementation: Supports rapid implementation of highest-need programming while guiding design for future programming.

- Ease of replication: Although designed to support STEM TCC, this framework can be adapted to support career attainment for students who transfer to other sectors.

Program evaluation continues, but early outcomes show promise. One hundred percent of S-CTR participants in Cohorts 1 and 2 were in good academic standing after one year, and all participants successfully obtained degree-related experiential learning within one year of university matriculation. S-CTR participants were more likely to declare a minor program of study (72%) than nontransfer COS undergraduates (31%). Pre- and post-assessment data from Transfer Bridge reflected considerable growth in percentages of students pursuing experiential learning during the first year at GMU (31% pre-assessment vs. 76% post-assessment). Awareness of undergraduate research as integral to STEM career readiness grew from 29% pre-assessment to 92% post-assessment. As of December 2021, 12 of the 15 initial S-CTR scholars had completed a STEM baccalaureate, and two remained undergraduates. Six of them self-reported admission to graduate or health professions programs, and five were employed in degree-related positions.

To maintain a transfer-responsive TCC intervention model, COS periodically revisits the framework and interventions and reaffirms the needs and priorities of COS students and partner institutions. This formative assessment proved critical as COS pivoted to virtual services during the COVID-19 pandemic, requiring re-evaluating existing service models to reflect pandemic-era courses, limited experiential learning, and STEM-sector career landscapes. Future programming efforts include virtual expansion of S-CTR to the pre-transfer stage, accelerating the development of TCC, and access to STEM experiential learning, including a flexible summer STEM research initiative for recent community college graduates.

Conclusion and a Call to Action

Natalia's limited TCC led her back to her community college to seek career support. With guidance, Natalia settled into a full-time STEM education career, securing a full-time position in STEM outreach while serving as an adjunct instructor. She currently teaches science at the secondary level. While Natalia is happy and prosperous, she admits STEM education was not the career path she had planned to pursue.

Natalia was a talented, resourceful, and driven student, yet her limited TCC derailed her STEM career plan. Her story is just one example of the career experiences of too many STEM students who transfer, who complete their degrees only to struggle to achieve their postbaccalaureate professional goals. Our design thinking analysis similarly uncovered many startling barriers to TCC for GMU COS students but justified the need for investment in students who transfer.

Limited TCC, if not addressed, can lead to lifelong inequities in STEM career attainment. These largely unrecognized structural inequities do not only limit career attainment and upward mobility for the students who transfer. They also delay (and sometimes prevent) many highly qualified, diverse candidates from joining the nation's scientific and technical workforce. Given the strong intersectionality of community college populations with groups minoritized on the basis of race and ethnicity, disability and neurodiversity, income, and basic needs insecurity, investment in the STEM transfer pipeline is a sound strategy to broaden access to and representation in STEM workforce pathways.

Significant strides have been made in improving transfer pathways. However, these interventions have focused on academic pathways reform at community colleges. It is long past time that universities stop deferring responsibility for equitable STEM career outcomes to two-year partners. Research universities are well-structured and resourced to support STEM-sector interventions, yet even flagship institutions with robust transfer supports fail to mitigate gaps in TCC. Investment in STEM-sector-based career readiness for future students who transfer directly supports institutional commitments to access, justice, diversity, equity, and inclusion.

Our DT approach generated multiple tools to enhance TCC, articulating the transfer lifecycle and a five-pillar model that guided student interventions and justified the need for systemic change. These tools and interventions serve as a roadmap for other universities to reach within and beyond their campuses to proactively support their future students, broadening engagement in STEM for students who transfer and paving pathways to graduate study and STEM-sector employment. Universities have the obligation to ensure that all their transfer graduates depart with fully developed transfer career capital in their chosen fields. Only then will we truly move the equity needle for career readiness.

References

American Association of Medical Colleges. (n.d.). *How to get research experience.* https://tinyurl.com/3pkk7r65

Bates, L., & Hayes, H. (2017). Using the student lifecycle approach to enhance employability: An example from criminology and criminal justice. *Asia-Pacific Journal of Cooperative Education, 18*(2), 141–151. https://eric.ed.gov/?id=EJ1151139

Bettinger, E. (2010). To be or not to be: Major choices of budding scientists. In C. T. Clotfelter (Ed.), *American universities in a global market* (pp. 33–68). University of Chicago Press. https://www.nber.org/system/files/chapters/c11593/revisions/c11593.rev0.pdf

Chakraverty, D. (2019). Impostor phenomenon in STEM: Occurrence, attribution, and identity. *Studies in Graduate and Postdoctoral Education, 10*(1), 2–20. https://doi.org/10.1108/SGPE-D-18-00014

Coker, J. S., Heiser, E., Taylor, L., & Book, C. (2017). Impacts of experiential learning depth and breadth on student outcomes. *Journal of Experiential Education, 40*(1), 5–23. https://doi.org/10.1177/1053825916678265

Conley, D. T. (2007). *Redefining college readiness.* Educational Policy Improvement Center. https://eric.ed.gov/?id=ED539251

Dobrow, S. R., Chandler, D. E., Murphy, W. M., & Kram, K. E. (2012). A review of developmental networks: Incorporating a mutuality perspective. *Journal of Management, 38*(1), 210–242. https://doi.org/10.1177/0149206311415858

Eismann, L. (2016, November 1). First-generation students and job success. *NACE Journal.* https://tinyurl.com/msfpys2r

García, H. A., & McNaughtan, J. (2019). "Why not?": How STEM identity development promotes Black transfer and transition. *The Journal of Negro Education, 88*(3), 343–357. https://doi.org/10.7709/jnegroeducation.88.3.0343

Garoutte, L., & McCarthy-Gilmore, K. (2014). Preparing students for community-based learning using an asset-based approach. *Journal of the Scholarship of Teaching and Learning, 14*(5), 48–61. https://doi.org/10.14434/josotlv14i5.5060

Goldrick-Rab, S. (2010). Challenges and opportunities for improving community college student success. *Review of Educational Research, 80*(3), 437–469. https://doi.org/10.3102/2F0034654310370163

Griffin, P., McGaw, B., & Care, E. (Eds.). (2012). *Assessment and teaching of 21st century skills.* Springer. http://doi.org/10.1007/978-94-007-2324-5

Hu, X., & Ortagus, J. C. (2019). A national study of the influence of the community college pathway on female students' STEM baccalaureate success. *Community College Review, 47*(3), 242–273. https://doi.org/10.1177%2F0091552119850321

Jang, H. (2016). Identifying 21st century STEM competencies using workplace data. *Journal of Science Education and Technology, 25*(2), 284–301. https://doi.org/10.1007/s10956-015-9593-1

Jenkins, P. D., Lahr, H. E., & Fink, J. (2017). *Implementing guided pathways: Early insights from the AACC pathways colleges.* https://doi.org/10.7916/D86D608W

Kazi, A. S., & Akhlaq, A. (2017). Factors affecting students' career choice. *Journal of Research & Reflections in Education, 11*(2), 187–196. https://tinyurl.com/2p8z9nxt

King, M. C. (2002). *Two-year college advising.* NACADA Clearinghouse of Academic Advising Resources. http://www.nacada.ksu.edu/tabid/3318/articleType/ArticleView/articleId/131/article.aspx.

Kuh, G. D. (2008). *High-impact educational practices: What they are, who has access to them, and why they matter.* Association of American Colleges and Universities.

Laanan, F. S., Starobin, S. S., & Eggleston, L. E. (2010). Adjustment of community college students at a four-year university: Role and relevance of transfer student capital for student retention. *Journal of College Student Retention: Research, Theory & Practice, 12*(2), 175–209. https://doi.org/10.2190/CS.12.2.d

Labov, J. B. (2012). Changing and evolving relationships between two- and four-year colleges and universities: They're not your parents' community colleges anymore. *CBE—Life Sciences Education, 11*(2), 121–128. https://doi.org/10.1187/cbe.12-03-0031

Lee, H., Anderson, C. B., Yates, M. S., Chang, S., & Chakraverty, D. (2020). Insights into the complexity of the impostor phenomenon among trainees and professionals in STEM and medicine. *Current Psychology, 41*, 5913–5924. https://doi.org/10.1007/s12144-020-01089-1

Maietta, H. (2016). Unfamiliar territory: Meeting the career development needs of first-generation college students. *NACE Journal, 77*(2), 19–25. https://tinyurl.com/4wyk59az

Maliszewski Lukszo, C., & Hayes, S. (2019). Facilitating transfer student success: Exploring sources of transfer student capital. *Community College Review, 48*(1), 31–54. https://doi.org/10.1177/0091552119876017

Musoba, G. D., & Nicholas, T. (2020). Pathways and potholes: Transfer student experiences at a four-year university. *College and University, 95*(3), 2–9.

Nicholson, B. A., Pollock, M., Ketcham, C. J., Fitz Gibbon, H. M., Bradley, E. D., & Bata, M. (2017). *Beyond the mentor–mentee model: A case for multi-mentoring in undergraduate research.* The College of Wooster Open Works. https://openworks.wooster.edu/facpub/373

Packard, B. W. L., Gagnon, J. L., & Senas, A. J. (2012). Navigating community college transfer in science, technical, engineering, and mathematics fields. *Community College Journal of Research and Practice, 36*(9), 670–683. https://doi.org/10.1080/10668926.2010.495570

Packard, B. W. L., & Jeffers, K. C. (2013). Advising and progress in the community college STEM transfer pathway. *NACADA Journal, 33*(2), 65–76. https://doi.org/10.12930/NACADA-13-015

Rios, A. L. (2019). *Examining the impacts of intrusive advising on the retention and academic success of first-year, at-risk, community college students* (Paper 397) [Doctoral dissertation, St. John Fisher College]. Fisher Digital Publications. https://fisherpub.sjfc.edu/education_etd/397

Roberts, J. (2018). Professional staff contributions to student retention and success in higher education. *Journal of Higher Education Policy and Management, 40*(2), 140–153. https://doi.org/10.1080/1360080X.2018.1428409

Rodriguez, S. L., Hensen, K. A., & Espino, M. L. (2019). Promoting STEM identity development in CCs & across the transfer process. *Journal of Applied Research in the Community College, 26*(2), 11–22. https://tinyurl.com/2zd5y4tt

SOC Policy Committee. (2019, June). *Options for defining STEM (Science, Technology, Engineering, and Mathematics) occupations under the 2018 Standard Occupational Classification (SOC) system.* Bureau of Labor Statistics. https://www.bls.gov/soc/attachment_a_stem_2018.pdf

Starobin, S. S., Smith, D. J., & Santos Laanan, F. (2016). Deconstructing the transfer student capital: Intersect between cultural and social capital among female transfer students in STEM fields. *Community College Journal of Research and Practice, 40*(12), 1040–1057. https://doi.org/10.1080/10668926.2016.1204964

Steinke, J., & Tavarez, P. M. P. (2018). Cultural representations of gender and STEM: Portrayals of female STEM characters in popular films 2002–2014. *International Journal of Gender, Science and Technology, 9*(3), 244–277. https://tinyurl.com/36vm95bb

Thomas, L., Quinn, J., Slack, K., & Casey, L. (2002). *Student services: Effective approaches to retaining students in higher education.* Institute for Access Studies, Staffordshire University. https://tinyurl.com/mu7fe3vx

Wang, X. (2021). *On my own: the challenge and promise of building equitable STEM transfer pathways.* Harvard Education Press. https://tinyurl.com/meethuzp

Ward, T. (2020). *Design thinking: Classroom integration to increase critical thinking, communication, collaboration, and creativity* (Publication No. 28087188) [Doctoral dissertation, Lamar University–Beaumont]. ProQuest Dissertations and Theses Global.

Whitehead, A. (2018). Examining influence of family, friends, and educators on first-year college student selection STEM major selection. *Journal of GMU Graduate Research, 5*(2), 58–84. https://doi.org/10.13021/G8jmgr.v5i2.1963

Wyner, J., Deane, K. C., Jenkins, D., & Fink, J. (2016). *The transfer playbook: essential practices for two- and four-year colleges.* Aspen Institute & Community College Research Center. https://eric.ed.gov/?id=ED565894

CHAPTER SIX

The Impact of Early and Integrated Career Support for Students Who Transfer

Miranda Atkinson and Rachel Allen

"The SOJC Transfer Student Seminar helped ground me at the University of Oregon and sparked my growth there. It gave me a community and an understanding of the community I had just stepped into."

—Jodi A.

Student success, a term used in higher education to focus primarily on educational outcomes such as time to degree, retention, and academic performance, has broadened recently to include career development. For example, the Complete College America's (2019) report *College, On Purpose* connected traditional student success factors and career development support. However, most institutions provide few strategic interventions focusing on career development for students who transfer.

This deficit becomes increasingly significant when considering the added barriers and limitations students who transfer often face. For example, because students who transfer have higher associations with other nontraditional and minoritized student identities (Cataldi et al., 2018), time and attention often go to academic progress, navigating institutional barriers, and meeting other critical needs, such as caretaking and earning income. The result is that students who transfer often navigate their career journeys independently, seeking career resources when time allows and leaving critical career development too late in their academic tenure.

Strada Education Network and Gallup's (2017) examination of current students and their preparation for the workforce proved that advising and career services are helpful for underrepresented and traditionally underserved student populations and that students receive academic support from advisors. However, career and postgraduate advising is offered less often. These data further suggest that student access to career resources affects equity in higher education. Because students who transfer often share minoritized and historically underserved identities, career interventions for students who transfer are essential for supporting equitable career development. With academic advisors serving as a helpful resource for minoritized and underserved students, integrating career support into academic advising, which students need, becomes a key strategy for addressing inequity in career support for students who transfer within higher education.

Institutional and School Context

Students who transfer to the University of Oregon (UO) face many barriers and challenges outlined above. The UO is Oregon's public flagship research university, founded in Eugene in 1876. According to the UO Office of Institutional Research, students who transfer comprised 17.2% of the undergraduate population in Fall 2021 (UO Office of Institutional Research, 2020a). They also share nontraditional and minoritized identities, with 35% of students who transfer at the UO identifying as first generation and 40% qualifying as Pell eligible for need-based federal funding (UO Office of Institutional Research, 2020b).

In the School of Journalism and Communication (SOJC) at the UO, students who transfer comprise 15% of the undergraduate student population, making the demographics of the group germane to the services and strategies for supporting students in the SOJC. The curricular structure within the SOJC places additional pressure on students who transfer. Sequential course requirements, restrictions on accepting journalism transfer credit from other institutions, and a 2.9 UO GPA for admissions mean that academic progress is especially critical for students who transfer, and barriers that affect it can result in delayed time to degree and possibly even attrition. Furthermore, as a professional school with a heavy emphasis on career preparation and outcomes, career development, including experiential learning, is essential for successful career outcomes. Because students who transfer arrive at the UO after already starting their undergraduate degrees, they have less time to obtain these experiences, seek career development resources, and make degree progress than students who matriculate as first-years. Tailored career interventions for students who transfer are essential for affecting career development and supporting this population's unique needs. Furthermore, given the demographic composition of students who transfer at the UO, equitable educational and career outcomes cannot be achieved without these tailored and targeted career interventions.

The UO institutional landscape of career services informed the strategy, structure, and approach for career services within the SOJC, including career interventions for students who transfer. While the central Office of Academic Advising and the University Career Center are key components of the student support services structure, individual schools, colleges, and departments have advising units that offer varying academic and career support degrees. Because the SOJC is an accredited professional school, industry-specific career guidance is essential, and students are primarily encouraged to seek career development support within the school through SOJC Student Services and faculty mentoring.

The SOJC student services unit provides integrated academic and career advising to all pre- and full majors in the SOJC and strategic outreach programming to engage students.

Students often discuss academic and career goals in the same advising interaction, which allows more commonly sought academic advising to become the hook for engaging students in early career development work. Career advising focuses on necessary skills, interests, and values and demonstrates to students how they can be applied in both media-related and nonrelated industries. Programming and interventions include courses, such as the Journalism Transfer Seminar.

Journalism Transfer Seminar Course Structure

The primary early career intervention implemented within the SOJC for students who transfer is the Journalism Transfer Seminar (J399). Since 1999, the SOJC has offered a fall transfer seminar course as part of campus-wide initiatives. Advisors who instruct the course facilitate a highly interactive experience with content tailored to meet individual student needs in 25-person class cohorts. This course was designed to orient students who transfer to the university, school, and profession. A former transfer seminar alum serves as a student teaching assistant to provide peer-to-peer advice about transitioning successfully at the UO. In addition, the peer assistant facilitates group discussions and collaborative activities. Peer assistants receive a monetary stipend for their work. Early iterations of the course were heavily resource driven, introducing students to academic engagement strategies and other campus departments.

In 2016, the Student Services unit within the SOJC at the UO intentionally integrated career development modules into the J399 seminar course. These career modules recognized the experience nontraditional students bring to their education and tailored content accordingly. Rendòn's (1994) validation theory emphasizes that students approach their education as whole persons with diverse experiences that make them capable of success. This perspective is especially critical for nontraditional students and students of color, who are often told overtly and through systems of oppression that their experiences are less relevant than those of traditional students and students who identify with the dominant culture.

Furthermore, the course presented career content in a format designed to support students' transition and help students frame career strategies in the context of individual student identities and experiences. Schlossberg's (1995) transition theory emphasizes that students who transfer experience multiple transitions simultaneously, including the transition between institutions. A career advisor who understands a student's situation and experiences can create a structure that helps the student feel more confident about their transitions and frame strategies for moving forward. This approach can alleviate a seemingly overwhelming situation by building students' self-efficacy and creating support structures.

Transfer course participants gained access to integrated advising focused on academic and career outcomes. These outcomes included faster progression through their majors (including the progression from pre-major to full major and time to degree), strategies to improve their GPAs, and better use of career support resources throughout their enrollment at the UO, compared to students who transferred into the SOJC and did not take part in the course. The outcomes fostered in the transfer seminar stress that timely career advising and engagement in career programs can improve academic and career outcomes.

The 2016–2018 course goals were as follows:

- Identify campus resources designed to help students who transfer succeed.

- Articulate academic requirements and time to degree for chosen majors/minors.

- Identify opportunities to become involved in the SOJC community.

- Interpret university and SOJC academic requirements and policies.

- Create tailored, well-written, and marketable resumes and application materials.

- Develop job and internship search strategies to help students who transfer gain experience relevant to professional endeavors.

The career focus offered in the seminar included advisor-guided self-reflection, resumes, cover letters, and job and internship search strategies. Students reflected on their interests, strengths, and values to gain a foundational understanding of themselves and their goals. The course focused on career interviewing and collaborative class conversations rather than career assessment instruments, which allowed advisors to better understand students' unique experiences and to tailor career content and advice to meet the needs of each unique cohort. These conversations also provided space for discussion of multiple dimensions of identity. Intersections between interests and major/minor pathways were evaluated and used as starting points to discuss ways to build experience and obtain jobs or internships. This self-reflection allowed students to articulate valuable transferable skills gained from experiential learning opportunities, jobs, military service, clubs, organizations, volunteer service, and other activities. The skills students identified assisted in creating industry-appropriate resumes that articulated the National Association of Colleges and Employers' (2014) career-readiness competencies. The result was an approach to career interventions that confirmed the unique identities of students who transfer and allowed them to capitalize on their experience.

Students also learned how to search for and create internships and portfolio-building opportunities. Discussions of strategic and intentional networking encouraged students to learn about potential career paths, gain industry advice, and build strong professional connections. Empowering students to identify their existing professional networks and expand on them served as an anchor for the course. Finally, students created professional development plans to express their goals and identify tangible action steps to achieve them.

Because students who transferred were facing acute time pressures for completing academic requirements and making career development progress, creating a space for them to feel comfortable discussing concerns and asking questions was critical to the success of the course. As one alum said, "The transfer seminar class was probably the one class where I felt comfortable asking questions about resumes and career development, more than any other classes." The emphasis on validating earlier experience in a setting in which students could safely express concerns was essential to bolstering student confidence and helping students identify actionable next steps in their career development. The course helped students overcome their apprehensions and apply for student group memberships, internship opportunities, and part-time jobs. Thus, they avoided delays in pursuing critical experiential learning opportunities.

Another critical part of the course was SOJC faculty sharing personal stories, their course curriculum, and the importance of experiential engagement. Students built faculty connections and accessibility points in their first term that continued throughout their college tenure and after. One alum stated,

> The relationship with my professors is something that I still hold close to this day. Speaking with them during office hours or in the hallways of Allen Hall is something that I always keep with me. Through those relationships, I gained more confidence, but more importantly, awareness of the outside world and job market. I learned that careers do change and shift, and that's normal and not something to be met with fear or anxiety.

Students also met peers and alumni through student leadership and alumni panels facilitated by the teaching assistant. An alum of the course shared,

> Having currently enrolled students speak up about their personal trials and successes was extremely enlightening. Having the students discuss how they overcame hardships or confusing times in the college experience made me feel much more comfortable not being 100% certain about my own path.

Alumni commentary on the transfer experience and early career progress authentically bridged the gap between college and career. An alum noted,

> Having the different jobs or career paths explained when I hadn't heard of many of them was super humbling. I was afraid to ask questions, as I didn't even know what to ask coming from an entirely different school that didn't go into depth of my potential abilities left me lost. I loved having maps to different, real careers presented to me!

For a final course requirement, students completed a graduation plan to better understand the UO's major requirements, time to graduation, potential experiential learning opportunities, and additional major/minor options. Because time to degree is often a stressor for students who transfer, the academic planning appointment provided a clear path to graduation. During these academic planning sessions, advisors also engaged students in individual conversations about career goals, identity and experiences, personal and professional networks, and actionable next steps. Individual recommendations for career development progress were made and incorporated into the academic planning process, helping students build in time for career progression. Such recommendations considered individual student needs to help students who transfer create achievable goals while identifying and offering support to make progress.

Program Evaluation

Assessment of the career interventions in the transfer seminar course includes preliminary positive outcomes in academic impact, career development, and the student experience, aligning with the intervention goal: to positively affect student academic and career development. While standard measures of academic success such as degree progress and GPA are important measures, time-to-full-major status from pre-major is an essential metric in this case. Because of the curricular structure of the SOJC, progress from pre-major to full major indicates persistence in the major and persistence between first and second term in the SOJC. Career development measures involved seeking career support from faculty and SOJC Student Services and participating in experiential learning, directly connecting to the course content and focus. The career interventions in the course heavily focused on networking and gaining experience and emphasized tailored support that can remove barriers students who transfer often face. The objective measures allowed for quantitative analysis of the early career intervention impact on these academic successes and career development markers for students who transferred.

The quantitative analysis included a series of two-sample *t* tests on data from students transferring to the UO who, at some point in their academic tenure, declared a major in the SOJC in 2016, 2017, 2018, 2019, and 2020. Analyses compared students who took the J399 seminar with those who did not, focused specifically on academic success and career engagement measures.[1] A J399 Transfer Seminar alum survey supplied subjective qualitative and quantitative data on the impact of the course, in particular if and how the course content shaped their career development.

These measurements covered the years during which intentional career development interventions became elements of the course. While correlation does not imply causation,

---

[1] First-year students and seniors were eliminated from the analysis as outliers.

the analyses clearly illustrate a correlation between participation in the J399 seminar and academic success and career development markers. Moreover, significant correlations illustrate the connection between early career interventions and these success markers.

Academic Success

The following markers for academic success were found to determine the impact of early career interventions with students who transferred via the J399 Transfer Seminar course:

- Admission time to full major from pre-major status

- First-term and at-graduation GPA

Because multiple cohorts with different matriculation terms at the UO were used in the analysis, comparing time to degree was a less meaningful indicator of academic progress and would result in small cohort sizes that would make finding statistical significance a challenge. Instead, admission time to full major from pre-major is a better indicator of persistence from first to second term.

Admission Time to Full Major From Pre-Major

Academic progress in the major for students who transfer is significantly affected by how quickly and how successfully students can move through the pre-major curriculum and achieve full-major status. Quantitative analysis of the correlation between participation in the transfer seminar and time to full major showed a significant correlation, with $p < .05$ in 2016, 2017, and 2018.[2]

Table 6.1 outlines the average transition time, in number of terms, from pre-major to full major for students who took the transfer seminar and those who did not. In 2016, 2017, and 2018, the difference in transition time was significant, and correlated with the intentional implementation of career development. The difference in transition time remained through 2019 but became progressively smaller. Co-occurring factors that could, in part, explain the progressive reduction include an increase in institutional interventions, such as mandatory advising for students who are struggling academically, that would have supplied increased academic support for all students who transfer, including those who did not take part in the seminar.

---

[2] The 2019 cohort sample size was too small to achieve statistical significance.

Table 6.1.

Average Tranisition Time to Full-Major Status, by Cohort

Cohort year	Terms required to transition to full major (J399)	Terms required to transition to full major (no J399)	*p*
Fall 2016	1.23	2.09	< .001***
Fall 2017	1.26	1.86	.001***
Fall 2018	1.26	1.81	< .001***
Fall 2019	1.22	1.47	.059

University of Oregon GPA, First Term and at Graduation

GPA is also an indicator of the impact of the transfer seminar on academic success. With the academic support focus of the course delivered in tandem with regular access to advisors, students in J399 had access to more support resources and a better understanding of policies and procedures than students not enrolled. Additionally, introductions to faculty through the transfer course also helped to make reaching out to faculty accessible, which can also help improve academic success.

Table 6.2 shows average UO GPA at graduation for SOJC students who transferred and who took the J399 seminar and students who transferred in the SOJC but did not take the seminar. Average GPA for students enrolled in the seminar was higher in 2017, 2018, and 2019 than students who were not enrolled, though the difference was only statistically significant ($p = .041$) in 2019. This finding likely reflects small sample size.

Table 6.2.

Average GPA at Graduation, by Cohort

Cohort year	GPA (J399)	GPA (no J399)	*p*
Fall 2017	3.44	3.27	.098
Fall 2018	3.33	3.21	.136
Fall 2019	3.35	3.19	.041*

Because small sample sizes made it difficult to establish statistical significance, aggregate data on UO GPA for cohorts 2017, 2018, and 2019 were also evaluated. The GPA at graduation was, on average, 3.36 for students who took the J399 seminar, compared to 3.22 for those who did not. This difference was statistically significant, $p = .005$, with a strong correlation between GPA at graduation and participation in the course.

Table 6.3.
Average GPA at Graduation, All Cohorts

Cohort year	GPA (J399)	GPA (no J399)	*p*
Fall 2017- Fall 2019	3.36	3.22	.005***

Because many students who transfer experience a drop in first-term GPA and a strong first-term GPA is necessary for forward progress into the major, an evaluation of first-term GPA was conducted. Analyses compared pre-major students who transferred and took the course with students who transferred but did not take the course. The results were similar to those showing UO GPA at graduation. As Table 6.4 illustrates, the average first-term GPA within the SOJC for each cohort was slightly higher for students who took the course. This finding, however, was not statistically significant, again likely because of the small sample size for each cohort.

Table 6.4.
Average First-Term GPA, by Cohort

Cohort year	Terms required to transition to full major (J399)	Terms required to transition to full major (no J399)	*p*
Fall 2016	3.32	3.17	.251
Fall 2017	3.33	3.18	.174
Fall 2018	3.39	3.20	.115
Fall 2019	3.38	3.31	.555

Table 6.5 includes aggregate data of those cohorts, revealing a statistically significant difference between the average first-term GPA (3.35) for students who transferred and took the J399 seminar and students who did not take the seminar (3.21). This difference was statistically significant, *p* = .013. Together, these analyses show that students who took the Journalism Transfer Seminar were more likely to make timely academic progress by persisting from pre-major to full major and had higher GPAs after their first term and at graduation than students who transferred but did not take the seminar. Both findings support the argument that early career intervention for students who transfer positively affects academic success.

Table 6.5.
Average First-Term GPA, All Cohorts

Year	GPA (J399)	GPA (no J399)	*p*
2016–2019	3.35	3.21	.013**

Career Development

With career resources for SOJC students primarily residing within the department in the form of both faculty and professional advising support, measures of student engagement in the career development process focused on activity within the SOJC. The markers for career development engagement included

- Student perception of career impact from the J399 Transfer Seminar career content

- Student participation in career advising with faculty and professional advising in the SOJC

- Participation in experiential learning opportunities such as internships, work, volunteer experiences, and project development

Subjective student perception was obtained through the Journalism Transfer Seminar alumni survey, which asked students to provide quantitative and qualitative feedback on the impact of the course on their career development. Objective measures of the impact focused on student behavior, specifically engagement in key career development activities. Because career interventions in this course emphasized the importance of seeking support from advisors and faculty and engaging in experiential learning, these measures are important indicators of the impact of specific form of intervention on students who transfer.

Student Perception of Career Impact From Transfer Seminar and Career Content

To measure student perceptions of the J399 Transfer Seminar and the career content within the course, we surveyed alumni, asking them to reflect on their experiences. One hundred and sixty-six alumni who graduated from the SOJC after taking J399 were contacted through LinkedIn, with 54 respondents (30%). When asked, "Did the SOJC transfer seminar positively impact your career readiness (ability to gain relevant experience, build professional contacts, create/refine professional materials) during college and afterwards?", 89% said yes. Qualitative descriptions explained what was most helpful and included networking with faculty and peers through guest speakers, connecting with experiential learning opportunities early on, and forming relationships with academic and career advisors through the seminar.

One alum spoke about the benefit of receiving support through the transfer seminar and identified the clarity it helped provide for academic and career planning: "First and foremost, the transfer seminar set me up with relevant advisors and course paths for my major. It gave an immediate light to my path through the SOJC. This seminar also made me feel confident in starting at UO as a transfer. It's hard to start classes at a new (and much bigger!) university, but this seminar encouraged me as I no longer felt alone. This is a great social networking opportunity for both classmates and SOJC staff!" This student directly spoke to the emphasis on the importance of networking offered in concert with opportunities to engage in networking with faculty, peers, and staff.

Another alum articulated that the course connected them to a key experiential learning opportunity, the Media in Ghana internship abroad program: "As a nontraditional student (veteran) moving to a new state/school where I knew nobody. The transfer seminar helped me meet others while also giving me insight into the school I was now attending. Specifically, it introduced me to the Media in Ghana program, which has helped shape the trajectory of my journalism career." This student's response speaks to the role of the course in helping the student engage in experiential learning and addresses the impact of that experiential learning opportunity on their career development.

One key feature of the course introduced students to integrated academic and career support through the SOJC Student Services unit for their entire time at UO. The survey asked students how this integrated support network affected their use of career resources. When asked, "While you were in the SOJC, advisors provided academic and career advising. Did having access to academic and career advising support in the same office make it easier for you to reach out for career support?", 83% of students responded yes.

In their qualitative answers, many students found the ability to plan academic and career trajectories together as a key feature of that support. One alum wrote, "It was very valuable to me when I was in the SOJC to not only have help from advisors with my scheduling but also career advice. The advisors were already well acquainted with the programs and different courses offered through the SOJC, which I believe helped with career advising as well." Another alum commented, "I feel like having academic and career advising together is a natural fit. It helped talking about my career with someone who had known me and checked in with me throughout my time at UO."

Many alumni spoke to the trust and confidence that was built because support resources were housed together. For example, an alum wrote that the course "allowed me to build a relationship with the same people and resources in one place and build trust." Student comments highlight the importance of integrated career and academic support that existed both in the framework of the course and in the advising support students could access throughout SOJC. This feedback aligns with Strada Education Network and Gallup's (2017) data on the benefit of coupling a service students access regularly, academic advising, with needed but less often accessed career support.

Student Participation in Career Advising with Faculty and SOJC Student Services

Because specialized career support for SOJC students primarily resides within the school, the two key measures of student career development that were evaluated were career advising with faculty and career advising with SOJC Student Services advisors. The career content presented in the J399 Transfer Seminar focused on introducing students to the importance of early and frequent career development, key steps in that development, and support in building connections with faculty. These measures reflect the effectiveness of those career interventions. Graduation survey questions asked students about career support resources they used during their time at the UO, specifically if they sought career advising from faculty and/or career and academic advisors, neither of which are mandatory.

Table 6.6 reflects the percentages of students who, at graduation, reported accessing these support services. Students who transferred and took the J399 seminar reported accessing career advising from faculty at a higher rate (96%) than students who transferred and did not take the J399 seminar (89%). The same was true of students accessing career advising from SOJC Student Services (94% compared to 86%). Because this survey was recently developed, the data reflect the experiences of only two graduation cohorts; as a result, the small sample size did not provide an opportunity to aggregate data and evaluate statistical significance.

Table 6.6.
Percentages of Students Accessing Career Services From Two Sources, Aggregated Across All Cohorts

	Percentage of J399 participants ($n = 48$)	**Percentage of non-J399 participants ($n = 97$)**
Career advising (SOJC faculty)	96%	89%
Career advising (SOJC Student Services)	94%	86%

Qualitative feedback from alumni about the impact of the course reflects these conclusions. "The connections I made with professors was crucial. They helped me make the connections that have landed me jobs, and I still reach out for their thoughts and guidance 3+ years after graduating," wrote one alum. Another alum focused on the support they received from advisors and said, "Throughout my time at SOJC, advisors helped me manage an internship that not only helped me get credits toward my degree but actually led to a job after graduation." Finally, while more cohorts would provide a larger sample of the population, the differences between students who took the J399 seminar and those who did not, in concert with qualitative student feedback, suggest that the career intervention in the course affected the ways in which students engaged in this career development behavior.

Participation in Experiential Learning Opportunities: Internships, Work, Volunteer, and Project Development

Another key measure of student engagement in career development is experiential learning. The J399 course emphasizes the value of engaging in internships and other forms of experiential learning for future career success. This emphasis was coupled with an emphasis on the value of both prior and current work experience that so many nontransfer students have. Students accessed many different forms of experiential learning to find opportunities without compromising other key commitments, such as caretaking and work.

Table 6.7 shows that students who took part in the J399 Transfer Seminar engaged in internships while at the UO at a higher rate (54%) than students who transferred but did not take the J399 seminar (49%) and had higher rates of internship and employment opportunities post-graduation (44% vs. 29%). Once again, the data was obtained with the graduation survey, and the sample sizes were small.

Table 6.7.

Internship and Post-Graduation Employment Rates, All Cohorts

	Percentage of students who had taken J399 ($n = 48$)	Percentage of students who had not taken J399 ($n = 97$)
Internships (# at UO)	54%	49%
Job/internship post-graduation	44%	29%

Data gathered from course outcomes has several limitations. The career outcomes survey used to gather this information from students was first implemented in 2018, repeated in 2019, and not implemented in 2020 during the COVID-19 pandemic. Therefore, the sample size from this time point was smaller than the aggregate data available from 2016, 2017, 2018, and 2019 cohorts. Additionally, these data are from students who responded to the career outcomes survey and therefore not necessarily representative of the entire student population. Finally, the career outcomes survey was completed by each cohort one month prior to graduation. Therefore, job and internship opportunities do not include opportunities students secured one month or more after graduation. Additional measures of career outcomes at these points after graduation could paint a more accurate and nuanced picture of the impact of the transfer seminar career interventions post-graduation.

While analysis of more cohorts is needed to generalize beyond the sample with confidence, the difference in rates is compelling. Not only are students who transfer more likely to engage in experiential learning if they take part in the transfer seminar, but they are also more likely to report having a job or internship post-graduation. These outcomes suggest that the early career interventions in the transfer seminar affect students' career development after graduation and may influence employment rates.

Conclusions and Recommendations for Future Research and Practice

The J399 Transfer Seminar course is an example of a programmatic intervention with preliminary positive assessment outcomes. The specific interventions implemented with an emphasis on the needs of students who transfer provide a framework grounded in theory for other institutions to implement. Qualitative and quantitative data suggest that early career interventions for students who transfer in the J399 Transfer Seminar course affect essential academic and career development outcomes. While these first findings are promising, limitations of the study, such as small sample sizes, heavy reliance on post-graduation assessment, and limited access to student data, prevent more expansive discussion of the findings and their implications. Future assessment of additional cohorts may address some of these limitations and point to the need for data analysis of larger cohorts over longer periods of time. Nevertheless, these first findings and study limitations lead to strong recommendations that future study assess more measures to find empirically supported recommendations for expanded application.

Objective measures, in particular with aggregate data, suggest an effect of participation in the course on academic success markers (progress within the major and GPA). Similarly, objective career development measures, including seeking career support from faculty and advisors and engaging in experiential learning, were more likely for students participating in the transfer seminar. However, with small sample sizes, the generalizability of this effect is unknown. Additionally, because data from each cohort were aggregated, the contextual factors of each cohort, such as the job market and economy, could not be controlled for. In future studies, larger cohort sizes and additional cohorts could address these concerns. Such adjustments to future applications of this or similar interventions are key for creating objective measures of career development in addition to academic success markers.

Direct measures of the course impact support these conclusions, with the alumni who responded to the survey overwhelmingly reporting that the career content in the course positively affected their career development. Qualitative feedback specified the components of the career interventions that were most valuable and reiterated their importance and impact. These data were gathered from alumni three to six years after completing the course and depended on alumni agreeing to respond. More comprehensive data might be gathered during the course, after its conclusion, or after students obtain their degrees and seek employment. Such adjustments would likely engage more students in responding, allow them to consider the impact on different career development outcomes as they transpire, and prepare them for follow-up surveys at graduation.

Survey data also showed that continued access to integrated career and academic support through SOJC Student Services and faculty affected the overall experience in SOJC for students who transferred. For example, an alum wrote, "The SOJC offers support for both academic and individual well-being. Transferring can be overwhelming, and the advising team was always there to lean on and offer guidance through it all." This finding was intriguing, and additional research may show whether the interventions in the transfer seminar drove student use of those resources and if such an intervention would have been equally successful in the absence of those integrated resources throughout students' academic tenure. Future research efforts could focus on comparing career interventions in transfer seminar courses with and without the additional support of an integrated academic and career advising center, thus assessing how these two career interventions compare with regard to supporting career development in students who transfer.

Additional research is also needed to identify key components of career support interventions and to distinguish their impact from other high-impact educational practices. For example, because this research did not compare the impact of a transfer seminar course that excludes career content with this course (a course like this does not exist within the SOJC), future research is needed to separate the impact of the course overall from the specific career interventions used. However, the data explicitly gathered on career course content, combined with the objective measures of career development actions, suggest that the career interventions in this course were important and affected student career development. The difference in the rates of career and internship opportunities at graduation suggests that the reach and impact of this early career intervention can affect these students beyond their academic tenure. Finally, because students have access to integrated career and academic advising following seminar participation, future research could examine the impact of different integration strategies, separating the effect of early career interventions like the ones in this course from ongoing integrated support.

Finally, this career intervention took place in a professional school of journalism and communication, and the findings are therefore not necessarily generalizable to other fields of study. However, there is great promise for application in other academic and professional areas.

Overwhelmingly, this analysis of the impact of early career interventions for students who transfer to the SOJC at the UO suggests that early career intervention matters and may affect academic and career outcomes and, perhaps most important, the student experience itself. What did students truly feel they were provided by the course? As one student said, "Hands-on support and a sense of community … It always felt as if you had these advisors in your corner because they were literally in your corner of the world. There also seemed to be a greater sense of integration/understanding between the students, professors, and counselors because we were all housed in the same environment." Given the compelling student testimonials such as this one, and the promising early data analysis included in this chapter, the SOJC transfer seminar serves as a model for intentional and strategic early career advising interventions for students who transfer.

References

Cataldi, E. F., Bennett, C. T., & Chen, X. (2018, February.) *First-generation students: College access, persistence, and post bachelor's outcomes* (Statistics in brief series). U.S. Department of Education: National Center for Education Statistics [NCES]. https://nces.ed.gov/pubs2018/2018421.pdf

Complete College America. (2019). *College, on purpose.* https://completecollege.org/wp-content/uploads/2019/03/PurposeFirst_Report_Full.pdf

National Association of Colleges and Employers. (2014). *Career readiness competencies: Employer survey results.* https://www.naceweb.org/career-readiness/competencies/career-readiness-competencies-employer-survey-results/

Rendòn, L. I. (1994). Validating culturally diverse students: Toward a new model of learning and student development. *Innovative Higher Education, 19,* 33–51. https://doi.org/10.1007/BF01191156

Schlossberg, N. K., Waters, E. B., & Goodman, J. (1995). *Counseling adults in transition: Linking practice with theory* (2nd ed.). Springer Publishing.

Strada Education Network & Gallup. (2017). *Crisis of confidence: Current college students do not feel prepared for the workforce: 2017 college student survey.* https://cci.stradaeducation.org/report/crisis-of-confidence-current-college-students-do-not-feel-prepared-for-the-workforce/

University of Oregon Office of Institutional Research. (2020a). *Student data: What's new* [Unpublished report]. https://ir.uoregon.edu/students

University of Oregon Office of Institutional Research. (2020b). *Transfer* (Report No. 202010127) [Unpublished report].

CHAPTER SEVEN

"This Sounds Just Like Me": Higher Education–Nonprofit Partnership Offers Targeted Supports To Help Launch the Careers of Students Who Transfer

Aimée Eubanks Davis

In my early work as an educator and Teach For America executive, I was troubled to see promising students, particularly those from low-income backgrounds, thrive academically through college but fail to secure a strong career. To address this, I founded Braven, a non-profit that focuses on preparing college students to land quality economic opportunities upon graduation that could put them on a path to the American promise. Braven runs an "Accelerator Course" on college campuses to address that education to-employment gap. Although the class has no selection or admissions requirements, it is geared toward sophomores and juniors who transfer and who are first-generation college students, students of color, and/or students from low-income backgrounds.

The course aims to help students, called "Fellows," gain the networks, professional skills, experiences, and confidence that will lead to strong first opportunities and provide pathways for future career growth. Unlike traditional college classes, professors do not teach the Accelerator Course in lecture halls. Instead, Braven staff recruit, train, and carefully manage volunteer professionals to facilitate the course in small groups/cohorts. Braven also works closely with faculty members who serve as the professors of record from each partner institution. Braven strives to help students earn what the organization defines as a "strong first opportunity" that would help build long-term wealth and financial health. Braven defines these strong first opportunities as full-time positions requiring a bachelor's degree and typically providing a combination of promotion pathways, employee benefits, and a market-competitive starting salary or enrollment in graduate school. When students finish the course, they receive additional career support throughout college.

Braven launched in 2013, and in 2014, we piloted our course on the San José State University (SJSU) campus as a 17-student, non-campus-affiliated pilot "boot camp." Several SJSU associate deans learned about our work and connected with me and my team to build an inaugural campus partnership. Initially marketed to transfers, SJSU decided to formally offer a credit-bearing Accelerator Course to all students.

Since then, Braven has expanded. Today, we continue to seek to work with institutions that are eager to innovate and willing to be flexible on behalf of their students, offering Braven's course for credit. As of late 2022, Braven had partnered with six colleges and universities: Lehman College (CUNY); National Louis University; Northern Illinois University; Rutgers University–Newark; San José State University (CSU); and Spelman College, and would soon be launching at City College of New York (CUNY). Many of these institutions offer a variety of intensive career preparation supports and are open to partnering with an organization like ours to help ensure career success for all student populations, including students who transferred. By connecting with Braven, colleges and universities give students access to additional career resources.

At each of these institutions, Braven's credit-bearing course is formally listed in the course catalog, and a faculty member from the institution is the professor of record, who works in close partnership with the Braven team. They ensure Braven follows institutional policies and academic standards while elevating concerns about any student who may benefit from additional support. At some campus partners, Braven staff and the institution publicize the course through emails, social media, webpages, and on-campus events to recruit students for whom the course may fill a gap. In particular, these promotional efforts focus on students who have recently transferred to the institution and may need to accelerate their career preparation as they are already midway through their four-year college careers. At Spelman College, the Accelerator Course is a requirement for all sophomores. Braven continues to scale up the capacity of its partnerships, aiming to enroll as many as 1,000 students per campus per year. We've found that Braven can be particularly helpful for students who transferred. This chapter holds the story of that impact.

The Fellows

When Alysyn Martinez talks about her future, she talks about helping others. She knew, growing up, she wanted to go to college but knew it would be expensive. For that reason, Martinez attended a community college close to home after high school graduation. However, she soon realized that a four-year college would provide more opportunities. Martinez transferred to SJSU, a public university in San José, California. She was thrilled to be at a university highly ranked for social mobility—over half of first-time SJSU undergraduates enrolled in 2019 were students who transferred (San José State University, 2019). Although Martinez received a warm welcome, she felt initially overwhelmed. Like many students who transfer, she found herself disconnected from much of what she called the "traditional college experience," sororities and fraternities, close-knit friend groups, and clubs. Students who transfer lose valuable time and relationship building by not participating in traditional campus engagement such as first-year orientation or, for those who commute, living in the residence halls on campus. Furthermore, as a student from a low-income background,

Martinez worked while taking a full course load and living at her mother's house, which meant commuting instead of living on campus. Her busy schedule left her with less time to engage in college experiences.

Despite the obstacles, Martinez was determined to be the first in her family to graduate with a bachelor's degree and land a job post-graduation that felt worthy of the resources she spent acquiring her degree. One day, a childhood friend and SJSU classmate told Martinez about a class she had just taken: Braven's Accelerator Course. Martinez signed up. Doing so could possibly widen Martinez's postgraduate options and expand her economic and career opportunities.

Not Alone

Martinez was not alone in her ambition or her challenges. Many students transfer each year and encounter the same obstacles in the transfer process. For example, more than one million students enrolled in postsecondary institutions in Fall 2020 had transferred from one institution to another (National Center for Education Statistics [NCES], 2020). Transferring from a two-year to a four-year college can be a crucial step in economic mobility, as graduates with bachelor's degrees have lower unemployment rates and greater earnings than those without degrees (Abel & Deitz, 2014). However, it can also be a steep climb. For example, of the students who started at a community college in 2012, around 30% transferred to a four-year institution, and only 13% earned a bachelor's degree within six years (Shapiro et al., 2019). In contrast, the overall six-year graduation rate for students who started at a four-year college in 2012 was 62% (NCES, 2019).

Across the country from Martinez, Ajani Compton was also determined to beat the odds. Compton transferred from a community college in New Jersey to Rutgers University–Newark (RU–N). Like Martinez, Ajani was eager to continue his education and expand his career options. Compton entered RU–N pursuing a degree in public and nonprofit administration. Though he was skilled, engaged, and dedicated, the transition was difficult. Compton did not live on campus, which contributed to a difficult transition. Many students who transfer face this same challenge (Shayestehpour, 2020). Compton reflected,

> The transfer process was extremely hard because it felt as though the people in my class knew a lot more about the public and nonprofit sector than me … I was going to have to study twice as hard. In addition to that, I was a commuter, so it was hard for me to see relationships being built on campus that I was not exposed to because as soon as class ended, I was heading home. (A. Compton, personal communication, September 19, 2020)

Claudia Saavedra had a similar experience. She graduated from high school at the top of her class, with full scholarships to colleges nationwide. However, these awards were insufficient to absorb the financial burden for Saavedra to attend a four-year out-of-state college. So instead, she opted to attend her local community college, where she received free tuition because of her academic ranking. When she finished, Saavedra transferred to RU–N. Despite her academic record, transitioning was difficult. She explained,

> When you go to community college, you develop friends, you develop relationships with professors. And then, your two years or so are up, and you transfer to a large institution. You must start that process all over again … Who is the right professor? How do I make friends? A lot of the people in my classes were already roommates and were together throughout first-year student orientation and all that. It was a huge challenge. (C. Saavedra, personal communication, September 13, 2020)

Making the Adjustment

As Martinez, Compton, and Saavedra shared, many students who transfer nationwide struggle to connect to classmates at their receiving institutions. This connection is further complicated if students commute or work while attending school. As a result, they may have fewer opportunities to build peer, faculty, and staff relationships to help navigate difficult academic or career decisions. College becomes lonelier and more complicated to navigate.

Many students who transfer also face intricate complexities stemming from social, economic, and racial inequities in the United States. As of 2016, the largest share of students at community colleges reported family incomes of less than $20,000 (Community College Research Center, 2020), and community colleges hold the largest share of first-generation students (Beer, 2018). Black, Latinx/o/a, and Asian students are more likely to enroll in community colleges than their White peers (Community College Research Center, 2020). Students may encounter barriers that affect persistence after transferring, such as working full time, struggling to pay tuition or rent, and systemic racism. In the national cohort that started at two-year public institutions in 2012, White students were around twice as likely as Black and Latinx/o/a students to graduate with a four-year degree within six years (Shapiro et al., 2018), and students from high-income families were more than twice as likely as students from low-income families to graduate within six years (Shapiro et al., 2019). Saavedra, for instance, worked several jobs while attending college. She is an example of the many students who pursue degrees while juggling multiple responsibilities and overcoming tremendous barriers to degree completion.

Colleges and universities are aware of the challenges faced by students who transfer and the ways in which these challenges can hinder graduation rates and job prospects. In response, many institutions design specific programs to support the transfer process. However, Tobolowsky and Cox (2012) found that while schools often wish they could do more for students who transfer, as one staff member put it, "We just do not have the resources and staff and time to do it" (p. 399). SJSU, for example, had long offered a targeted transfer orientation and a Success for Transfer Students course, and they initially decided to partner with Braven to supplement this support for students who had transferred. As a result, the Accelerator Course became the main course to help students who had transferred, just as Success for Transfer Students had been.

Designing the Course: What Employers Seek

In part, Braven's team designed the Accelerator Course content by examining hiring rubrics from top employers, including the corps member selection model at Teach For America. The team used these rubrics as guides, designing a curriculum based on the competencies, skills, and assets they saw employers seeking in new hires. In doing so, they created a course that aims to explicitly help students develop those strengths and frame their assets to speak directly to employer needs. Braven's team also sought feedback from college faculty, students, and employers and adjusted their support in response to their expressed needs.

The Accelerator Course centers on competencies. Braven defines "competency" as the knowledge and behaviors that can lead a Fellow to achieve a goal. For Fellows in the Accelerator Course, that goal is to secure a strong first opportunity and thrive in it. The Braven team determined five competencies were key to professional success: leadership, working in teams, problem solving, and two paired sets of competencies with overlapping skills, "networking and communicating" and "operating and managing." Braven selected these competencies based on broad research into employment and what it takes to thrive in a job, their prior work as educators through teacher training, coaching, experiences at Teach For America leading learning and development work, and the input of consultants. They next considered the skills associated with each competency and defined these skills as the specific abilities a Fellow would need to develop and demonstrate to show they are competent at something. They linked skills with competencies formally in their curriculum, so Fellows could build toward their competency with clear steps and markers.

Based on the research and experiences of their team, Braven's definition of "leadership" includes skills such as students owning their personal growth and taking the initiative to achieve their goals. Braven defines "networking and communicating" as skills such as actively building a network and presenting ideas clearly and concisely. The competency of working in teams requires skills in managing projects effectively and handling interpersonal challenges. The competency of problem solving involves approaching challenges as opportunities and creatively finding solutions. Braven's competency of operating and managing requires students to effectively plan and prioritize their time to achieve their goals and utilize feedback to reach stronger outcomes.

As they developed this structure, the Braven team, many of whom identified as first generation college students, students from low-income backgrounds, and/or students of color, drew on their educational, professional, and personal journeys. They considered concepts such as the gradual release of responsibility, through which an instructor moves from demonstrating a task to shared practice and then to allowing the student to take full responsibility for that task (Pearson & Gallagher, 1983). Fellows practice the skills within these competencies with a gradual increase of intensity, first in online modules in which Braven's team delivers key information and Fellows engage in lower stakes practice, then in their weekly cohort meetings in which they practice as a group, and finally in higher stakes team and individual interactions with professionals from the workforce.

The Course

The Accelerator Course comprises three parts that help Fellows move from simply exploring the career paths that interest them to preparing to embark on those careers and engaging in real-life networking opportunities: Design Your Career, Launch Your Career, and the Capstone Challenge. Braven's staff leads some group events, but most class sessions meet in small groups/cohorts, led by off-campus professionals who serve as Leadership Coaches. Leadership Coaches apply to volunteer their time to facilitate Braven's curriculum with a cohort and to mentor the Fellows. Many of the Leadership Coaches are early in their careers, allowing Fellows to have a meaningful sense of connection through early career mentors who have been in the workforce for only a few years. Martinez's Leadership Coach, Allison, worked at Facebook, and they had much in common. Martinez noted:

> What was cool about it was that you were not really with a professor, you were with a more approachable person … Allison was also a San José State alum … She went to a rival high school of mine. She grew up near where I did. She was someone I resonated with. (A. Martinez, personal communication, September 12, 2020)

Part 1: Design Your Career

The first section of the course, Design Your Career, helps Fellows think through their assets, passions, and career goals. Fellows identify their strengths and practice telling their own stories, critical skills for succeeding in an interview and thriving in a job. They explore authentic leadership and how they can embody it. To do so, they engage in activities designed to help them gain confidence themselves and their ability to persist in the face of difficulty, as well as to identify their existing leadership skills. The course reminds students that employers are often looking for qualities and strengths the students already have—they need to frame those strengths to resonate with an employer. Fellows complete an assignment in which they reach out to the people who know them well and ask them to share a time when these people saw the Fellows at their best. Fellows then use this feedback to write a narrative of their strengths. Fellows also create a core value story: They tell how they overcame a challenge;

here, the program aims to help them feel empowered regarding the difficulties they may have faced. These difficulties may have hindered their career preparation in traditional ways but can be seen as valuable experiences, such as juggling serious responsibilities and managing time wisely. For example, Braven's coaches might guide a student who supported their siblings by working two jobs instead of taking a prestigious unpaid internship to talk about the leadership skills and flexibility they were building by taking responsibility for others and adjusting to multiple environments.

Part 2: Launch Your Career

Through the next part of the course, Launch Your Career, Fellows prepare the concrete tools they will need for applying for jobs and obtaining them. Coaches encourage Fellows to connect with the career services centers at their institutions because they often have key resources, such as lists of internships and job opportunities. Fellows create resumes, LinkedIn profiles, and cover letters, and they turn their personal stories into elevator pitches about themselves to later share with interviewers or job representatives. They then present those pitches in mock interviews with professionals who volunteer their time. Because they are explicitly taught how to use these tools and given opportunities to practice using them in a low-stakes setting, Fellows feel more prepared in the career search and transition process. Saavedra reflected,

> I never knew that a lot of corporations or organizations use a basic framework when they are conducting interviews. Braven teaches you "PAR"—problem, action, result—and when you start speaking to companies and organizations, you want to frame answers to questions that way. (C. Saavedra, personal communication, September 13, 2020)

Part 3: The Capstone Challenge

The course concludes with the Capstone Challenge, in which cohorts solve an existing company's problem, allowing them to bring all their new competencies to the table. As Quoc Nguyen, who became a Fellow at SJSU after transferring from a community college, explained,

> We might help a Fortune 500 company solve a challenge. We split into teams. We have a cohort leader, a product manager, a marketer, an audio-visual designer—we have so many different positions so that we can delve into different categories and business processes, so everyone learns communication, teamwork, and leadership. (Q. Nguyen, personal communication, September 20, 2020)

The Capstone Challenge requires students to create and use a project plan, manage work over multiple settings, and problem-solve using design thinking. They must also hone communication and networking skills in interactions with the working professionals who review their presentations.

Braven Model Outcomes

The aim of the three parts of the course is to help Fellows gradually develop across the competencies Braven's team had identified as key to employers. The skills, networks, and experiences that Fellows gain then support them in launching their careers in ways both intangible—like a sense of confidence and self-efficacy—and tangible—like a more extensive professional network.

Skill Development and Confidence

Braven's course includes multiple group projects to help Fellows build teamwork skills that are critical in the workplace. The projects also serve as opportunities to hone leadership skills, as Fellows take turns assuming different roles (e.g., lead presenter, slide deck designer) and identifying their strengths through the process. In addition, the course requires Fellows to pace their own time in online modules to help them practice operating and managing skills such as time management and organization. Finally, the mid-course mock interviews help Fellows build networking and communication skills.

Braven's course was designed with the understanding that Fellows—many of whom are students of color, students from low-income backgrounds, and/or students who have transferred—face ongoing obstacles that many other job applicants may not have. The course materials are explicit about this reality, noting that Fellows may enter workplaces in which their colleagues do not share their racial or economic backgrounds. By addressing this outright, the program help Fellows prepare, process, and gain confidence that starting at a community college, for instance, does not make them "less than" their peers or future colleagues. Braven helps Fellows see their ability to confront these obstacles as part of their powers as people and professionals. For Quoc Nguyen, this confidence was powerful:

> Braven really helps you understand that … you have all these different strengths that you can use. Even though we are poor, and even though we may see ourselves as not as capable as others, which does not mean anything—because what you do now, and what you believe in now will help change your future. With Braven, they teach you to be confident … to help you see that you are not beneath anyone. (Q. Nguyen, personal communication, September 20, 2020)

Braven's curriculum aims to build this type of confidence by directly addressing the concept of *stereotype threat,* a term that Steele and Aronson (1995) coined to refer to "being at risk of confirming, as self-characteristic, a negative stereotype about one's group" (p. 797). When people feel a performance stereotype applies to them, their belief may undermine their confidence and unintentionally hinder their performance. The course dedicates a complete learning module in which Fellows are explicitly taught tools to combat self-efficacy within themselves to address the possibility that they will experience workplace bias and to have the chance to explore and embrace their identities within the classroom context. This process also offers a bridge to practicing communication and networking skills. Fellows tell their own stories in authentic and empowering ways, both on their own and in groups. Saavedra, for instance, eventually saw the financial difficulties and family obligations that kept her from starting at a four-year college as building professional expertise in time management:

> I had to help raise my five-year-old niece, so I was taking on a very parental role while in college. And then being a full-time first-gen student, and then working two to three jobs at a time and trying to maintain that academic standard—I just had a lot of time management under my belt. (C. Saavedra, personal communication, September 13, 2020)

Saavedra felt that this process, paired with the more concrete skills she gained through the Capstone Challenge and other projects, placed her on the path to her job.

> You start focusing on hard technical skills, like how to essentially do a market analysis on a problem, and then do more soft skills like working with a team or pitching to a panel of judges who are executives of large government agencies or corporations … and that's what led me into consulting—now I'm a consultant in New York. (C. Saavedra, personal communication, September 13, 2020)

Saavedra's reflections mirror some of Braven's internal data addressing Fellows' self efficacy, a quality defined by Bandura (1997) as people's beliefs in their capabilities to produce desired effects based on their actions. Job search self-efficacy (JSSE) is the belief that one can successfully perform specific job search behaviors. Individuals with higher JSSE receive more job offers, are unemployed less frequently, and are more likely to obtain employment overall than individuals with lower JSSE (Saks et al., 2015). JSSE is measured along two dimensions: job search behaviors and job search outcomes..

Braven measures job search self-efficacy using three measures from the JSSE scale developed by Saks et al. (2015). Measures include "I feel certain about my ability to get the job I want," "I have what it takes to get a good job," and "I am certain that my job search will be successful." These measures relate to students' confidence in job search outcomes; they are asked in pre-course and post-course surveys and recorded on a 7-point Likert-type scale from *strongly disagree* to *strongly agree.* All Braven Fellows take pre- and post-course surveys as required coursework assignments, and Braven measures the extent to which students' self-reports of JSSE changed over the semester. Survey results from 2017 to 2020 indicate that Fellows who had transferred began the course with JSSE 12% lower than students who had not transferred (1.0 compared to 1.13 on a scale ranging from –3 to 3). However, they ended the course with JSSE that was 6% higher than students who had not transferred.

Network Building

Braven's Fellows build their professional networks and networking skills as another aspect of their coursework. As with other aspects of the job search, the course offers direct instruction on the importance of connections, knowing that applicants referred to a job are more likely to be hired than applicants without referrals and have higher starting salaries (Brown et al., 2014). Fellows are encouraged to use their class assignments as networking opportunities. They receive explicit and measurable networking tasks. For example, during Launch Your Career, Fellows create a LinkedIn profile and make a minimum of 50 connections in Braven's LinkedIn group. In addition, they must engage in two informational interviews with leaders from Braven's online database of professionals. Practicing these skills allows Fellows to expand their networks and strengthen their ability to continue doing so throughout their careers.

Experiences

Fellows finish the course having undertaken key pre-professional experiences. The mock interviews and Capstone Challenge are built-in opportunities to develop leadership skills and to get to know professionals throughout the course. Sometimes, these experiences lead to job offers or fruitful connections. Fellows must apply to internships, volunteer roles, and leadership positions in campus clubs. For students who transfer, these applications are crucial, as adjusting to their new schools may have left little time to apply to such opportunities, and these experiences provide professional opportunities, bolster resumes, and help foster a sense of belonging. Their Leadership Coaches and cohort also support the Fellows through a weekly check-in ritual regarding their applications and progress to earning a role. This experience of applying is valuable and designed to help Fellows prepare to apply for future jobs.

Community

The course is designed to help Fellows build community and a sense of belonging as they engage in these experiences and skill-building opportunities. *Sense of belonging* refers to a feeling of connectedness, that a person matters or is important to others (Rosenberg & McCullough, 1981). McMillan and Chavis (1986) viewed a sense of community as a "feeling that members matter to one another and to the group, and a shared faith that members' needs will be met through their commitment to be together" (p. 9). Once students establish a sense of community, underrepresented minoritized and first-generation college students attain more successful outcomes (Gopalan & Brady, 2019). Transferring from a two-year to a four-year school may be especially jarring because a student loses the community they built at their community college. A study at the University of California at Berkeley showed that 26.5% of students who transferred experienced rejection because of their identity as a transfer (Alexander et al., 2009). This finding is consistent with that of Laanan and colleagues (2010), who posited that students seek to socialize quickly to lose the stigma or label of being a "transfer."

Braven accomplishes community building in part through its cohort model; each Leadership Coach has a cohort of five to eight Fellows. This small group structure helps create a sense of community and belonging. Martinez, speaking of her time after arriving at SJSU said,

> I started feeling like I was not connecting with people very well. And that is one of the things that Braven was great at. We had this small cohort of people that we saw every week. Braven was an opportunity for us to just kind of … be college kids together. (A. Martinez, personal communication, September 12, 2020)

The community that develops in these cohorts reflects Shayestehpour's (2020) belief: "When community college transfer students developed social connections at the four-year university, they reported feeling supported enough to be able to navigate the institution and persist" (p. 12).

A credit-bearing course that can build a sense of community allows classes to serve as both social and learning time, which may be particularly important for many students that transfer. D'Amico et al. (2013) suggested that for students that have transferred from community college, "it is possible … that a factor such as participating in class, traditionally considered an academic activity, may serve as both an academic and a social outlet" (p. 394). Students with family obligations and multiple jobs, like Saavedra, or who leave campus immediately following class, like Compton, may need to maximize their class time as social time. "I think most of my cohort were transfers. It was one way to feel much more connected to school and other people on campus," Martinez said.

Braven also helps students connect through specific rituals. One such ritual is "Roses and Thorns," an activity sharing weekly highlights and struggles. Cooper (2009) wrote, "higher education professionals can purposefully address the need for a sense of belonging through consciously developing traditions and rituals that promote shared values and by cultivating collective identities among the students that celebrate those shared values" (p. 7). In reviewing the literature on transfer and a student's sense of belonging, Shayestehpour (2020) found that relationships can help young people not just feel better in college but perform and persist better.

The social connections the Fellows fostered in their cohorts may have helped to maintain a sense of community in the face of COVID-19. When the virus shut down college campuses, Braven was able to keep Fellows in supportive contact through virtual meetings with their preexisting cohorts. The continuation of these groupings and the rituals they had come to know may have added a sense of stability for students who had transferred during uncertain times.

Connections

Because the Accelerator Course offers opportunities to practice career skills among professionals, Fellows often end the course with expanded networks and connections. The mock interview process was one such opportunity for Compton. "Braven set up the platform for me to showcase my talents and skills to companies," he explained. Saavedra, too, reflected,

> Braven brought the network to the classroom. They brought in professionals in the workforce—many of them are higher-up directors, higher-up managers. And they are teaching you the steps of how to obtain a strong first job after graduation. You start building this natural relationship. (C. Saavedra, personal communication, September 13, 2020)

The course instructs Fellows to examine the ways in which their existing networks are robust and can be opportunities for professional connections. Fellows draw on their high school and college associations, religious networks or community affiliations, and the extensive Braven network. They connect with other students across cohorts, Leadership Coaches, mock interviewers, and other program volunteers. In doing so, they build relationships that can be resources for jobs, advice, and professional advancement.

Graduation and Career Impact

In surveys, anecdotes, essays, and other reflections, many Fellows report that Braven had an enormous impact on their lives, from building community and growing networks to launching careers. Though it cannot be attributed to Braven alone and cohort sizes limit in-depth conclusions, Fellows who have transferred have historically graduated at a rate more than 50% higher than the national six-year average for students who transfer (cf. Shapiro et al., 2019). However, their graduation rate remains lower than the projected four-and six-year rate for their Braven peers who started college as first-year students. Braven is focused on improving this graduation rate and, in doing so, continues to explore unique support for students who transfer.

After graduation, Fellows thrive. Braven's class of 2021, of whom almost half were students that had transferred, entered an unstable economy with a median starting salary of $56,000. Their earnings were above the most recent national median starting salary for graduates of 4-year public schools of the class of 2019: $51,468

(National Association of Colleges and Employers [NACE], 2021). Braven also tracks the number of Fellows who attain a strong first opportunity, which the nonprofit defines as enrollment in graduate school or a full-time job requiring a bachelor's degree, and including a combination of promotion pathways, benefits, and a market-competitive salary. Braven Fellows' outcome measures exceed the national figures reported by various sources for the latest available data. Based on these sources (Abel & Dietz, 2015; Burning Glass Technologies & Strada Institute for the Future of Work, 2018; NACE, 2019), 61% percent of Braven's 2021 graduates, including students from SJSU, RU–N, and Lehman College, obtained a strong first opportunity by their measure, outpacing the pre-COVID-19 pandemic national benchmark set by the class of 2019, which had graduated in a surging economy.

In comparison, based on these sources (Abel & Dietz, 2015; Burning Glass Technologies & Strada Institute for the Future of Work, 2018; NACE, 2019), 46% percent of 2019 graduates of color from public four-year colleges nationwide and 54% of graduates from all four-year schools attained markers of the "strong first opportunity" standards established by Braven. The 2021 class of Braven graduates also had, on average, a higher percentage (61%) of students with Pell grant eligibility than the classes of 2020 at their colleges at large, the last class for which institutional data are available (NCES, 2022). We cannot rule out the presence of selection bias in these job-attainment results; however, many of Braven's Fellows opt into the program and may already have characteristics that correlate with student success in college (e.g., persisting in and graduating from college, strong academic record, obtaining leadership roles and/or meaningful internship experience).

Looking Forward

Post-pandemic challenges continue to affect the landscape of education and the workplace nationwide, and Braven's team is concerned about the pandemic's lingering effect on college enrollment, graduation rates, and job attainment. Personal, familial, and financial responsibilities may take additional tolls on Fellows who transfer. Braven's team believes that their auxiliary support for colleges and their students, both when it comes to career preparation and in providing a sense of community, is significant in this moment of continued fluctuation. Braven's team and coaches have leveraged their strong relationships with Fellows to stay responsive to evolving needs.

After completing the Accelerator Course, the four students who had transferred—Martinez, Nguyen, Saavedra, and Compton—all made strong progress in their career journeys. Martinez used the resume she prepared in the Accelerator Course to earn her first post-college job. She later used it to complete her law school application and was accepted and entered law school in the fall of 2020. After law school, Nguyen went into business development in the cybersecurity industry; he believes Braven's interview prep helped him land the job. Saavedra is a management consultant, and Compton is an associate manager at a media/entertainment company, a role he worked toward after receiving an entry-level position through the connection with a Braven volunteer.

Martinez reported that even though she started amidst a pandemic, she uses the skills she developed in the Accelerator Course to network with her classmates online. She said that she still feels Braven's support, reflecting that "even in the years after Braven, you have Braven people reaching back out, and it validates what you're doing. People are interested in your success, care about your success, and want you to do well." (personal communication, September 12, 2020). These young people believe Braven's impact extends beyond their own experiences. Saavedra felt that the support Braven offers might have economic and social benefits for society beyond the individual benefits she experienced. She reflected,

> I think if every college in the nation had Braven … more students would be pursuing graduate education, more students will be obtaining their dream job or their first strong first job … and that in turn starts creating this cycle of economic mobility, because the more you're able to sustain yourself financially, the more you're able to give back to others … Students will end up persisting and passing their parents' income, especially those from lower economic groups. And, so, they are starting to live this American Dream that they once thought was never possible. (C. Saavedra, personal communication, September 13, 2020)

Colleges and universities wanting to offer comprehensive and tailored career support for students from low-income backgrounds, who have transferred, or who are the first in their families to attend college can leverage Braven's network of volunteers and employer partners to support their efforts. Integrating Braven's course into academic structures can complement existing career services by offering students a community to develop skills, make connections, and access supportive coaching. To provide more students with opportunities like those mentioned by Martinez or to kick off the ripple effect Saavedra described, colleges and universities may consider building partnerships to create these additional supports. They could also consider offering a formal program, like Braven's, which allows students to gain these valuable skills and to connect with volunteer mentors and employers while still earning credit toward their degrees. Such programs, courses, and partnerships should be responsive to the unique experiences of students, especially the challenges of transferring from a two-year institution or facing financial challenges, discrimination, or stereotype threat.

Students who have transferred must quickly absorb many new written and unwritten rules and protocols on a new campus. By partnering with programs like Braven, colleges and universities can deepen or help unveil the practices that can help young people with diverse backgrounds and life experiences enter their careers with clarity, opportunities, and an awareness of their unique strengths.

References

Abel, J. R., & Deitz, R. (2014). Do the benefits of college still outweigh the costs? *Current Issues in Economics & Finance, 20*(3), 1–11. https://www.newyorkfed.org/medialibrary/media/research/current_issues/ci20-3.pdf

Abel, J. R., & Deitz, R. (2015, December). *Underemployment in the early careers of college graduates following the Great Recession* (Staff report no. 749). Federal Reserve Bank of New York Staff Reports. https://www.newyorkfed.org/medialibrary/media/research/staff_reports/sr749.pdf?la=en

Alexander, S., Ellis, D., & Mendoza-Denton, R. (2009). *Transfer student experiences and success at Berkeley* (Research & Occasional Paper Series CSHE.3.09). Center for Studies in Higher Education, University of California at Berkeley. https://escholarship.org/uc/item/4973x119

Bandura, A. (1997). *Self-efficacy: The exercise of control.* W. H. Freeman.

Beer, A. (2018, June). Diversity of community college students in 7 charts. *ACCT Now.* http://perspectives.acct.org/stories/diversity-of-community-college-students-in-7-charts

Burning Glass Technologies & Strada Institute for the Future of Work. (2018). *The permanent detour: Underemployment's long-term effects on the careers of college grads.* https://www.burning-glass.com/wp-content/uploads/permanent_detour_underemployment_report.pdf

Brown, M., Setren, E., & Topa, G. (2014). *Do informal referrals lead to better matches? evidence from a firm's employee referral system* (Discussion Paper 8175). The Institute for the Study of Labor (IZA). https://papers.ssrn.com/sol3/papers.cfm?abstract_id=2441471

Community College Research Center. (2020). *Community college FAQs.* Teachers College Columbia University. https://ccrc.tc.columbia.edu/Community-College-FAQs.html

Cooper, R. (2009). Constructing belonging in a diverse campus community. *Journal of College and Character, 10*(3), 1–10. https://doi.org/10.2202/1940-1639.1085

D'Amico, M. M., Dika, S. L., Elling, T. W., Algozzine, B., & Ginn, D. J. (2013). Early integration and other outcomes for community college transfer students. *Research in Higher Education, 55*(4), 370–399. https://doi.org/10.1007/s11162-013-9316-5

Gopalan, M., & Brady, S. (2019). College students' sense of belonging: A national perspective. *Educational Researcher, 49*(2). https://doi.org/10.3102/0013189X19897622

Laanan, F. S., Starobin, S. S., & Eggleston, L. E. (2010). Adjustment of community college students at a four-year university: Role and relevance of transfer student capital for student retention. *Journal of College Student Retention: Research, Theory & Practice, 12*(2), 175–209. https://doi.org/10.2190/CS.12.2.d

McMillan, D. W., & Chavis, D. M. (1986). Sense of community: A definition and theory. *Journal of Community Psychology, 14*(1), 6–23. https://doi.org/10.1002/1520-6629(198601)14:1<6::AID-JCOP2290140103>3.0.CO;2-I

National Association of Colleges and Employers. (2019, October). *First destinations for the college class of 2018: Findings and analysis.* https://www.naceweb.org/uploadedfiles/files/2019/publication/free-report/first-destinations-for-the-class-of-2018.pdf

National Association of Colleges and Employers. (2021). *First destinations for the college class of 2019: Findings and analysis.* https://www.naceweb.org/uploadedfiles/files/2021/publication/free-report/first-destinations-for-the-class-of-2019.pdf

National Center for Education Statistics. (2019). *Table 326.10 – Graduation rate from first institution attended for first-time, full-time bachelor's degree-seeking students at 4-year post-secondary institutions, by race/ethnicity, time to completion, sex, control of institution, and percentage of applications accepted: Selected cohort entry years, 1996–2014.* https://nces.ed.gov/programs/digest/d21/tables/dt21_326.10.asp

National Center for Education Statistics. (2020). *Trend generator: Student enrollment: How many students are enrolled in postsecondary institutions as transfer-in students in the fall?* [Data set]. https://nces.ed.gov/ipeds/TrendGenerator/app/answer/2/4

National Center for Education Statistics. (2022). *Compare institutions.* [Data set]. https://nces.ed.gov/ipeds/datacenter/InstitutionByName.aspx?goToReportId=1

Pearson, P. D., & Gallagher, M. C. (1983). The instruction of reading comprehension. *Contemporary Educational Psychology, 8*(3), 317–344. https://doi.org/10.1016/0361-476X(83)90019-X

Rosenberg, M., & McCullough, B. C. (1981). Mattering: Inferred significance and mental health among adolescents. *Research in Community Mental Health, (2),* 163–182.

Saks, A. M., Zikic, J., & Koen, J. (2015). Job search self-efficacy: Reconceptualizing the construct and its measurement. *Journal of Vocational Behavior, 86,* 104–114. https://doi.org/10.1016/j.jvb.2014.11.007

San José State University. (2019). *University snapshot.* Retrieved October 16, 2020, from http://www.iea.sjsu.edu/

Shapiro, D., Dundar, A., Huie, F., Wakhungu, P. K., Bhimdiwala, A., & Wilson, S. E. (2018). *Completing college: A national view of student completion rates – Fall 2012 cohort* (Signature Report No. 16). National Student Clearinghouse Research Center. https://nscresearchcenter.org/signaturereport16/

Shapiro, D., Dundar, A., Huie, F., Wakhungu, P. K., Yuan, X., Nathan, A., & Hwang, Y. (2019). *Tracking transfer: Measures of effectiveness in helping community college students to complete bachelor's degrees—2019 data update* (Signature Report No. 13) [Data set]. National Student Clearinghouse Research Center. https://nscresearchcenter.org/wp-content/uploads/Sig13Update_Fall-2012-1.xlsx

Shayestehpour, A. (2020). *Addressing transfer shock: How community college transfer students develop peer-to-peer social connections at a four-year university.* [Doctoral dissertation, University of California, Los Angeles]. https://escholarship.org/uc/item/5g8632zk

Steele, C. M., & Aronson, J. (1995). Stereotype threat and the intellectual test performance of African Americans. *Journal of Personality and Social Psychology, 69*(5), 797–811. https://doi.org/10.1037/0022-3514.69.5.79

Tobolowsky, B. F., & Cox, B. E. (2012). Rationalizing neglect: An institutional response to transfer students. *The Journal of Higher Education, 83*(3), 389–410. https://doi.org/10.1080/00221546.2012.11777249

CHAPTER EIGHT

UCLA's Career Programming for Students Who Transfer

Alejandra De Alba and Heather Adams

For a nontraditional transfer student like myself, I found the UCLA Early Career Engagement Certificate Program (ECECP) for transfer students to be extremely helpful in exploring my career interests and building on my previous work experience in concrete ways. Because this program was specific for transfers and had resources relevant to my unique life experience, I felt appreciated, welcomed, and part of a community! [Above] is a photo of my ECECP cohort. I am in the back, holding up my certificate." (ECECP 2018 transfer student)

Universities tend to design their career programming with the full-time, first-time college student in mind—a student whose educational path takes them from high school directly to a four-year university or college as a full-time student (Burbank et al., 2021; Larkin et al., 2007; National Association of Colleges and Employers [NACE], 2016; Reha et al., 2009). Programming exclusively for a youth-centered, full-time, residential student population excludes students from other academic pathways and life backgrounds and who may lack the transferable skills and social and cultural capital associated with these experiences (Burbank et al., 2021; Kasworm, 2012; NACE, 2016; Stephenson, 2012). This narrow focus meets the needs of only a small portion of today's college-going populations excluding a diverse student body. This gap programming can leave some students with feelings of isolation or that their academic needs are inadequately being addressed. Moreover, it does not capture the needs of the more seasoned student who has workforce experience and specialized career needs (Chen, 2017; Kasworm, 2010; NACE, 2016; Soares, 2013; Soares et al., 2017; Wang, 2020).

The average age of students attending community college is 27 nationally, 62% of all full-time community college students work while in school (21% full time and 41% part-time), and 72% of all part-time students work (38% full time and 43% part-time; American Association of Community Colleges [AACC], 2022). Additionally, one in five undergraduate students is a parent, most of whom take the community college pathway to pursue education (Reichlin Cruse et al., 2019)—despite enrollment drops compounded by the COVID-19 pandemic (White & Reichlin Cruse, 2021). Students who transfer from community college are diverse and have varying life experiences; among these students are veterans returning to school after a stop-out, immigrants, and Pell grant recipients (AACC, 2021; Community College Research Center, 2021). Many community college students who transfer, even those who attend community college straight out of high school and then attend four-year institutions with no gaps in their higher education journeys, have prior life experience that adds to their unique career exploration journeys (AACC, 2021; Contreras-Mendez & Reichlin Cruse, 2021; Herrera et al., 2020; Soares, 2013; Soares et al., 2017).

Consequently, workshops focusing on "crafting a resume with *no* work experience" or "how to get your *first* job" overlook the substantial number of students who have had lives full of workforce engagement and other involvements. Programs framed purely through a first-time lens can be exclusionary, less impactful, or impractical. Students who transfer need career exploration and support navigating the workforce; however, this support is often different from that needed by a student delving into the topic for the first time. Additionally, students who transfer have a shorter time to degree completion than their peers who did not transfer and therefore have less time to thoroughly take advantage of resources and professional networks at their sending and receiving institutions. Providing effective career services and support requires an individualistic, nuanced approach that considers students' unique life experiences. When developing a transfer-receptive culture, it is important to engage career service professionals as change agents in the transfer process (Herrera et al., 2020). Without this engagement, the transfer process lacks support and a career and workforce post-transfer connection.

Supporting Students Who Transfer to UCLA

Students who have transferred account for 36% of all incoming students to UCLA, and approximately 3,200 new students transfer in to UCLA each fall. Ninety-two percent transfer from the 104 California community colleges, and half of all admitted transfer students identify as first generation (UCLA, 2019). With thousands of students who experience transfer enrolling simultaneously, UCLA faces the challenge of addressing gaps in career services for such a large and diverse community.

Unlike most students who experience a transfer, many students who transfer to UCLA have extensive work experience yet are still exploring career options. Regardless of the diversity of backgrounds, a common refrain heard by professional staff at the UCLA Transfer Student Center (TSC) and UCLA Career Center (CC) is the discouragement students feel when they attend general first-time, full-time, youth-centric, early-career-experience student programming. Instead, the UCLA students who have transferred desire (and need) career programming and services that speak directly to their unique experiences. Therefore, career developmental support designed to speak to their career trajectories and varied professional aspirations is critical for these students.

In 2014, in direct response to student feedback, the TSC and the CC began collaborating to originate transfer-specific career-ready programming. At the time, national data illustrated a misalignment in the competencies employers needed and the ones demonstrated by graduates as they entered the workforce. For example, only 11% of business leaders felt graduates were prepared for the workforce, versus 96% of chief academic officers (Gallup & Lumina Foundation, 2013). This shocking data illustrated the gap in necessary competencies desired for successful workplace integration and influenced TSC/CC to develop career services specifically for the large population of students who have transferred in to UCLA. Most significantly, the reality that these students had limited time to make the most of the UCLA experience added to the urgency.

The TSC/CC Partnership

The initial efforts by the TSC and the CC included cohosting workshops for transfers who categorized themselves as veterans, first-generation students, and individuals with extensive work experience. Collaboration also included general career development and workforce preparation workshops explicitly designed for transfers on a short timeline. In addition, guests from across campus participated in topical discussions on academic-to-career scenarios intended to spark interest in various industry college-to-career options. The effort generated participants from divisions such as UCLA's School of Law, the Alumni Association, and the Academic Advancement Program, the nation's largest university-based student diversity program (AAP, 2021). Transfer-specific, one-on-one drop-in sessions with career counselors were also available, and weekly drop-in group conversations with graduate school students working on their degrees to be career specialists were a bonus for students interested in advanced degrees.

Marketing Efforts

Like many students, students who transfer face challenges in locating appropriate resources because services are decentralized. Therefore, broad-based and transfer-specific social media outreach was employed to spread the word that Career Services had tailored support for the transfer community, which helped combat low resource utilization. These efforts successfully disseminated the messages: The campus transfer social media accounts daily reached well over 32,000 current and former students who transferred to UCLA as well as students considering a transfer to UCLA. In addition, work with other campus partners extended the program awareness to the entire transfer community.

Innovative Programming

Two specific career programming initiatives became scaling targets for transfer-specific support to address competencies desired for successful workplace integration: the Career Ready Bootcamp (CRB) and the Early Career Engagement Certificate Program (ECECP). These two previously existing programs were modified to be more relevant and valuable for students who had transferred to UCLA.

The Career Ready Bootcamp

I am a pre-business economics student who transferred. Before coming to the U.S., I worked in Indonesia for eight years as a high school language teacher. I also owned and managed a boutique shop. I understand that I need to develop my network, but with a lot of classwork and family responsibilities, it is difficult to spend time in school clubs to build a network and learn about careers. I believe the boot camp will help me tremendously because it focuses on the fields I needed the most: career advice, interview skills, and networking. (CRB 2018 student)

Transferring to UCLA was hard. I have had to hit the ground running. I am tired of getting random jobs that do not benefit me, but I lack the skills I need to interview. I was never taught how to speak to professionals. Most of the jobs I have had were in retail, where I did not have to interview with the owners. This camp would really help me learn how to interact with professionals and improve my chances of getting the job. (2020 CRB student)

The CRB is a three-day career and professional development overnight immersion program for up to 50 undergraduate students, with 25 of the seats reserved for students who had transferred. The CRB was developed to foster community between the participants, CC staff, and the UCLA community while significantly elevating the career readiness of students who had transferred. CRB career-readiness goals align with the definition of career readiness from the National Association of Colleges and Employers (NACE, 2021): attaining and demonstrating requisite competencies that broadly prepare college graduates for a successful transition into the workplace. CRB focused on helping students who had transferred develop one of eight career-readiness competencies, the career and self-development competency (NACE, 2021). This competency requires the ability to develop self and career proactively through continual personal and professional learning, awareness of one's strengths and weaknesses, and networking to build relationships within and without one's organization. It includes the following sample behaviors (from NACE, 2021):

- Show an awareness of one's strengths and areas for development.

- Identify areas for continual growth while pursuing and applying feedback.

- Develop plans and goals for one's future career.

- Professionally advocate for oneself and others.

- Display curiosity: Seek out opportunities to learn.

- Assume duties or positions that will help one progress professionally.

- Establish, maintain, and leverage relationships with people who can help professionally.

- Seek and embrace development opportunities.

- Voluntarily participate in further education, training, or other events to support one's career.

The CC works closely with the Office of Residential Life, Alumni Affairs, Student Affairs Development, Parent and Family Programs, TSC, First to Go programs, and numerous academic units to connect current UCLA students who transferred with professionals (alums, parents, and employers). These connections serve as guest speakers and instructional experts on topics including etiquette dinner behaviors, communicating skills and strengths, interviewing, resume writing, storytelling, and networking. In addition, students apply and practice their skills through interactive exercises in small groups and one-on-one settings, receiving immediate feedback and guidance from participating professionals. More details on the design for the CRB program are provided in the following sections.

CRB Curriculum Design. While not initially designed exclusively for students who transfer, elements of the curriculum were adapted to meet the unique needs of the transfer experience. The camp is structured across three days, Friday through Sunday. CRB is hosted purposely on weekends and during winter break so that it does not interfere with class or other potential responsibilities during the week—this structural element was a direct and intentional response to feedback regarding the timing of events. The two-day, off-site event includes guest speaker presentations, career and self-development workshops, and community-building activities. Students are provided roundtrip transportation from the

UCLA campus and back, and all their meals and supplies are covered. These expenses are accounted for to alleviate the logistical and financial burden an overnight program might create for students—a particular concern for students transferring in to UCLA. When selecting guest speakers, programmers deliberately select UCLA staff and alumni who understand and/or identify with the transfer experience.

The curricular theme changes year over year based on student and alumni feedback. In recent years, the CRB focused on mentorship and finding authenticity and confidence in sharing one's "true self" in career and professional settings—this topic was selected based on feedback from past CRB participants, particularly first-generation participants. First-generation college students rank lower than non-first-generation college students in self-efficacy and experience feelings of not belonging or impostor syndrome (Maietta, 2016; Tate et al., 2015). Moreover, past participants emphasized the value of the mentoring opportunities provided through CRB, considering their limited access to professional mentors. Recent research confirms the value of mentorship in reducing instances of impostor syndrome in marginalized communities (Wilkerson & Reynolds, 2021). Thus, mentorship is always a major part of CRB, and because students who transfer have extra challenges when attempting to connect and make the most of the university experience post-transfer, it is essential to ensure students who transfer are paired with UCLA alumni mentors.

Moreover, CRB seeks to empower students to recognize their strengths and values and the importance of fostering professional relationships in one's career. CRB participants engage in meaningful self-reflection, group processing facilitated by UCLA staff trained in guiding career conversations with first-time, full-time students who transfer, and active networking with UCLA alumni, parents, and employers while receiving guidance and feedback. As a result, participants report that putting themselves out there and being receptive to supportive and constructive feedback is empowering. Through the program, students demonstrate that they can network with confidence and learn that professionals value the unique perspectives and experiences they bring to the table.

CRB Outcomes. In 2019, pre- and post-program surveys were administered, allowing students to self-assess selected sample behaviors from the NACE career and self-development competency (NACE, 2021). The CC staff translated these behaviors into interviewing skills, networking, articulating abilities, strengths, experiences, and understanding steps necessary to pursue opportunities. These topics focused heavily on developing oral communication skills with employers and understanding how to translate unique, lived experiences into a networking situation.

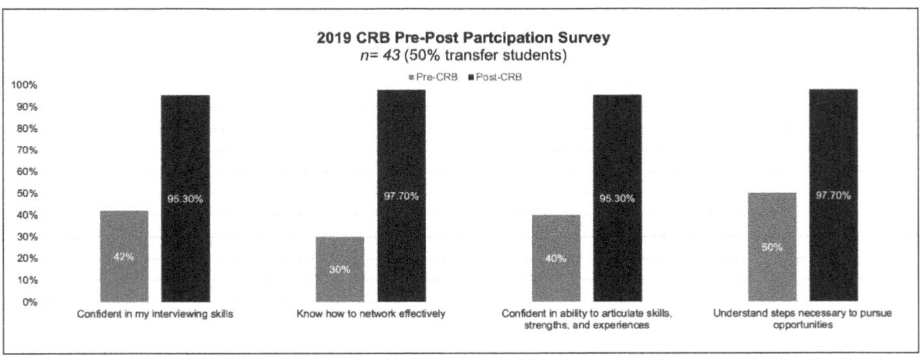

Figure 8.1. Percentage of students agreeing that they have mastered key career skills before and after participating in 2019 CRB

The 2019 survey data show how students self-reported on a four-point scale [strongly agree, agree, disagree, and strongly disagree] on the following components:

- Networking effectively: 30% of students reported strongly agree/agree on the pre-program survey, and 97.7% on the post-program survey, yielding a 67.7% gain.

- Confidence in articulating skills, strengths, and experiences: 40% of students reported strongly agree/agree on the pre-program survey, and 95.3% on the post-program survey, yielding a 55.3% gain.

- Confidence in interviewing skills: 42% of students reported strongly agree/agree on the pre-program survey, and 95.3% on the post-program survey, yielding a 53.3% gain.

- Understanding steps necessary to pursue opportunities: 50% of students reported strongly agree/agree on the pre-program survey, and 97.7% on the post-program survey, yielding a 47.7% gain.

Overall, survey data showed that increased to over 95% of participants agreed or strongly agreed they were confident they mastered the selected career and self-development competency behaviors. It was evident that participation had a significant positive impact on improving students' career and self-development competency. These outcomes prompted UCLA to develop the ECECP, a 100% fully focused program for students who transfer.

The ECECP Pilot Program

> I am a first-generation student and the first in my family to pursue a STEM major. I have only been living in the United States for five years, making me unfamiliar with careers here in my field. I feel lost sometimes and unsure about what is there after graduation. I am certain that I love studying engineering; however, I would also like to be certain about the future career I am working for. I believe having a sharp goal set ahead of me will increase my motivation in studying to pursue it. (ECECP 2020 transfer, international, and first-generation college student. Aerospace Engineering major)

In 2018 the CC piloted the ECECP for students who transferred to UCLA. The ECECP pilot provided a five-session, once-a-week, noncredit course that appealed to students who transferred to UCLA and had limited availability for extracurricular engagement. The program focused on self-assessment, career exploration, strengths identification, navigating job options, and prepping for postgraduate transition. The ECECP sessions fully supported and developed eight behaviors addressed by the career and self-development competency. The program started with an introduction to career development and planning. It concluded with students developing their one- to two-year action plans based on their identified academic and professional growth areas. In each session, the instructors closely considered the students' unique life experiences, prompting relevant questions for discussion and demystifying commonly held assumptions about careers and degrees as well as other limiting beliefs that can derail progress.

The program was piloted in 2018 during the first term for newly admitted students transferring into UCLA. The purpose of students' participation in ECECP was to engage newly admitted transfers early in their university experience and promote career planning and career readiness across eight career and self-development concepts. Students who participated in ECECP evaluated their skills, interests, personalities, values, and career options and developed career plans. The application clearly stated these learning outcomes to help students understand the program. Because of budget cuts and reduced staffing resources resulting from the COVID-19 pandemic, the ECECP was offered online during the Spring 2020 term.

ECECP Pilot Outcomes. An intake question and pre- and post-program surveys were distributed to assess the effectiveness of the ECECP pilot. The intake question was included as part of the application process. The question posed was "Why are you interested in participating in ECECP?" Typical responses from more than 100 applications revealed that the students who transferred into UCLA wanted

- To receive support navigating campus services
- To get help choosing a major or career path

- To expand their peer and professional network

- To enhance their resume, cover letter, and interviewing skills

- To understand the steps to enter diverse industries

One student shared,

> Even though it is my first year as a transfer, it feels like the end of my time in school is approaching so fast, and I still feel lost about what I am going to do after graduation. I have been exploring my options and reflecting on the experiences I have had, so I have some ideas of what I could pursue, but I'm really hoping this workshop can give clarity on what to do next. (ECECP 2020 transfer student, psychology major)

ECECP discussion topics centered on the student feedback from the intake questionnaire. Sessions were designed to promote student confidence in navigating resources, building professional and academic networks, and creating a roadmap to navigate the college-to-career journey for those on a condensed timeline.

Online surveys assessed students' career and self-development competency (NACE, 2021) at the start and end of the ECECP. The pre- and post-program surveys consisted of students ranking themselves on a scale (1 = *beginner*; 2 = *basic*; 3 = *intermediate*; 4 = *advanced*; 5 = *expert*) regarding the following concepts:

- Familiarity with the career development process

- Ability to identify personal attributes (values, skills, interests, and personality)

- Ability to identify careers related to personal attributes (values, skills, interests, and personality)

- Ability to research careers of interest

- Ability to search strategically for jobs/internships

- Quality of job search materials (resume/cover letter)

- Interviewing skills

- Confidence in ability to navigate career post-UCLA

The pre- and-post-program assessment data for the 2020 virtual cohort show how students self-reported on the 1–5 scale for the following components of career and self-development competency, ordered by greatest to least difference:

- Ability to search for jobs/internships strategically: The average pre-program score was 2.31, and the average post-program score was 4.26, yielding a 45.8% gain.

- Familiarity with the career development process: The average pre-program score was 2.34, and the average post-program score was 4.13, yielding a 43.3% gain.

- Confidence in ability to navigate career post-UCLA: The average pre-program score was 2.31, and the average post-program score was 3.8, yielding a 39.0% gain.

- Quality of job search materials (resume/cover letter): The average pre-program score was 2.43, and the average post-program score was 3.83, yielding a 36.6% gain.

- Ability to research careers of interest: The average pre-program score was 2.95, and the average post-program score was 4.5, yielding a 34.4% gain.

- Ability to identify careers related to attributes (values, skills, interests, and personality): The average pre-program score was 2.73, and the average post-program score was 4.1, yielding a 33.4% gain.

- Interviewing skills (oral communication): The average pre-program score was 2.58, and the average post-program score was 3.76, yielding a 31.0% gain.

- Ability to identify attributes (values, skills, interests, and personality): The average pre-program score was 3.04, and the average post-program score was 4.16, yielding a 26.9% gain.

The results demonstrate that students who completed the program felt more confident, with an average 57% increase in career and self-development competency.

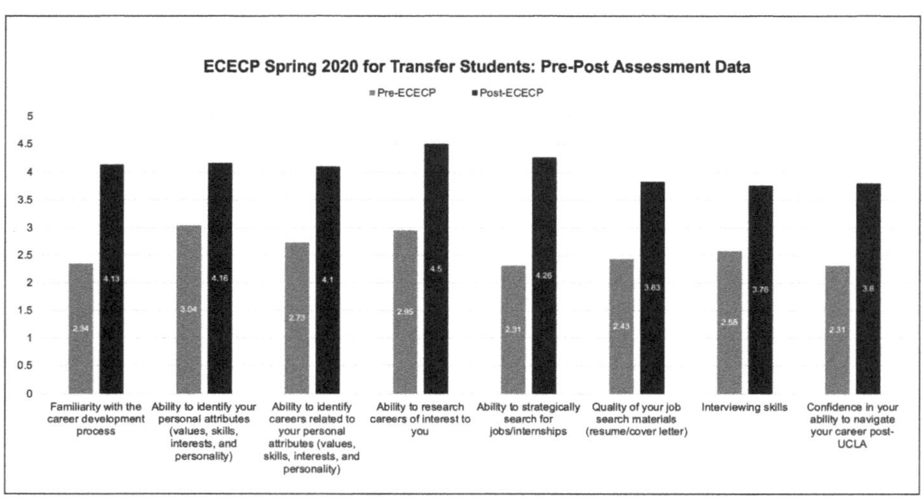

Figure 8.2. Student ranking of their abilities on key career and self-development competencies before and after ECECP

Offered once per year, ECECP continuously reached an enrollment capacity of 50. In 2018–2019, the program engaged 50 students, 20 of whom completed the program in person and 20 who attended all five required sessions. The program ran virtually in the 2019–2020 academic year. Of 53 admitted transfer students, 30 completed the program virtually, and 33 attended all five required sessions. Based on direct student feedback, the reason for student attrition was that ECECP was not a credit-based course. With limited time at UCLA, students needed to and felt pressure to prioritize credit-bearing courses. COVID-19 also contributed to the drop in numbers for the session held in Spring 2020. However, even with the move to remote learning in the 2019–2020 academic year and the effects of the pandemic, students continued to commit to the program.

Students who participated in the 2020 cohort completed a program evaluation in which they rated the likelihood that they would recommend the ECECP and instructors on a Likert scale [*very likely, likely, not likely, definitely will not*]. This evaluation also provided the option to share comments and recommendations about their experience in the virtual ECECP. The program evaluation shows the effectiveness of the program and the instructors—100% approval ratings from students who completed the program, with students reporting they were likely or very likely to recommend the program and instructors to their peers. Also, students made no negative comments or recommendations, and plenty of responses indicated students had a positive experience:

> "I loved how open they were to our questions and how much they really cared about our learning inside and outside of class. I felt like I learned a lot from their teaching and their slides. Their advice was very practical."

> "I liked the resources provided because I didn't know that many of these resources could help me in the future."

> "My favorite activity was the personality assessment because it helped me understand my strengths and how I could best apply those in my career."

Overall, the results, student approval ratings, and feedback from follow-up meetings are encouraging. The growth in career and self-development competency and the students' experience in the program emphasize the positive impact of transfer-specific career-readiness programs and the need for more transfer-specific career programming at the institution. By collaborating with the TSC, the CC effectively promoted the program to thousands of students navigating a transfer event via their social media platforms and arranged to split the costs to pay for career assessments, padfolios, printed certificates, a shopping spree giveaway to purchase professional wear, and food for an end-of-year celebration. The total money spent on the program for 20 students was $1,200. This budget covered the costs for padfolios, career assessments, and end-of-year celebrations. Participation in these transfer-specific career programs built student confidence to explore new campus resources rather than relying solely on the TSC to access opportunities—a common occurrence for new, first-year transfers at UCLA who are unfamiliar with campus resources.

Innovating Programming: Lessons Learned and Recommendations

The CRB and ECECP provide insight into how the university might effectively address career exploration and workforce preparation for the many students who transfer. The ongoing challenge is to scale transfer-specific, high-touch programs with direct access for all students navigating transfer at UCLA. The UCLA transfer-specific career programs, particularly CRB, are resource intensive, which prohibits the school from scaling to serve more students who transfer. Initiatives such as CRB and ECECP will require university support and external funding to reach the thousands of students who transfer. However, the COVID-19 pandemic and the rush to remote learning provided UCLA the opportunity to try online programming earlier than expected. In the next section, we discuss our observations and recommendations for growth of transfer-receptive career programming.

Student Feedback

If you are not regularly having a conversation with your institution's transfer community, find ways to make this happen. UCLA learned from asking and listening. Students who transfer can have difficulty viewing their past life and work experience as relevant to their college pursuits. For example, when meeting with a student for a 15-minute resume advising appointment, a career advisor asked, "Are there experiences left off your resume because you questioned relevance?" The student shared that they worked full-time for two years as a truck driver while serving in the Korean military. The student had not included this experience on his resume or in his career conversation with the advisor. By asking about the student's military history in more detail, the advisor was able to learn what past military work experience had taught him and how he envisioned those skills translating to the next phase of his career. The advisor provided the student with language for communicating this valuable element of work. This story is an example that many students who navigate transfer bring rich, compelling experiences ripe for showcasing on resumes, cover letters, interviews, and graduate school applications. They need career professionals to support them in finding the language and context to communicate these experiences with employers.

Transfer-Specific Career Programming

With 100% approval ratings from students who completed the ECECP and 95% of participants reporting agreed or strongly agree they mastered selected career and self-development competencies, the UCLA transfer-specific career programming positively impacted students. In addition, the data show that developing intentional programming centered on the needs of the transfer experience, rather than merely using a model that works for all students, is an effective strategy.

Transfer-specific career programming can be budget friendly and low cost, depending on the institution, resources, available staffing, and the level of student need. Ideas to get started include

- Hosting career office hours, work sessions, and conversations at the transfer center or in the spaces and places these students congregate.

- Working with student staff, student organizations, and the staff designated to support the transfer process to build programs specific to the unique transfer needs.

- Building digital engagement and career resources to expand accessibility. The COVID-19 pandemic has proved that online and asynchronous programming and digital community building can be accessible, affordable, and impactful and can be used effectively if in-person and on-campus events are too expensive or resource heavy.

Collaboration Is Key

Transfer-receptive career development is not one person or department; it requires a collaborative effort. Without joint effort, neither the UCLA TSC nor the CC would have effectively addressed career needs or built strong career development programs for students who transfer. The ECECP and CRB partnerships allowed staff to combine knowledge and experience and educate each other, decreasing resource overlap. In addition, the centers united in purpose and funding, maximizing intentional programming.

TSC and CC also forged collaborative relationships with the UCLA Alumni Association, offering alumni participation in transfer networking and career exploration events and providing a wider network of professional support for the UCLA transfer community. After participating in a number of these transfer-specific career-focused events, the Alumni Association gained knowledge regarding the transfer community's career needs. As a result, the Alumni Association began to intentionally search out transfer alumni mentoring and coaching opportunities and developed an official Transfer Alumni Network affinity group within the Alumni Association to focus on building relationships and supporting current students who have transferred in their college and career journey. Presently, the Transfer Alumni Network is a regular partner in all transfer-specific career programming hosted by the TSC and CC.

Opportunities to collaborate with other campus departments, offices, and schools are available: Law school, medical school, business school, external partners, and regional employers can affect students who transfer successfully and powerfully. Invite faculty, staff, graduate students, and alumni to serve on career development panels. Ask who on campus is already doing excellent career-related work, and develop relationships to serve and reach more students who transfer. To continue developing and transforming the institutional culture, provide transfer-specific training, resources, and best practices to ensure that colleagues and other staff are transfer receptive when partnering and co-collaborating (Herrera et al., 2020). Many transfer centers and programs offer transfer advocacy training to help close the gap in awareness and need (Adams & Greathouse, 2021).

Offer Incentives and Resources

Students who transfer have varying and demanding schedules, and many have limited time to juggle responsibilities, so high-touch/high-impact career practices must be worth their effort. Otherwise, they will discontinue taking advantage of support, as we saw with ECECP. Advocate for providing course credit, internship hours, scholarships and grants, and other incentives for students to incentivize career exploration. If funding is an issue, incentives might include flexible timelines or schedules and accessing materials online or asynchronously rather than in real time. These incentives promote consistency and follow-through, giving the program legitimacy and popularity with students and campus leaders. Recommending such measures and securing them on campus will often require making a case that transfer-specific programming is vital. The TSC and CC could advocate and educate regarding the moral and economic imperative to prioritizing transfer, the unique transfer experience, and the importance and impact of transfer career programming. This advocacy adds to the campus culture and transfer receptivity (Herrera et al., 2020).

Conclusion

From this book and this chapter, we know that engaging students in career development early in their college experience has an enormous impact, with the first six months being critical, particularly for students who have transferred and have limited campus exposure. This impact is particularly true on a campus like UCLA: large, decentralized, and with many students navigating transfer. We know that the transfer and student mobility between higher education institutions is a reality in the journey to a baccalaureate for millions of students (National Student Clearinghouse, 2020). The baccalaureate degree is an avenue for upward social mobility, increased economic advantage, and equity (Carnevale et al., 2018; Georgetown University Center on Education and the Workforce, 2021). We urge institutional partners to consider piloting transfer-specific early career engagement programs, career-ready boot camps, or other career development initiatives explicitly built for students who transfer. Regardless of the format, budget, or institutional support, continue to leverage the resources and opportunities available to develop and sustain transfer-receptive programs while proactively seeking opportunities to increase the career development impact (Herrera et al., 2020).

The following recommendations are provided to develop and sustain transfer-receptive career programming:

- Talk to students who transfer and ask them about their unique work, life, and career experience.

- Build in transfer-specific career programming and guidance.

- Collaborate with transfer programs and professionals.

- Add additional incentives or resources to transfer career programs to increase participation.

Implementing transfer-specific career development programming provides students the career-readiness competency required to achieve their goals post-graduation, benefit talent development nationally, and fuel economic sustainability in the long term.

References

Academic Advancement Program. (2022). *Home page.* UCLA Undergraduate Education. Retrieved on April 30, 2022 from https://www.aap.ucla.edu/

Adams, H., & Greathouse, T. (2021). *Transforming culture and empowering change agents through transfer advocate training* [Video]. National Institute for the Study of Transfer Students. https://www.youtube.com/watch?v=kn1Mw-lWsmQ

American Association of Community Colleges. (2022). *Fast facts 2021.* https://www.aacc.nche.edu/research-trends/fast-facts/

Burbank, C., Romanillos, R., Williams, L., & Williams, B. (2021). *Equity in CTE & STEM root causes and strategies.* NAPE Education Foundation, Inc. https://napequity.org/root

Carnevale, A., Strohl, J., Rideley, N., & Gulish, A. (2018). *Three educational pathways to good jobs.* Georgetown University Center on Education and the Workforce. https://cew.georgetown.edu/wp-content/uploads/3ways-FR.pdf

Chen, J. C. (2017). *Nontraditional adult learners: The neglected diversity in postsecondary education.* Sage Open. https://doi.org/10.1177/2158244017697161

Community College Research Center. (2021). *Community college facts.* https://ccrc.tc.columbia.edu/Community-College-FAQs.html

Contreras-Mendez, M. A., & Reichlin Cruse, L. (2021, March). *Busy with a purpose: lessons for education and policy leaders from returning student parents.* Institute for Women's Policy Research. https://iwpr.org/wp-content/uploads/2021/03/Busy-With-Purpose-v2b.pdf

Gallup & Lumina Foundation. (2013). *What America needs to know about higher education redesign.* http://www.luminafoundation.org/files/resources/2013-gallup-lumina-foundation-report.pdf

Georgetown University Center on Education and the Workforce. (2021). *COVID-19's impact on education and the workforce.* https://cew.georgetown.edu/cew-reports/covid-research/

Herrera, A.R., Bernal Melendez, S.N., & Jain, D. (2020). *Power to the Transfer: Critical Race Theory and a Transfer Receptive Culture.* Michigan State University Press.

Kasworm, C. E. (2010). Adult learners in a research university: Negotiating undergraduate student identity. *Adult Education Quarterly, 60*(2), 143–160. https://doi.org/10.1177/0741713609336110

Larkin, J., LaPort, K., & Pines, H. (2007). Job choice and career relevance for today's college students. *Journal of Employment Counseling, 44,* 86–94. http://doi.org/10.1002/j.2161-1920.2007.tb00027.x

Maietta, H. (2016). *Career development needs of first-generation students.* National Association of Colleges and Employers. https://www.naceweb.org/career-development/special-populations/career-development-needs-of-first-generation-students/

National Association of Colleges and Employers. (2016, February 24). *Addressing the career readiness of nontraditional students.* https://www.naceweb.org/career-readiness/best-practices/addressing-the-career-readiness-of-nontraditional-students/

National Association of Colleges and Employers. (2021). *What is career readiness?* https://www.naceweb.org/uploadedfiles/files/2021/resources/nace-career-readiness-competencies-revised-apr-2021.pdf

Reha, L., Lufkin, M., & Harrison, L. (2009). *Nontraditional career preparation root causes and strategies.* National Alliance for Partnerships in Equity.

Reichlin Cruse, L., Holtzman, T., Gualt, B., Croom, D., & Polk, P. (2019, April). *Parents in college: By the numbers. Facts sheet, IWPR #C481.* The Institute for Women's Policy Research and Ascend at the Aspen Institute. https://iwpr.org/wp-content/uploads/2020/08/C481_Parents-in-College-By-the-Numbers-Aspen-Ascend-and-IWPR.pdf

Soares, L. (2013). *Post-traditional learners and the transformation of postsecondary education: A manifesto for college leaders.* American Council on Education.

Soares, L., Gagliardi, J. S., & Nellum, C. (2017). *The post-traditional learner's manifesto revisited: Aligning postsecondary education with real-life for adult student success.* American Council on Education.

Stephenson, M., (2012). Listening to their voices: Career development for nontraditional students. *The Vermont Connection, 33,* Article 13. https://scholarworks.uvm.edu/tvc/vol33/iss1/13

Tate, K. A., Caperton, W., Kaiser, D., Pruitt, N. T., White, H., & Hall, E. (2015). An exploration of first-generation college students' career development beliefs and experiences. *Journal of Career Development, 42*(4), 294–310. https://doi.org/10.1177/0894845314565025

Wang, X. (2020). *On my own: The challenge and promise of building equitable STEM transfer pathways.* Harvard Education Press.

White, C., & Reichlin Cruse, L. (2021, November 30). *Supporting students' parents through state policy: Lessons from Georgia, Texas, and Washington state* (Report IWPR #C509). Institute for Women's Policy Research. https://iwpr.org/wp-content/uploads/2021/11/Supporting-Student-Parent-Recovery-through-State-Policy_FINAL.pdf

Wilkerson, P., & Reynolds, S. (2021, February 1). The value of intentional cross-identity mentorship: Examining the benefits of shared and differing-identity mentors. *NACE Journal.* https://www.naceweb.org/career-development/organizational-structure/the-value-of-intenIonal-cross-identity-mentorship-examining-the-benefits-of-shared-and-differing-identitymentors/

CHAPTER NINE

Lasting Impressions: Why Immediate Support Has Long-Term Career Impact

Tasia Cerezo

> "I realized I could one day be them."
> —Ava

For many students, transferring from one college to another can be challenging—a lack of knowledge regarding academic requirements, college processes, and campus procedures affects the transition from the sending to the receiving institution. Given the short-term challenges of a transfer combined with a lack of long-term understanding about how transfer affects one's academic and professional pursuits, students who transfer are likely to face career decision-making complications.

An ongoing challenge in navigating the transfer experience is linking a course of study and career choice while maintaining open lines of communication between academic support and auxiliary career services. When academic advising and career services operate as separate support functions, a gap in understanding for students unfamiliar with connecting college to career emerges. Gati et al. (1996), in their adaptation of decision theory, acknowledged that career decision-making is an unconventional process that creates difficulties, often leading to an inability to decide or, if not executed with proper direction, creates undesirable consequences. Often students cannot describe their skills, interests, or values and do not have a personal reference point to evaluate academic and career options. Critical career conversations occur in isolation from academic advising, leaving a disconnect between one's course of study and the world of work. Gati and colleagues explained that the "ideal career decision-maker is a person who is aware of the need to make a career decision, is willing to make such a decision, and is capable of making the decision" (p. 332). Disconnected career conversations can leave new graduates in difficult situations, uncertain of their future, and directionless post-graduation.

Decision Theory

Decision theory is concerned with the reasons underlying choice, whether that choice is inconsequential or substantial. In this theory of choice, beliefs, desires, and attitudes play roles as these preferences cohere together (Steele & Stefánsson, 2020). Decision theory applied to career decision-making possesses the following elements: (a) the student making the decision has several alternatives to select from, (b) a wealth of information is available to the student for each alternative, (c) occupational characteristics, such as educational requirements and employment options, can be attributed to each alternative, (d) the student can articulate preferences related to each available alternative in a meaningful way, and (e) the student is uncertain about their future career alternatives (Gati, 1990; Gelatt, 1989).

Students who engage with academic advisors and career services are more likely to make early connections between their major and career options, increasing their decision-making capabilities. In contrast, students who postpone decision-making until senior year or after graduation are more likely to make uninformed or misinformed decisions and fail to develop a basic understanding of their career preferences (Gordon, 2006). Lack of readiness, an absence of information, and conflicting information are challenges in the career decision-making process, and delaying or failing to seek career support puts students at a disadvantage professionally (Gati et al., 1996). Along with challenges discussed in previous chapters, these challenges position many new graduates underprepared for entry-level workforce requirements and employer expectations.

First-Generation Students Who Transfer

Historically, community colleges have laid the foundation of academic preparation for students to transfer into four-year institutions (Rath et al., 2013), and they are one alternative for individuals looking to make career changes, particularly students from nontraditional backgrounds (Barrington, 2017). Conflicting definitions attempt to identify "first-generation" students; however, this book follows the definition from the National Center for Education Statistics [NCES] at the U.S. Department of Education: First-generation students are those whose parents never enrolled in postsecondary education (Nunez et al., 1998).

According to the Postsecondary National Policy Institute ([PNPI], 2020), first-generation students are more likely to be

- students from low-income backgrounds
- part-time students
- caregivers to others
- persons of color

The previously mentioned definition and identifiers are important to note while acknowledging the barriers to persistence, including course attendance, transferring, and degree completion (Falcon, 2015). An additional identifier of first-generation students, according to PNPI (2020), is that they are more likely to attend community colleges for their career and social development (Ayala & Striplen, 2002). Combining the differences in students' educational experiences with the documented barriers noted previously points these students toward at-risk career trajectories.

Questionable college readiness creates barriers to degree completion (Gati et al., 1996) and reduces confidence in students' ability to persist through transfer. Doubt in one's ability to succeed at the community college level can influence academic self-efficacy that, without intervention, is likely to affect a first-generation student's decision to continue their education at a four-year institution (Crisp et al., 2021; Jenkins et al., 2009). Low self-efficacy manifests itself in career decision-making situations and affects short- and long-term career and professional goals (Taylor & Betz, 1983). In these instances, institutions and students could benefit from coordinated efforts of academic and career advisors, improving the chances for successful transfer and improving students' understanding of their academic courses of study and related career pathways.

This chapter presents findings from research with first-generation community college alumni. Findings suggest that the challenges students face while attending community college have lasting impacts on their decision to transfer and their career decision-making efficacy post-transfer. The chapter presents implications for colleges and the workplace as well as recommendations for collaborative efforts.

The Unguided Academic Journey

First-generation community college students are less likely to seek virtual or campus-based resources related to career advising, financial aid, and academic advising (Cerezo, 2020). Many of these students transfer, and their postgraduate transition represents "a significant issue for higher education leaders in general and career services professionals in particular, making research into their attitudes, behaviors, and outcomes critical" (Eismann, 2016, para. 1). Often, community college students have limited understanding of the financial aid process or how financial aid coincides with credits; therefore, many take courses that do not count toward their programs of study or transfer articulations between institutions or do not connect to their career interests (Moore & Shulock, 2011; Toyokawa & DeWald, 2020). In addition, first-generation students who research career opportunities are often unaware of the information related to their specific educational journey and interests. This uninformed or misguided direction leaves career opportunities unexplored or prolongs workforce entry (Taylor, 2019).

Revealing Institutions Strengths and Challenges (RISC) 2017 and 2018 fall surveys captured the experiences of approximately 50,100 U.S. community college students, identifying key challenges faced by these student cohorts (Porter & Umbach, 2019). Challenges included paying expenses, taking online and developmental courses, and engaging in the rigor of college-level work. Approximately 53% of students who identified online courses as a challenge discussed the difficulty associated with self-directed learning compared to guided and structured learning. Absent or inconsistent advising exacerbated these challenges and created barriers to persistence, complicating transfer potential. In a separate study on the impact of academic advising on student development at the postsecondary level, Pargett (2011) found that first-generation students who had a positive experience with an advisor and discussed topics such as academic deadlines and career options were more satisfied with their postsecondary experience. These positive experiences are essential when considering the impact they could also have on persistence. It is clear from these studies that advising is an essential instrument in achieving career goals.

As previously mentioned, the struggles affecting first-generation students who transfer are not new. These students arrive on campus and face the challenge of identifying a course of study without knowing how career interests intersect or how to seek out available resources to support this process (Toyokawa & DeWald, 2020). First-generation students also lack the social networks and connections to provide resources and support in making important career decisions (Levine & Aley, 2021; Maietta, 2016, 2021).

In evaluating factors influencing first-generation students' job success, Eismann (2016) found a slight difference between first-generation and non-first-generation students in selecting career-oriented majors or academic majors. Career-oriented majors prepare students for a specific occupational area, such as engineering or computer science, whereas academic majors do not prepare students for a specific occupational field, such as mathematics or social/behavioral science. However, a deeper look revealed that the most significant difference exists in engineering and social/behavioral science majors. The number of non-first-generation students majoring in engineering was nearly double the number of first-generation students, and fewer non-first-generation students chose social/behavioral majors than first-generation students. The variation may be attributed to challenging prerequisite courses for engineering majors or unfamiliarity of first-generation students with engineering as a career path. Higher enrollment in social science majors is important because many fields require graduate education beyond a bachelor's degree. Students may not receive guidance about these expectations during the academic selection or during the transfer process, causing long-term implications (Newlin, 2021).

There are benefits of connecting a major to a professional career and engaging students early in discussions of how careers relate to selected majors (Burnett, 2017). In the absence of social capital, first-generation students often make career decisions without association with their academic major. Eismann (2016) emphasized a common finding in the National Association of Colleges and Employers (NACE) annual report that "career-orientated majors tend to secure jobs earlier and out-earn academic majors," also stating, "one could posit that first-generation students either do not recognize this dynamic or are not focused on it" (para. 7). While not all first-generation student experiences are the same, research suggests first-generation students are not aware of this dynamic, and studies indicate that disparities persist for this population long after they graduate from college.

The Experience of Being a First-Generation Student

In this chapter, I discuss findings from a qualitative phenomenological study designed to investigate the individual journey and successful degree completion of a small group of first-generation community college alumni (Cerezo, 2020). Focused on the individual journeys and successful degree completion of participants, the study rendered three noteworthy findings related to the topic of career decision-making:

- Pre-college experiences informed students' decisions to apply to college, their perceptions of their ability to perform academically, and the absence of career clarity.

- First-generation college students attributed their successes to themselves, including to their determination and resiliency.

- Influencers recognizing a student's potential helps them realize their ability to succeed.

Sixty-one percent of the respondents in this study were female, 46% were White, and 50% identified as parents of children under 18. In addition, 46% of the sample had completed their two-year degrees before 2014. Although of varying backgrounds demographically, participants reported similar experiences as first-generation students who had attended a community college.

Pre-College Experiences Informed Students' Decisions

Participants pointed to the factors that influenced their decision to attend a community college. Over 50% of participant stories ended in similar sentiment: They pursued their education through a desire to do something different with their lives to ensure gainful employment. However, like many first-generation students who transfer, most of the participants in this study did not know what they wanted to do after their educational journey, and none used "career" when referring to employment or discussing "what was next."

All participants in the study discussed challenges that affected their initial decision to attend community college (e.g., financial difficulties, family obligations). In addition, participants spoke of their decision to transfer and the life events that led them to believe they could achieve success, with one exception being academic advisement pre- and post-transfer. The low self-efficacy related to academic and career decision-making was evident. These marginalized feelings align with the findings of Taylor and Betz (1983), who posited that career indecision is common among students with less self-efficacy. Conversely, students with higher levels of self-efficacy are more secure in their career intent. These findings are also consistent with Allen et al.'s (2013) claim that academic advising before and after transferring enhances the success of baccalaureate degree-seeking students who begin at community colleges. Mary, a study participant, mentioned her lack of confidence in decision-making about academic and career choices and the desire for better guidance before making educational and career decisions that affected her career trajectory. Mary acknowledged that it would have been beneficial for her to discuss a career pathway plan, take advantage of existing campus resources, and understand the transfer process in greater detail before entering college, during college, and heading into the workplace.

Mary also spoke of the relationship with her mother and its impact on her success, indicating how her mother had different views on education. Mary remembered an art history professor who saw potential in her and urged her to continue her education after her mother became terminally ill. Although Mary initially deferred her transfer, she eventually returned to school, acknowledging the push from her professor as part of her reason to keep going. She, like other participants, spoke of positive and negative interactions with individuals who had affected how she felt about herself and her ability to perform academically. Many participants shared not feeling prepared academically at the onset of college, stating that they could not "write papers" or "do well in math." A few participants shared the emotional and mental toll of enrolling in remedial courses and their inability to process how the course(s) would benefit their major or career, which led to frustrations of "being behind before [they] even started." These events affected time to degree completion and students' career choices, steering them away from potential career paths because they identified a self-perceived weakness. Miguel, a cancer survivor, spoke openly about his pre-college challenges being in the hospital receiving treatment and the importance of having an educator point him toward college as an option he had not considered for himself. He attributed his decision to pursue social work to the community college faculty and staff who "took me under their wing." The self-efficacy theme ran throughout these conversations, confirming the literature that low levels of career decision-making self-efficacy are usually associated with vulnerability to stress and depression (Bandura et al., 2001) and specific career decision-making difficulties, often leading to career indecision (Gati et al., 2011). Conversely, higher levels of career decision-making self-efficacy are usually associated with positive career attitudes, high self-esteem, and clear vocational identity (Choi et al., 2012). The opportunity to combat self-efficacy issues and work through self-identified weaknesses by evaluating skills and knowledge early on and connecting these to academic and career decisions is a powerful influencer in navigating healthy transfer transitions.

First-Generation College Students Attributed Their Success to Themselves

Gaps in support services, difficulty understanding and navigating the transfer process, and navigating the experience without support from family were three barriers mentioned by participants in this study. The challenge of balancing work, school, and family obligations frequently surfaces in literature as a barrier to persistence for students who transfer, especially first-generation students (Bers & Younger, 2011; Lester et al., 2013). For example, Alicia was a single parent while attending community college, then transferring to a 4-year institution. During her interview, she discussed the continued feeling of alienation from her family:

> The other issues that come along with being a first-gen and being successful in a family where your family feels like, "Oh, you think you better than we are" is playing down the fact that I am a little educated.

As a primary source of social support, family influences career development and decision-making (Whiston & Keller, 2004). While a college degree increases the chances of upward mobility for first-generation students (Falcon, 2015; Hébert, 2017), family members often do not recognize their influence on individuals' career development, positively or negatively (Keller & Whiston, 2008). Family structural features (socioeconomic status) and process-oriented features (parental support and family members' interactions) influence the development of career aspirations, career exploration, and perceived self-efficacy (Metheny & McWhirter, 2013). These features can positively or negatively affect students' decision-making, including the transfer transition. For example, studies with agricultural laborers and rural migrant workers that address family structural features have suggested that low socioeconomic status harmed process-oriented features. Specifically, these parents had low career expectations of their children and provided limited support for their career development (Chu et al., 2015; Deng et al., 2013). Because of a lack of resources and support, these students experienced low career decision-making self-efficacy.

Alicia recalled her challenges related to daycare and transportation as a college student with two children. Managing multiple roles caused her to question her probability of success during the transfer. While Alicia described herself as resilient, she spoke of these experiences as defining moments in her educational journey, being happy when the TRIO director at her community college began to advise her on the transfer process. Those early discussions related to education, transferring, and career helped Alicia realize that support was available when she needed to make decisions related to her education. In addition, she recalled benefitting from direct training through TRIO, which gave her confidence to pursue a career in higher education.

Both Mary and Alicia's experiences align with findings by Owens et al. (2010), Parks-Yancy (2012), and others who discuss how first-generation college students experience a constant push and pull, sometimes estrangement from family and peers, and a lack of support from their communities. The separation from their home base can often negatively affect their short and long-term success.

Influencers Recognizing a Student's Potential Helps

During interviews, participants reflected on how their pre-college experiences prepared them academically or otherwise and spoke highly of professionals or *influencers* who recognized their potential for success. This support triggered an interest in following a career path similar to that of these influencers. As one participant stated, "I realized I could one day be them." This data point and the feedback from other study participants echoed the benefits of career shadowing and mentorship. However, an absence of career guidance and needed support resources as well as absence of a foundational understanding of the higher education landscape foreshadow academic pitfalls for community college students who transfer. For some, being cut off from career resources leads to a decision to step out of college: Some students may return, others do not.

Limited career knowledge eventually caused Maria to take a semester off so that she could work. In her interview, Maria stated, "… once I started at the community college, I was not sure of my direction in life, and so I took a semester off to go to work." For Maria, the support of her family and time for self-reflection provided an opportunity to regroup and return to school. Maria recalled thinking during her time away from the classroom, "Is this really going to be the rest of my life?" She continued, "And, so, that is when I went back to college. Okay, I'd rather be sitting in class than sitting in a job that had no future." Without guidance, students make decisions based on their limited past experiences and the experiences of those they know, whether to their benefit or not. Fouad et al. (2010) indicated that the individuals closest to the student affect the student's career development and interests. For Maria, her immediate family members were her influencers. These individuals alleviated Maria of her home responsibilities while reminding her of the importance of focusing on her academics and influenced her decision to go back to school.

Maria's story of influencer support continues. When she began college, Maria knew that writing would be challenging, but after she faced many writing challenges during her first year, an instructor encouraged her to consider an evaluation. After being diagnosed with a learning disability, Maria's confidence and perspective on education changed. She sought assistance from the center for students with disabilities and signed up for additional campus support that helped her understand her transfer options and future career prospects.

This campus support influenced her to choose her current professional role as an academic advisor. Had these additional influencers not taken the time to support Maria, she may not have persisted in transferring and beyond.

Implications for Early Intervention

Students who transfer often make long-term, life-impacting career decisions with inadequate information. Jenkins et al. (2009) suggested that early intervention is the best way to ensure that immediate support positively affects first-generation students who think they may transfer. Early intervention must emphasize the necessity of career decision-making, which is often absent due to a lack of experience with higher education and career identification. Multiple interventions may be necessary to help mitigate the challenges associated with the transfer. One strategy is for institutions to engage students considering transfer well before students engage in the transfer process (see Chapter 5 in this volume). Earlier exposure to career planning resources may increase a student's self-efficacy beliefs related to career decision-making. Additionally, to help alleviate the long-term impact of uninformed or misinformed decisions relating to transfer and career, first-generation students who transfer would benefit from mentors (influencers) to aid in laying the foundation for students' professional development. According to the U.S. Department of Education Office of Postsecondary Education (2020), support programs—such as TRIO—close the gap in services for individuals with marginalized backgrounds and assist as they move through their educational journey, including the transfer experience.

Another perspective suggests that balancing social integration and appropriate advising throughout the educational journey enhances a students' experience and positively affects their transfer experience and career development. Although research suggests that challenges regarding transfer and career vary, students are more likely to persist and transfer in ways that support their professional goals and motivation (Ryan & Deci, 2000). Therefore, it is essential to develop capital-building opportunities that help first-generation students understand what social and cultural capital means and how it affects decision-making as a student and in the professional world.

Holistic Approach and Support

In or out of higher education, no single group or individual can fully prepare first-generation students who transfer for the workforce. A comprehensive approach involving all constituents is necessary, most notably along with the student's willingness to seek and receive support. Academic advisors and career service professionals who understand this population's limited access to internship and co-op positions due to work or family obligations could meet with first-generation students who have transferred to identify and plan alternative career pathways. To be workforce ready, first-generation students who transfer benefit from using existing campus resources, especially those in partnership with industries willing to assist in filling gaps in these students' knowledge and experiences. Higher education institutions provide career resources and experiences, including multiyear career support programs, early internships, professional networking opportunities with employer and alumni partners, student professional associations, and individual career advising. Students who transfer often miss an introduction to these services as they are made during first-year orientation, or they may not avail themselves of these resources in the urgency of completing their degree. Without those services, resources, and guidance, one can assume the negative impact of not understanding industry expectations and needs on students' acquisition of tools and knowledge in their career transition.

Two areas in which higher education and industry could focus their collaborative efforts to support first-generation students who transfer throughout their educational journey are experience and mentorship. Workforce experience and mentorship are key in helping first-generation transfers navigate the transition from sending to receiving institution and the college-to-career transition more successfully.

Conclusion

The plethora of literature regarding the barriers to success for first-generation students is well documented; however, the impact beyond the immediate college experience, especially as it relates to transfer and career, is less well understood. Although there is already increased awareness of the challenges many students face at community colleges during matriculation and completion, the impact of the 2020 COVID-19 pandemic exacerbated those challenges and shed light on the growing gaps in access and education. Now is a pivotal time for higher education to redefine its transfer support model and engage in ongoing, impactful processes to address the challenges a lack of advising creates for students who transfer and to encourage seamless transfers via early intervention and continuous career development. It is time to stop taking a passive ride in the journey of career exploration and advising of community college students and engage in a quickly evolving economy through the education of students. In a world with so many decisions and so many paths to consider, higher education institutions should lead the charge to lessen the complications, increase knowledge, and aid in supporting transfer experiences in the journey of career exploration.

References

Allen, J., Smith, C., & Muehleck, J. (2013). What kinds of advising are important to community college pre- and posttransfer students? *Community College Review, 41*(4), 330–345. https://doi.org/10.1177%2F0091552113505320

Ayala, C., & Striplen, A. (2002). A career introduction model for first-generation college freshmen students. In G. R. Walz, R. Knowdell, & C. Kirkman (Eds.), *Thriving in challenging and uncertain times* (pp. 57–62). https:files.eric.ed.gov/fulltext/ED469991.pdf#page=61

Bandura, A., Barbaranelli, C., Caprara, G. V., & Pastorelli, C. (2001). Self-efficacy beliefs as shapers of children's aspirations and career trajectories. *Child Development, 72*(1), 187–206.

Barrington, K. (2017, July 19). *Switching careers? Consider going to community college.* Community College Review. https://www.communitycollegereview.com/blog/switching-careers-consider-going-to-community-college

Bers, T., & Younger, D. (2011). The role of feeder community colleges. In M. A. Poisel & S. Joseph (Eds.), *Transfer students in higher education, building foundations for policies, programs, and services that foster student success.* National Resource Center for The First-Year Experience and Students in Transition.

Burnett, R. I. (2017). *It's a major decision: The process of choosing a major by first-generation college students in a scholarship program* (Publication No. 10275478) [Doctoral dissertation, Regis College]. ProQuest Dissertation and Thesis Global.

Cerezo, T. L (2020). *Factors attributing to success: Perceptions of first-generation, community college alumni's journey to degree attainment* (Publication No. 28000141) [Doctoral dissertation, Regis College]. ProQuest Dissertation and Thesis Global.

Choi, B. Y., Park, H., Yang, E., Lee, S. K., Lee, Y., & Lee, S. M. (2012). Understanding career decision self-efficacy: A meta-analytic approach. *Journal of Career Development, 39*(5), 443–460. http://doi.org/10.1177/0894845311398042

Chu, X., Li, Z., Yan, B., Han, J., & Fan, F. (2015). Comparative study of regular and vocational high school students on family socioeconomic status, social support, self-efficacy and well-being. *Open Journal of Social Sciences, 3*, 61–68. http://doi.org/10.4236/jss.2015.38006

Crisp, G., & Nuñez, A. (2014). Understanding the Racial Transfer Gap: Modeling Underrepresented Minority and Nonminority Students' Pathways from Two-to Four-Year Institutions. *The Review of Higher Education 37*(3), 291-320. doi:10.1353/rhe.2014.0017.

Deng, D., He, G., & Zhao, Y. (2013). Parents' occupational expectations of primary and junior high school students and influencing factors. In X. Lu, P. Li, G. Chen, W. Li, & X. Xu (Eds.), *Chinese research perspectives on society* (Vol.1, pp. 139–153). Brill.

Eismann, L. (2016, November 1). *First-generation students and job success.* NACE Community. https://www.naceweb.org/job-market/special-populations/first-generation-students-and-job-success/

Falcon, L. (2015). Breaking down barriers: First-generation college students and college success. *Innovation Showcase, 10*(6). https://www.league.org/innovation-showcase/breaking-down-barriers-first-generation-college-students-and-college-success

Fouad, N. A., Cotter, E. W., Fitzpatrick, M. E., Kantamneni, N., Carter, L., & Bernfeld, S. (2010). Development and validation of the family influence scale. *Journal of Career Assessment, 18*(3), 276–291. http://doi.org/10.1177/1069072710364793

Gati, I. (1990). Why, when, and how to take into account the uncertainty involved in career decisions. *Journal of Counseling Psychology, 37,* 277–280. https:/doi.org/

Gati, I., Gadassi, R., Saka, N., Hadadi, Y., Ansenberg, N., Friedmann, R., & Asulin-Peretz, L. (2011). Emotional and personality-related aspects of career decision-making difficulties: Facets of career indecisiveness. *Journal of Career Assessment, 19*(1), 3–20. http://doi.org/10.1177/1069072710382525

Gati, I., Krausz, M., & Osipow, S. H. (1996). A taxonomy of difficulties in career decision making. *Journal of Counseling Psychology, 43*(4), 510–526. https://doi.org/10.1037/0022-0167.43.4.510

Gelatt, H. B. (1989). Positive uncertainty: A new decision-making framework for counseling. *Journal of Counseling Psychology, 36,* 252–256. https:/doi.org/

Gordon, V. N. (2006). *Career advising: An academic advisor's guide.* Jossey-Bass.

Hébert, T. P. (2017). An examination of high-achieving first-generation college students from low-income backgrounds. *Gifted Child Quarterly, 62*(1), 96–110. https://doi.org/10.1177%2F0016986217738051

Jenkins, A. L., Miyazaki, Y., & Janosik, S. M. (2009). Predictors that distinguish first-generation college students from non-first-generation college students. *Journal of Multicultural, Gender and Minority Studies, 3*(1), 142-161.

Keller, B. K., & Whiston, S. C. (2008). The role of parental influences on young adolescents' career development. *Journal of Career Assessment, 16*(2), 198–217. http://doi.org/10.1177/1069072707313206

Lester, J., Leonard, J. B., & Mathias, D. (2013). Transfer student engagement: Blurring of social and academic engagement. *Community College Review, 41*(3), 202–222. https://doi.org/10.1177%2F0091552113496141

Levine, K., & Aley, M. (2021). Career barriers affecting first-generation college students: Can socializing messages increase career confidence? *Southern Communication Journal, 86*(5), 498–510. http://doi.org/10.1080/1041794X.2021.1970795

Maietta, H. (2016, November 1). Career development needs of first-generation students. *NACE Journal.* https://www.naceweb.org/career-development/special-populations/career-development-needs-of-first-generation-students/

Maietta, H. N. (2021). Career development needs of first-generation college students. In R. Longwell-Grice & H. Longwell-Grice (Eds.), *At the intersection: Understanding and supporting first-generation college students,* 244-259. Stylus Publishing, LLC.

Metheny, J., & McWhirter, E. H. (2013). Contributions of social status and family support to college students' career decision self-efficacy and outcome expectations. *Journal of Career Assessment, 21*(3), 378–394. http://doi.org/10.1177/1069072712475164

Moore, C., & Shulock, N. (2011). *Sense of direction: The importance of helping community college students select and enter a program of study.* Institute for Higher Education Leadership & Policy.

Newlin, M. (2021). *Employment trends of first-generation college students: A review of the literature.* National Student Employment Association. https://nsea.memberclicks.net/assets/docs/Employment%20Trends%20for%20First-Generation%20Students.pdf

Nunez, A. M., Cuccaro-Alamin, S., & Carroll, C. D. (1998). *First-generation students: Undergraduates whose parents never enrolled in postsecondary education* (Statistical Analysis Report, NCES 98-082). U.S. Department of Education, National Center for Education Statistics. https://nces.ed.gov/pubs98/98082.pdf

Owens, D., Lacey, K., Rawls, G., & Holbert-Quince, J. (2010). First-generation African American male college students: Implications for career counselors. *Career Development Quarterly, 58,* 291–300. http://doi.org/10.1002/j.2161-0045.2010.tb00179.x

Pargett, K. K. (2011). *The effects of academic advising on college student development in higher education.* [Unpublished master's thesis]. University of Nebraska. https://www.researchgate.net/publication/282229297_The_Effects_of_Academic_Advising_on_College_Student_Development_in_Higher_Education

Parks-Yancy, R. (2012). Interactions into opportunities: Career management for low-income, first-generation African American college students. *Journal of College Student Development, 53,* 510–523. http://doi.org/10.1353/csd.2012.0052

Porter, S. R., & Umbach, P. D. (2019, January). *What challenges to success do community college students face?* Percontor, LLC. https://www.risc.college/sites/default/files/2019-01/RISC_2019_report_natl.pdf

Postsecondary National Policy Institute. (2020, November 6). *Factsheets: First-generation students.* Retrieved on January 10, 2022 from https://pnpi.org/first-generation-students/

Rath, B., Rock, K., & Laferriere, A. (2013). *Pathways through college: Strategies for improving community college student success.* Our Piece of the Pie. https://opp.org/wp-content/uploads/2017/06/Pathways-through-College-OPP-April-2013.pdf

Ryan, R. M., & Deci, E. L. (2000). Self-determination theory and the facilitation of intrinsic motivation, social development, and well-being. *American Psychologist, 55*(1), 68–78. https://doi.org/10.1037/0003-066X.55.1.68

Steele, K., & Stefánsson, H. O. (2020). Decision theory. *The Stanford Encyclopedia of Philosophy.* Edward N. Zalta (Ed.). Retrieved on January 15, 2021 from https://plato.stanford.edu/archives/win2020/entries/decision-theory/

Taylor, C. P. (2019). *Influence of career services on time to undergraduate degree completion* [Unpublished doctoral dissertation]. The University of Southern Mississippi.

Taylor, K., & Betz, T. (1983). Applications of self-efficacy theory to the understanding and treatment of career indecision. *Journal of Vocational Behavior, 22,* 63–81. https://doi.org/10.1016/0001-8791(83)90006-4

Toyokawa, T., & DeWald, C. (2020). Perceived career barriers and career decidedness of first-generation college students. *The Career Development Quarterly, 68*(4), 332–347. http://doi.org/10.1002/cdq.12240

U.S. Department of Education. (2020, December 8). *TRIO Home Page.* Federal TRIO Programs—Home page. Retrieved on December 15, 2020 from https://www2.ed.gov/about/offices/list/ope/trio/index.html

Whiston, S. C., & Keller, B. K. (2004). The influences of the family of origin on career development: A review and analysis. *Counseling Psychologist, 32*(4), 493–568. http://doi.org/10.1177/0011000004265660

CHAPTER TEN

The Impact of Forced Transfer on Students' College Transition

Heather N. Maietta

> "I would say that there are still a lot of things that I am uncertain about. There are still a lot of things I have not accurately processed."
>
> —Kendra

Higher education faces financial and demographic challenges threatening many small nonprofit and for-profit colleges. In 2016, the Parthenon identified 800 colleges vulnerable to economic challenges such as financial inefficiencies, increasing market competition, and skepticism about the value of higher education (Kelchen, 2018). Moody's Investor Service (2015) predicted college closures would triple and mergers would double after years of tuition increases, particularly with small private colleges that have "less capacity to support their operating costs through tuition revenue alone" (Eide, 2018, p. 37). These declines were forecasted to be more significant in the northeastern and midwestern United States, two areas home to a large share of private nonprofit colleges (Grawe, 2018). Moody's upgraded their projection in 2019, estimating that one out of every five institutions would encounter unsustainable financial hardship due to enrollment, financial instability, and campus climate issues (Cohn, 2019; Moody's Investor Service, 2019). In addition, deep losses to higher education due to the coronavirus pandemic of 2020 threatened to deplete the resources across the industry, including those colleges that were in a reasonable financial condition before the pandemic (Baker et al., 2020; Bauer-Wolf, 2020; Fernandez & Shaw, 2020). Amidst these predictions and discussions, more than 40 colleges and universities closed their doors between 2016 and 2019 (Witt & Coyne, 2019). According to the Institutional Viability Metric, which uses publicly available data from the Integrated Postsecondary Education Data System (IPEDS) to assess institutional risk levels, approximately 20% of four-year institutions were "at risk" in both 2019 and 2020, and another 20% was flagged as "monitor." Sixteen of the 26 institutions that closed in 2020 and 2021 were flagged as "at risk" (Lundy & El-Baz, 2022). Post-pandemic uncertainty and its impact will continue to alter the future of small colleges and prolong the heightened awareness and concern surrounding the stability of American higher education.

A detailed literature search on college closures over the past five years revealed that most institutions cite financial and administrative disruptions as the cause (Higher Ed Dive, 2022; National Center for Educational Statistics, 2018). As Sapiro (2019) noted, many of the small schools that have recently closed "lived close to the financial margin for a long time" (p. 20), depending heavily on tuition dollars as their primary source of revenue. Tuition dependency will continue to affect college health, impacted by the impending traditional-age college student population decline and the COVID-19 pandemic period, which saw more than one million fewer students enrolled in college than before the pandemic began (Nadworny, 2022).

Parthenon EY Educational Practice (2016) argued that higher education as an industry is in a developmental downturn marked by "diminished state and federal spending, lagging personal incomes of college-going families, and increased accountability around outcomes, particularly the view that the role of colleges is to prepare graduates for a job" (p. 3). These sentiments were echoed by LeSane (2020), who argued that the decreasing number of families with the income needed to finance education and the increasing number of potential college-aged students from previously underrepresented or unenrolled populations are reasons that enrollment has declined and may continue to decline in the coming years. Kelchen (2020) cited predicting factors that may result in closure, such as sharp enrollment declines, deteriorating facilities and services, and inferior performance and graduation outcomes, points that families pay attention to when seeking college admissions for their prospective students. Parthenon's (2016) finding that the role colleges play in the lives of those they employ and educate is essential when considering closure and its effect on students forced to transfer.

When colleges close, students are unwillingly removed from their learning environments before degree completion. Students are given two choices: quit school or transfer. Vasquez and Bauman (2019) analyzed federal data that shows over half a million students were displaced from closed institutions from 2015-2019 in the past five years (from the time of publication), with institutions failing their responsibility to mitigate the impact of the closure on students. Institutional irresponsibility manifested in failing to alert students well before the closure dates or to ensure support services were in place to assist with their transfer. Although Sapiro (2019) pointed out that the effects of a college's closure spread far beyond people directly involved with the institution, few articles mentioned how students who are displaced or thrust into unanticipated transfer navigate the closure. Less understood are the short- and long-term implications of the closure on undergraduate students who began college on a traditional academic path, many with no intentions of ever transferring, now forced to contend with an unfamiliar, unplanned, and often opaque process.

This chapter shares interview findings from 27 students left to reconsider and reframe their college journeys because of forced transfer. A qualitative descriptive inquiry was purposefully employed; I sought to understand participants' perceptions as unique individuals with similar experiences. Data from individual interviews and reflective questionnaires were analyzed to fully understand the impact of this forced transition and supports and strategies needed to navigate its outcome. Results introduced a new category: the *forced transfer*, a transition experienced by students not by choice. Such an event can occur from a college closure or a program discontinuation, forcing students to enroll elsewhere to fulfill their remaining degree requirements.

Transfers as Students in Transition

The typical undergraduate journey begins on the first day of college and continues through graduation. During this period, students confront different challenges and transitions, such as course of study indecision, residential to commuter status, loss or acquisition of a job, and for some, transferring from one college to another. Schlossberg (1984) defined transition as "events or nonevents resulting in change" (p. 43). Transitions, such as transferring from one institution to another, influence relationships, routines, assumptions, and roles in various settings (Anderson et al., 2012). In most cases, transferring is an anticipated event (Gere et al., 2017), but transferring can be unanticipated in certain circumstances, such as a college closure or program discontinuation.

Everyone experiences and manages transition differently, and the response depends on numerous factors, including their environment, background, gender, sex, and socioeconomic status (Schlossberg, 1984; Schlossberg et al., 1995). Transition theory facilitates an understanding of adults in transition and the coping mechanisms needed to move from one event to another in one's life (Goodman et al., 2006), eventually strengthening the resources around them to help them cope with the transition (Anderson et al., 2012). When students transition, they progress through these interrelated phases to move into, through, and out of life-changing experiences, such as a forced transfer. Understanding the progression of the interrelated phases provides students who transfer with a framework to navigate this transition.

In one study, students who transferred from one four-year school to another were 32% less likely to graduate than native students (Li, 2010), despite the extensive literature that exists to identify barriers and challenges in the transfer process. Self-efficacy, strategies, and supports are valuable in navigating transitions and needed to perform academic and career-related actions, yet many students who transfer do so without high self-efficacy, resources, or a support network. Unfortunately, students who transfer often struggle more than native students to adjust to their new institutions and fail to engage in academic and social activities (Ghusson, 2016). Career engagement, a critical and fundamental source of support for this transitional experience, is often absent yet necessary. Amundson and colleagues (2010) studied the attainment of career goals related to belonging. Findings suggested that decisions to pursue challenging career goals and reaching these goals were attributed to confidence gained by supportive persons, including community faculty, friends, and others. Amundson and colleagues found that negative emotions and decisional difficulties are directly associated with a lack of belonging. A sense of belonging or absence of belonging can affect confidence in career decision-making.

Unanticipated and unwanted transfer thrusts students and their families into unexpected, sometimes immediate chaos. Currently, the literature recognizes eight distinct transfer patterns: vertical transfer; lateral transfer; reverse transfer; reverse credit transfer; swirlers and alternating enrollees; concurrent enrollees, coenrollment, double-dipping, simultaneous enrollees; dual credit, dual enrollment; and transient (Poisel & Joseph, 2011; Taylor & Jain, 2017). Although transfer currently has many subcategories, students who experience transfer resulting from college closure do not fit any of these classifications. Therefore, forced transfer warrants a new category and definition. This research used the following definition of forced transfer:

> A student enrolled in an academic program at a degree-granting institution with plans to fulfill all academic requirements for degree completion at that institution; however, because of a discontinued program or institutional closure, the student cannot finish academic requirements necessary to earn that degree and is instead forced to seek education at another degree-granting institution.

To understand the impact of a transfer transition, observers need a more profound knowledge of students' perceptions as they maneuver through the process. For example, a student navigating a forced transfer might ask, "Was I expecting to transfer, or was this transition unexpected?" or "What strategies were in place for me when this transition occurred?" or "What supports were available to help me navigate this unexpected transition?"

The forced transfer may become more common in the coming years as institutions continue to struggle. The absence of research on forced transfer motivated this research. This chapter delineates early findings from our investigation of students' career-related challenges resulting from forced transfers.

Research Approach

A single question guided the research: What was the impact of forced transfer due to college closure on the career-related supports of students who experienced this event? I employed a qualitative descriptive approach to investigate students' shared forced transfer experiences due to college closure. Qualitative research best suits topics for which little is known and quantitative measurement is not likely to produce desired results or open new avenues of inquiry (Creswell & Poth, 2018; Merriam & Tisdell, 2015). Qualitative data are also rich and complex, offering a deep understanding of the phenomenon being studied (Patton, 2015). Schlossberg's (1984) transition theory was used for structure and consistency when collecting and analyzing data, including the 4-S system, which identifies transitional management elements: situational understanding, self-assessment, available supports, and choice strategies. According to Schlossberg's theory, situational understanding and a clear sense of self are essential in successfully managing a transition. Further, supports and strategies combine to identify resources and methods to work through a transition.

The study comprised one-on-one interviews with 27 students who met the definition of forced transfer. All 27 students transferred from one four-year institution that closed (sending institution) to another four-year institution (receiving institution). The researcher approached the study through an ontological lens, or understanding of the world, believing that the nature of the world is far from decided. Given that an existing body of research on forced transfer does not exist and participants in the study reported their experiences through different realities, an ontological lens provided "the use of multiple forms of evidence in themes using the actual words of different individuals and presenting different perspectives" (Creswell & Poth, 2018, p. 20). Thus, although participants shared the forced transfer experience, they viewed and lived the experience differently. Furthermore, employing a transformative framework, I sought to construct knowledge regarding forced transfer to give a platform for the students' voices, raise awareness of the implications of the forced transfer, and suggest change through knowledge (Creswell & Poth, 2018).

Instrumentation and Data Management

Participants were recruited using a purposeful sampling approach to target a specific group who experienced a forced transfer (Merriam & Tisdell, 2015). Additionally, participants were asked to invite others who met the criteria to join the study; this process is known as snowball sampling (O'Dwyer & Bernauer, 2014). Social media and word-of-mouth recruiting methods allowed for broad geographical participation. Students were chosen for study inclusion using a prequalifying questionnaire (van Manen, 1990, 2014); at this time they also completed an informed consent and demographics inquiry. See Table 10.1 for demographics details with pseudonyms. The final sample size of 27 reflected theoretical saturation: The subjective judgment was made that data collection would conclude when additional participants or new data no longer furthered the findings (Creswell, 2013).

Participant interviews followed a semistructured protocol using Rubin and Rubin's (2012) conversational model, in which main questions were combined with follow-up questions and probes. The interview guide used the 4-S model to organize a transitional understanding of forced transfer. Interviews were conducted between March 2019 and January 2020. Interviews lasted no longer than 60 minutes and were audio recorded to ensure attribution accuracy in using direct quotes to illuminate or exemplify powerful themes. Analytic memos captured emerging themes (Saldaña, 2021) using pseudonyms for privacy (see Table 10.1).

After completing all individual interviews, participants received a reflective questionnaire to elicit follow-up data and to allow for member checking or respondent validation (Lincoln & Guba, 1985). This second data collection method was employed to achieve triangulation, which involves sourcing multiple methods to develop increased comprehension of a phenomenon that a single method may not yield (Patton, 2015). Finally, data from interviews and reflective questionnaires were uploaded to Temi, a transcription software program for storage and early coding.

Table 10.1.

Demographics of Forced Transfer Participants

Participant (pseudonyms)	Gender	Ethnicity	Major
Lily	Female	White	Art history
Lauren	Female	White	Forensic science
Patricia	Female	White	Dental hygiene
Ben	Male	Hispanic	Sports management
Jennifer	Female	White	Dental hygiene
Anita	Female	White	Dental hygiene
Marchand	Male	Black	Business
Bri	Female	White	Dance
Hannah	Female	White	Humanities
Sabrina	Female	Black	Music therapy
Marcus	Male	Hispanic	Business
Kendra	Female	White	Dental hygiene
Dakota	Male	White	Outdoor education
Bridget	Female	White	Psychology
Brock	Male	White	Environmental science
Stella	Female	White	Early childhood education
Caroline	Female	White	Education
Deshaun	Male	Hispanic	Accounting
Shelly	Female	White	Music therapy
Kathleen	Female	White	History
Derek	Male	White	Marketing
Kelly	Female	White	Undecided
Tasia	Female	Black	Business

table continues on page 179

table continued from page 178

Participant (pseudonyms)	Gender	Ethnicity	Major
Priscilla	Female	White	Undecided
Conway	Male	Black	History
Camille	Female	White	Dental hygiene
John	Male	White	Undecided

Data analysis was an ongoing inductive process involving continual reflection. Lincoln and Guba (1985) noted that when using the method of constant comparison, "hypothesis generation begins with the analysis of initial observations, undergoes continuous refinement throughout the data collection and analysis process, and continuously feeds back into the process of category coding" (p. 335). Analysis of data employed Saldaña's (2021) levels of coding, generating themes to elicit participants' experiences, revealing how their experiences influenced transition, a process also known as a "structural description" (Creswell, 2013, p. 82). The structural description in this study focused on the participants' commonalities of experiences to present the study results.

Limitations

Although the sample size of 27 exceeds expected participant numbers for qualitative research (Creswell & Poth, 2018), the sample does not represent the population of students displaced as a result of college closure in the past five years. As such, the findings of this research are applicable only to the participants involved and cannot be assumed to represent other students in a comparable situation. Several strategies were employed to ensure the trustworthiness and credibility of the findings. First, an audit trail was maintained to avoid researcher bias. Second, member checking was employed to explore the credibility of early findings (Lincoln & Guba, 1985). Finally, data triangulation was employed, allowing comparison of data derived from interviews with those from post-reflective questionnaires (Creswell & Poth, 2018).

Results

Three themes emerged from interviews and post-reflective questionnaires to answer the research question: (a) sense of belonging, (b) redefining the academic and career journey, and (c) clarity and resiliency around postgraduate goal attainment.

Sense of Belonging

McMillan and Chavis (1986) stated that sense of belonging is a "feeling that members matter to one another and to the group, and a shared faith that members' needs will be met through their commitment to be together" (p. 9). Hurtado and Carter (1997) defined belonging as identification or positioning within a group that may yield cognitive and affective responses. The collegiate environment fosters belonging to a group of individuals whose purpose or goal is receiving an education for individual growth, contribution to society, and betterment of one's career. A 2021 representative sample of graduates affirmed their purpose for attending college was to qualify for a good job, be successful at work, make money, learn new things, and grow as a person (Strada Education Network, 2021). These responses aligned with Phillips et al.'s (2001) study, which illustrated that career decisions are, in effect, community events and that deciders navigate career decisions through belonging. Career decision-making is embedded within the life context of the whole person, and a sense of belonging is integral to decisions to join or remain in a particular group and/or place (Amundson et al., 2010).

Important to students who transfer is the need to socialize quickly into the receiving institution, a need that stems from the desire to lose the individualism of the "transfer" label (Laanan et al., 2010). By being accepted as part of the college community, students who transfer lessen the probability of standing out or being recognized as different, reducing the chances of not belonging.

Several students in the forced transfer study expressed positive affirmation when discussing their transition to their receiving institution, indicating they felt welcomed and included. Lily, an art history major explained,

> I love my [receiving] institution. It is a very welcoming community. Everyone I have met so far has been helpful and concerned with my well-being. I am involved in sign language, dance, and work-study—I actually like didn't know I qualified [for work-study] until I came to this campus. Being involved on [the new] campus has helped me acclimate to the community. I did not find it difficult to meet people and like feel comfortable here because I got involved right away.

When discussing the factors that led to choosing a receiving school, Dakota, an outdoor education major shared,

> I think that my community, um, really dictated my happiness because just the energy that [sending institution] had was just something that I admired and wanted to be around. And so, I just wanted to follow that community wherever they went. I knew I was going to be happy if I did this. … And so, I chose [receiving institution] with like 100 others from my [sending] community.

However, some students negated these assertions, stating they did not feel the same sense of belonging. Social self-concept at the time of matriculation from sending to receiving institution can affect a sense of belonging (Hurtado et al., 2007). Maestas et al. (2007)

reported that a sense of belonging could be further compromised by socialization factors that differed between student groups, such as racial, ethnic, transfer, and commuter status. Lauren, a forensic science major mentioned,

> I do not feel like I belong [at the receiving institution]. Everyone refers to us as the kids who transferred from [the school that closed]. I don't want to be known as the kid who transferred—I want to be a [receiving institution] student just like everyone else. But no one will let us forget where we came from.

Jennifer was acutely aware of her need for, and absence of, belonging as she sought acceptance into her new campus community. As she described,

> The rest of the students already know each other. They have already made their friends. I am one person starting school like by myself. And I am supposed to magically make friends. I do not feel like I belong here. I am a [sending institution] student going to classes at a campus that isn't mine.

When asked how the transition could have been navigated differently, Jennifer, who kept her dental hygiene major from sending to receiving institution, went on to explain,

> Other than my institution not closing? I don't know. I guess maybe [receiving institution] could have paired me with a buddy or someone who would have showed me around, introduced me to people, hung out with me. Now that I say that it sounds lame. But I still don't know where some things are. Are there other students who transferred? This college is big—I can't be the only student who transfer[red] here.

Students' proclivity to become engaged on a college campus is predicated on their sense of belonging at the institution (Strange & Banning, 2001). Jennifer's low self-efficacy in terms of belonging discouraged her from becoming involved.

Patricia, also a dental hygiene major, mentioned shedding the label associated with transferring and expressed an ardent desire to blend into the new campus environment:

> I am sick of talking about [the transfer]. I have to break into this like traumatizing story of like how my school closed because once people find out I was a student from [the school that closed] everyone asks me, "how are you feeling?" and "I can't believe they did that to you!" It is exhausting. I never wanted to go to school here, but now I am here so I wish people would just let me BE a [receiving institution] student.

Jennifer and Patricia's stories illustrate a need for the students to cast aside prior identities and acclimate into the receiving institution in a way that allows them to fully belong. Closures can be stressful to navigate because students must contend with clashing traditions, cultures, and priorities from sending to receiving institutions, which may affect their sense of belonging (Cartwright, 2007). Yet administrators at receiving institutions believe that students will adapt as time passes (Daltry & Mehr, 2016).

A student's perception of the transition affects their account of their assets and liabilities. Each time the student unwantedly recounts the experience, they are relabeled as "that student who transferred," triggering the transition yet again, catapulting the student back to the sending institution and initiating a loss of control (Anderson et al., 2012). The absence of belonging can cause various ill effects on adjustment and well-being (Baumeister & Leary, 1995).

Individuals are fundamentally and pervasively motivated by a need to form and maintain enduring interpersonal attachments—students who experienced a forced transfer reported losing interpersonal attachments with faculty, staff, and peers. Naz et al. (2014) noted peers have a positive impact on education, job search, and social organizations. Several students commented that although they adjusted well to the transfer process from a curricular standpoint, faculty and peer relationships were absent. As Deshaun, an accounting major, mentioned,

> They put us on the same floor in the same residence together, so we were all so like unified that I feel like it made such a different experience but also inhibited us. We had classes not with any other [receiving institution] students. We were very segregated. We didn't feel like we belonged.

And Bri, a dance major, confirmed this feeling in her interview:

> It was literally the worst year. Like it was not the best experience that a college student would want to have. I'm not graduating with my friends. It's like we're [students in the program] just going to go through—we are just going to graduate, and we don't even know anyone [at receiving institution]. It's just weird. We're not part of the community.

Sabrina, a music therapy major went on to explain,

> You learn who you are when you have been displaced, when you have to figure it out, when you lose your identity as a student from the college, which used to give you identity, which is how in your early twenties works. … You have to grow up faster than the degree you've bought was going to help you grow up.

For students to feel a keen sense of belonging to their receiving institution and community, frequent, positive interactions within the context of long-term, caring relationships would need to be demonstrated (Anant, 1966).

One requirement for effective student transitions is a campus that fosters a sense of community. As illustrated in the following statement from Bri, belonging to an institution starts before a student arrives at the institution and, if not orchestrated well, can have an immediate negative impact on how the student acclimates to the institution:

> I feel like I would have loved for [receiving institution] to be more involved in our transition and not give us the brush-off when we inquired about where to go to for [transitional] help … like they expected us to just know how to navigate around the campus because we had been on a college campus before … we hadn't been on the THIS campus before, so essentially we were new students again.

Sense of belonging—or lack thereof—persists long past graduation and affects career in ways many do not consider. As Patricia mentioned in her interview,

> I always think about having like my resume say like dental hygiene program and people being like, oh, like I didn't know [receiving institution] had a dental hygiene program.

It is critical for students who transfer to experience a sense of belonging at their receiving institution (McIntosh & Nelson, 2012). This need for belonging was evident in the student feedback gathered in this forced transfer study. Career and other support staff contribute to the positive experiences of students who transfer by fostering a sense of belonging through shared experiences like undergraduate research, seminar courses, career advisor meetings, and career-related programming.

Redefining the Academic and Career Journey

Tinto (1993) claimed that formal and informal academic activities have bearing on how students integrate into their institutions and that failure to integrate within a community system influences student departure. A key influencer of student persistence and degree completion is academic integration, which is linked to positive career decision-making. Integration is the function advisors use to aid students in connecting their curricular choices to academic, career, and life goals (Allen et al., 2013). Tinto's departure theory (1985) suggests that students committed to their academic goals and their institutions have a far greater likelihood of completing their degrees, whereas students who are not committed to their academic goals and institutions are more likely to withdraw. Students engaged in meaningful experiences that contributed toward academic integration (e.g., relationships with faculty and other advisors) and social integration (e.g., involvement in clubs and sports) improved their commitment to the institution, resulting in degree completion (Fauria & Fuller, 2015; Lopez & Jones, 2016; Tinto, 1993). The impact of the forced transfer on integration to the receiving institution and the students' (increased or decreased) commitment to their academic and career goals was shared across all interviews.

Forced transfer heightened awareness of the comparisons between academic processes and services. Several students spoke of the noticeable differences in institutional supports from sending to receiving institutions. Students who believed supports were abundant or had experienced high-touch services since moving through the transfer process spoke favorably of institutional commitment and resource utilization. Several students reported accessing academic and career resources far more at the receiving institution than at the sending institution. Ben, a sports management major, commented on his renewed attitude associated with academic supports post-transfer, stating,

> The academic programs are definitely more helpful—it feels like I have a lot more stability [at my new institution]. I have scheduled appointments with my success coach every week, which is not something I had before. In my opinion, my new institution has made me feel more successful in my [academic] progress and with exploring careers.

Ben's comment highlights the awareness of services and resources available at the receiving institution, which is a key to navigating the transition (Anderson et al., 2012). Ben also described an encounter with a success coach who helped him with academic and career exploration. According to Ghusson (2016), "a highly involved student is one who devotes considerable time and energy to studying, spends time on campus, participates in student life on campus, and has frequent interactions with faculty and peers" (p. 35). Given this positive, early exposure and that he is highly engaged, Ben will likely assume a favorable attitude toward seeking help for future career planning (Bernaud & Bideault, 2005).

In contrast, other students who experienced a forced transfer disengaged completely from all services at the receiving institution, reporting a desire to "get in and get out" of school as quickly as possible. In the literature, students who transfer often report low levels of satisfaction with the campus climate and their relationships with faculty members (Lester, 2006; Ma & Baum, 2016), struggles in a new academic environment (Handel & Williams, 2012), and low self-efficacy in navigating campus resources (Chin-Newman & Shaw, 2013).

Academic major selection aligned with participants' career and personal interests and the ability to transfer into similar programs with receiving institutions accepting all or the majority of earned credits were themes evident in all 27 forced transfer interviews. For example, Marchand, a business major, expressed gratitude for assimilating to a receiving institution with the same major and little credit transfer difficulty, stating,

> So, I don't necessarily think that [transferring] majorly changed like my career. … it's just nice to see another part of the country, and experience my major differently.

So, I, I've been trying to apply for a[n] internship in the adventure field for, um, for the summer.

Kendra, a dental hygiene major, touched on the organic supports she received from faculty and advisors from her sending institution. Specifically, she stated,

I'm just ridiculously lucky to have the teachers who I have and they're, they've been so amazing throughout this entire process, even though like they're, they're hurting as much as we are, if not more for some, and, and they're doing an absolute, incredible job.

This feedback illustrates that the student utilized situational strategies to cope with the transition (Schlossberg, 1984) by seeking familiar supports from her sending institution to help her navigate the transition. That she received supports from her former faculty— although they had also lost their jobs to the college closure—aligns with the notion that receiving positive encouragement will set up students for success in their transfer process (Lukszo & Hayes, 2020).

However, not all students felt supported by their sending or receiving intuitions in redefining their academic paths, which left their career journeys uncertain. In addition, several students discussed a strong disconnect with faculty, citing difficulty assimilating to the academic environment because faculty supports were lacking or absent. This conflicting feedback illustrates that the students' experiences were objective and subjective. Objectively, they had a shared experience as a cohort of students forced to transfer, yet subjectively, their personal experiences were internalized life circumstances unique to each student (Merriam & Tisdell, 2015). Situationally, for example, the transition proved difficult for Brock, an environmental science major, who discussed the mechanics of transfer:

Like the transfer process isn't as easy as people think it is. It's not just like a snap your fingers and I'm sending the transcript over to the other school. Like there's a process that goes along with it. And with that, it's like making sure that like your classes match and that your credits are transferring. So that was one thing that I really had to worry about was like, okay, I do not want to waste money because I've already paid for these classes. I have my career planned. I don't want to be set behind.

Several students shared challenges associated with fulfilling academic requirements for their degrees because of the transfer. Anita, a dental hygiene major, disclosed,

We felt very isolated. We couldn't find [volunteers for the practicum program we needed to run] to get credit for class. Volunteers would cancel, so we would lose points. We didn't know anyone on campus to say, "hey, come help me today." They didn't know what we were doing. We felt like we didn't belong. It didn't work—it hurt our grade.

Decision-making is only one step in the process of goal attainment. According to the agentic theory of decision-making, implementing a decision and sticking to it, particularly when difficulties arise, takes a fair amount of developed self-efficacy (Bandura, 1997). Students who are forced to transfer may receive the support needed during the initial transition or during early transfer; however, their continual need to make and act on their decisions repeatedly and over time requires high self-efficacy (Harré, 1983), and, as Kajstura and Keim (1992) posited, faculty support is highly important because it provides students with increased confidence needed for good academic performance. Lauren discussed implications related to lack of academic support and its impact on her career trajectory:

> I was a forensic science major. They didn't have that major at [receiving institution], so when I transferred, I became a psychology major. They didn't have a lot of faculty advising, no academic support services.

Shelly, a music therapy major, shared the challenges that arose because of disparities in academic and career services related to her major. When asked about receiving academic and career supports to complete a summer internship, Shelly replied,

> [Receiving institution] gave us like a resume template that I ha[d] to fill out and I mean like [sending institution] used to have students go on external site visits, which basically gives you like a real-life image of what you're going to be jumping into for your summer internship. Um, I mean that's not happening for me. I just have to fill out that resume template.

Research by Jabbar et al. (2021) indicated that students who experienced hurdles during transfer were frequently derailed in their decision-making, which resulted in lengthening of their transfer timeline. Furthermore, Jabbar et al. found that instead of linear decision-making, students who transfer repeat the process of academic and career decision-making multiple times, creating uncertainty and lengthening the time to degree completion.

Hannah, who was a classics major at her receiving institution, discussed the academic consequences of the transfer, the finality of her degree, and its impact on postgraduate outcomes, stating,

> I got, um, an arts degree. I don't even know the title of it. Like, um, it's just a piece of paper now. It has, it has lost its magic quality and it is just like, I think it's arts and letters. … there was no career development, even while I was a student there [receiving institution], there was no, let's get you a job.

Forced to declare a major as a humanities undergraduate because her previous major was unavailable, Hannah's feedback exemplifies that the transition from sending institution to receiving institution is more complicated than accepting transfer credits and approximate alignment to fulfill degree requirements.

Overall, results from finding two necessitate the importance of the faculty–student relationship and its positive impact on the student's academic and career experiences. The results also underscore the impact of targeted assistance (e.g., programs, advising, supports, resources) that helps to increase students' acclamation to the sending institution and throughout their remaining time at the institution.

Clarity and Resiliency Around Postgraduate Goal Attainment

Most participants expressed discomfort with the unfamiliarity of their unanticipated and unwanted transitions and the move to their new college settings. Early on, this discomfort heightened vulnerability as students negotiated stability and sought to refocus their goals in their new environments (Compas et al., 1986). The nature of this transition calls for consideration of career adaptability and resiliency to better understand the career development of students who are forced to transfer as they adjust to their new roles as displaced students in relation to other life roles. Career adaptability includes the dimensions of planning, exploring, and decision-making about one's future (Savickas, 1997). Overcoming unanticipated transition requires a high level of resiliency, defined as the capacity to respond and persevere despite life stressors or adversities (Beasley et al., 2003; Campbell-Sills et al., 2006; Mandleco & Peery, 2000; Munro & Pooley, 2009; Raphael, 1993). As students renegotiated the immediate and long-term career obstacles brought on by forced transfer, interactions between career adaptability and resiliency became prominent.

For some students forced to transfer, a sense of goal clarity crystallized as resiliency increased. Anita stated,

> I didn't use to be very confident, but this transition has made me more confident in my career path and my future goals. I had to decide to take this transfer positively or negatively. I've taken it in a positive way. I've taken things one step at a time, and my career experiences have grown in a positive way, so I trust there will be a better future for me.

Anita reconfigured the stress from the transition into resiliency, which led to increased goal clarity. Resiliency is a key trait required for high performance in today's uncertain and ever-changing workplace. Solving problems, facing challenges, and learning from mistakes exemplify how students will be challenged to show resiliency when they enter the world of work post-graduation.

Tasia, a business major, reflected on how the transition brought her clarity, confidence, and motivation to seek out support and how, upon doing so, she became more open to possibilities. Tasia's sudden, uncertain pivot required a certain amount of career adaptability, which was channeled into proactively exploring postgraduate career options:

> I am learning a lot about my skills from my work-study, and I've also been researching graduate school, something I never thought of before coming here [receiving institution]. My faculty advisor has been great in helping me with career questions. There are so many things I can do with my degree—I am in the exploration stage, so I am ready when graduation comes.

Tasia's experience aligns with several studies suggesting that when students felt their majors would lead them to secure careers, they were more likely to persist than were students who felt that their educations were not worthwhile (Killeen et al., 1999; Peterson & delMas, 2001). Tasia's faculty provided her with career support; her experience aligns with research by Laanan et al. (2010) and by Moser (2014), who found that interactions with faculty significantly affected the motivation and confidence of students who transfer. The divide between academic and career advising based on this student's experience furthers the argument that career services span the campus ecosystem and that one of the best ways to support students in their career-related needs is through comprehensive advising.

Tusaie and Dyer (2004) noted that individuals are considered resilient when they can overcome adversity and view the experience as beneficial toward future endeavors. Stella, an early childhood education major, talked about this resiliency in her interview:

> Long-term, whatever happens to me, whether I get rejected for a job interview or something scary like that, this closure will always be in the back of my mind. Like if I can get through this [transition], I think I can get through anything really.

Stella went on to say that

> [t]his situation made me a stronger person. No one ever told me what to do or how to get through it. I came here undeclared, but now I'm studying education. I never thought I could be a teacher, but now I know I can.

Personal characteristics such as optimism, self-efficacy, and adaptability can influence levels of resiliency (Prince-Embury, 2006), as seen in Stella's story. Ben corroborated Stella's thoughts, expressing how resiliency increased his goal clarity and future direction:

> This transition has made me more confident in my career path and my future goals. I've taken this transfer in a positive way because [receiving institution] offered me so much more opportunities than [sending institution] did. If I knew

all the opportunities [receiving institution] offered, I would have chosen [receiving institution] from the start. Since I transferred, my social, academic, and career experience[s] have grown in a positive way.

Ben's willingness to show resiliency and career adaptability increased his confidence in the future and opened his eyes to unrealized possibilities.

Although Stella and Ben discussed how the transfer helped them become more resilient, Stella did not experience goal clarity early on—for Stella, determination to reach a state of clarity grew as she sought supports to help her establish career goals. She shared,

> When the closure happened, I just thought that was like the end, I wouldn't graduate from college because I didn't see myself going to another college. I wouldn't finish my education and my life would consist of a different experience. But then I visited the career center [at the receiving institution] and they really spent time listening to me and, yah, just helping me figure it out. Now I'm really excited about my major.

Career decision-making affects, and is affected by, multiple facets of the college experience, and saliency in decision-making varies between individuals. Navigating a transfer carries its own unique set of short- and long-term challenges, and these challenges can be faced at any time during the transfer experience. Receiving academic and career advisors' support both holistically and comprehensively during the transition is just one strategy that can help students successfully traverse forced transfer.

Discussion

This study captured students' experiences navigating forced transfer due to college closure by investigating a single research question: What was the impact of forced transfer due to college closure on the career-related supports of students who experienced this event? The data suggest three findings that lead to the development of a working definition of this emerging transitional experience for which no previous research exists. Participants in this study expressed (a) challenges with a sense of belonging, (b) a need to redefine the academic and career journey, and (c) increased clarity and resiliency around postgraduate goal attainment. As Marcus, a business major shared,

> There's a lot of uncertainty. I was not thinking about transferring or planning to transfer. Um, I knew what might happen because of this, but I was not prepared. So, I think the term "force transfer" is good. I saw that. And I was like, yeah, that sounds about right.

Engagement continues to be lower for students who transfer than for native student peer groups (Lester et al., 2013), which is concerning because college closure forces students to transfer although they never intended to do so in the first place. As Handel and Williams (2012) declared, "The point to be gleaned here is that regardless of the receiving institution, students who transfer must make a transition in the middle of their undergraduate careers; a transition we almost never advise an undergraduate who begins college at a four-year institution to make (p. 51)." Moving from one institution where the student is accepted and part of a student majority to a new institution where the student encounters assumptions and stigmas can significantly affect whether the student successfully and fully acclimates.

Resiliency could be an ingredient that helps to mitigate the difficulties associated with transfer. Building resiliency could lead to a satisfactory adjustment to the receiving institution, increasing one's negotiation capacity for unexpected academic and career decisions and confidence in repositioning oneself in a new and unfamiliar community. Long term, this resiliency can translate to career resilience, which manifests itself in an individual taking charge of their career path and routinely developing new skills to remain relevant (Joubert, 2021).

The success of students who experience forced transfer depends on providing transitional support before, during, and after the transfer. Supports include a student's communal foundation, such as friends, family, mentors, academic and career advisors, and available institutional structures (Goodman et al., 2006; Lukszo & Hayes, 2020). For example, institutions might consider it beneficial for students who transfer to spend time with faculty and staff who had themselves transferred; this strategy could influence retention. Participants in the study noted that they lost some of their support systems through the transfer process, resulting in a need to create and maintain new foundations at the receiving institution. Awareness of and access to institutional mechanisms designed to facilitate transfer, group sessions, workshops, and educational materials could increase a student's sense of belonging to their receiving institution, foster a greater connection to the institution, and increase supports needed for successful transfer transition. How well supports are executed by the receiving institution and accepted by the students greatly influences their belonging to that institution and, in turn, their interest in deeper involvement. Increasing communication and collaboration between sending and receiving institutions may increase institutional supports and serve as a safety net for students whose external supports are less secure.

The impact of the forced transfer on academic trajectory was an influential strand that weaved through all the student interviews. Tinto (1993) recognized that academic "fit" between the student and the institution plays a role in persistence. The study participants reported that challenges with (a) establishing and maintaining faculty connections, (b) utilization of academic services, (c) degree conversion from sending to receiving institution, and (d) career clarity brought on by academic disruption all influenced some aspects of the academic transition. Students who demonstrated a "taking-charge" attitude and employed new strategies to manage and deal with the transition (Schlossberg et al., 1995; Anderson et al., 2012) were far more successful in managing the transfer. A transfer orientation and a transfer week are two of the more common strategies to ease the impact of a transfer experience because they allow students to control perceptions ("We belong!"), respond appropriately ("There are [resources] available to help me adjust"), and manage stress while changing ("I have [advisors] here to support me"). Ensuring students who were forced to transfer have these or equally supportive services during their transitions will help them take charge of available resources, which would result in strengthening their resiliency.

Students forced to transfer will move in, through, and out (Chickering & Schlossberg, 2001) of the college transfer transition. The questions are how they move through the transition, when they arrive, and who they will be when they reach the end of the transition. As Kathleen, a history major so eloquently put it,

> I hear people say a lot, like, oh, I want, like, I just want to get this many credits and graduate. And like, I'm not just looking for a degree. I'm like, I'm looking for rich educational experiences that teach[es] me things that I want to know. And so, like, I feel like honestly, I was pretty cheated.

Engaging students who are forced to transfer early on and throughout the transfer process will be essential for erasing deficits many of these students will face upon arrival, enhancing their acculturation to the campus environment, and helping them to reposition themselves onto a stable pathway to degree completion. The aftermath of the pandemic will cause an increase in disruption within higher education—to what extent is yet to be determined. However, financial concerns are real and can result in college closure, forcing more students into unexpected transfer.

Conclusion

In 2017, Harvard Business School professor Clayton Christensen predicted half of the colleges in America would close or go bankrupt in the next decade (Lederman, 2017), and a 2018 Moody's Investor Service rating estimated closures would increase 11% from that year (Moody's Investor Service, 2019). Hussar and Bailey (2020) predicted that college enrollment of students aged 14 to 24 would increase 6% between 2017 and 2028, but the COVID-19 pandemic affected those projections. According to recent data (Nadworny, 2022), undergraduate enrollment is 6.6% lower than it was before the pandemic, with many 2020 high school graduates choosing not to enroll in college after graduation. This finding is not surprising, given that only 25% said that "the traditional college model is the only pathway to getting a good job" (Burt, 2021, para. 2).

Whether these predictions and estimations are accurate, it is evident that disruption resulting from college closure is not slowing, and the next few years will reveal the impact the pandemic has had on higher education. Rising student loan debt, pressures to hold colleges accountable for student outcomes, and a declining number of high school graduates leave unanswered questions relating to the future of college closure and the students impacted by a forced transfer.

Further research should include quantitative inquiry based on the academic, social, and career impacts of students experiencing transfer. Many institutions in jeopardy of closure are small, private institutions; however, industry challenges also extend to larger private and public institutions, both nonprofit and for profit. Although institutions find themselves in a wide range of financial conditions, their reactions to the changing market need not be independent and isolated from one another. Executing a successful transfer is the responsibility of both the sending and the receiving institutions. In a few cases, the things we've learned from COVID offers tremendous opportunities for institutions to partner in new and innovative ways and, when it makes sense, to merge internally and externally. For these reasons, the lack of research focused on students affected by college closures should resonate with scholars and higher education leaders.

A forced transfer is outside the norm of the traditional transfer route. The experience of students forced to transfer is unique, and while quick assimilation is the goal, the students need an environment that offers different or tailored support sooner and longer than other types of transfer students may need. The alternative is that students forced to transfer are ignored and pushed through like all other students who have transferred—with little to no career guidance—and this situation creates additional complexity to a pre-existing problem that no one has the stamina to solve. The qualitative study presented in this chapter provides valuable findings on forced transfer. However, it only begins to raise awareness of this emerging transfer experience and provides leaders and support staff of sending and receiving institutions with information to create appropriate services for students affected by forced transfer. A key finding of this work is that more research is necessary.

References

Allen, J. M., Smith, C. L., & Muehleck, J. K. (2013). What kinds of advising are important to community college pre- and post-transfer students? *Community College Review, 41*(4), 330–345. https://doi.org/10.1177%2F0091552113505320

Amundson, N. E., Borgen, W. A., Iaquinta, M., Butterfield, L. D., & Koert, E. (2010). Career decision from the decider's perspective. *The Career Development Quarterly, 58,* 336–351. 10.1002/j.2161-0045.2010.tb00182.x

Anant, S. S. (1966). The need to belong. *Canada's Mental Health, 14,* 21–27. https://doi.org/10.1016/0001-6918(67)90035-2

Anderson, M. L., Goodman, J., & Schlossberg, N. K. (2012). *Counseling adults in transition: Linking Schlossberg's theory with practice in a diverse world* (4th ed.). Springer Publishing.

Baker, P., Hearn Moore, P., Byars, K., & Aden, C. (2020). Covid closing down colleges: How the Covid-19 pandemic accelerated nonprofit college closings. *BYU Education and Law Journal, 2020*(2), Article 4. https://scholarsarchive.byu.edu/cgi/viewcontent. cgi?article=1007&context=byu_elj

Bandura, A. (1997). *Self-efficacy: The exercise of control.* Freeman.

Bauer-Wolf, J. (2020, March 18). *Moody's lowers higher ed outlook to negative amid coronavirus crisis.* Higher Ed Dive. https://www.highereddive.com/news/moodys-lowers-higher-ed-outlook-to-negative-amid-coronavirus-crisis/574414/

Baumeister, R. F., & Leary, M. R. (1995). The need to belong: desire for interpersonal attachments as a fundamental human motivation. *Psychological Bulletin, 117*(3), 497–529. https://doi.org/10.1037/0033-2909.117.3.497

Beasley, M., Thompson, T., & Davidson, J. (2003). Resilience in response to life stress: The effects of coping style and cognitive hardiness. *Personality and Individual Differences, 34*, 77–95. https://doi.org/10.1016/S0191-8869(02)00027-2

Bernaud, J., & Bideault, A. (2005). Le déterminants de l'attractivité face á une démarche de conseil en orientation. *Carrièrologie, 10*(2), 289–303.

Burt, C. (2021, February 24). *Gen Z leery of 4-year degree paths, surveys show.* University Business. https://universitybusiness.com/gen-z-leery-of-4-year-degree-paths-surveys-show/

Campbell-Sills, L., Cohan, S. L., & Stein. M. B. (2006). Relationship of resilience to personality, coping, and psychiatric symptoms in young adults. *Behaviour Research and Therapy, 44*, 585–599. https://doi.org/10.1016/j.brat.2005.05.001

Cartwright, S. (2007). Are mergers always successful? Some evidence from the higher education sector. *European Journal of Work and Organizational Psychology, 16*(4), 456–478. https://doi.org/10.1080/13594320701606391

Chickering, A. W., & Schlossberg, N. K. (2001). *Getting the most out of college* (2nd ed.). Pearson.

Chin-Newman, S., & Shaw, S. T. (2013). The anxiety of change: How new transfer students overcome challenges. *Journal of College Admission, 1*, 5–21.

Cohn, S. (2019). *The other college debt crisis: Schools are going broke.* CNBC. https://www.cnbc.com/2019/12/03/the-other-college-debt-crisis-schools-are-going-broke.html

Compas, B. E., Slavin, L. A., Wagner, B. M., & Vannatta, K. (1986). Relationship of life events and social supports with psychological dysfunction among adolescents. *Journal of Youth and Adolescence, 15*(3), 205–221. https://doi.org/10.1007/BF02139123

Creswell, J. W. (2013). *Qualitative inquiry & research design: Choosing among five approaches* (3rd ed.). Sage Publications.

Creswell, J. W., & Poth, C. N. (2018). *Qualitative inquiry and research design: Choosing among five approaches.* Sage Publications.

Daltry, R., & Mehr, K. (2016). Examining mental health differences between transfer and nontransfer university students seeking counseling services. *Journal of College Student Psychotherapy, 30*(2), 146–155. https://doi.org/10.1080/87568225.2016.1140996

Eide, S. (2018). Private colleges in peril: Financial pressures and declining enrollment may lead to more closures. *Education Next, 18*(4), 34–42.

Fauria, R. M., & Fuller, M. B. (2015). Transfer student success: Educationally purposeful activities predictive of undergraduate GPA. *Research and Practice in Assessment, 10,* 39–52.

Fernandez, A. A., & Shaw, G. P. (2020). Academic leadership in a time of crisis: The coronavirus and COVID-19. *Journal of Leadership Studies, 14*(1), 39–45. https://doi.org/10.1002/jls.21684

Gere, A., Hutton, L., Keating, B., Knutson, A., Silver, N., & Toth, C. (2017). Mutual adjustments: Learning from and responding to transfer student writers. *College English, 79*(4), 333–357. https://www.jstor.org/stable/44806091

Ghusson, M. (2016). *Understanding the engagement of transfer students in four-year institutions: A national study* (UMI No. 10109010) [Doctoral dissertation, Seton Hall University]. ProQuest Dissertations and Theses database.

Goodman, J., Schlossberg, N. K., & Anderson, M. L. (2006). *Counseling adults in transition: Linking practice with theory* (3rd ed.). Springer Publishing.

Grawe, N. (2018). *Demographics and the demand for higher education.* Johns Hopkins University Press.

Handel, S. J., & Williams, R. A. (2012). *The promise of the transfer pathway: Opportunities and challenges for community college students seeking the baccalaureate degree.* The College Board Advocacy & Policy Center. https://secure-media.collegeboard.org/digitalServices/pdf/professionals/handel-williams-promise-of-the-transfer-pathway-2012.pdf

Harré, R. (1983). *Personal being: A theory for individual psychology.* Blackwell.

Higher Ed Dive. (2022). *A look at trends in college and university consolidation since 2016.* https://www.highereddive.com/news/how-many-colleges-and-universities-have-closed-since-2016/539379/

Hurtado, S., & Carter, D. F. (1997). Effects of college transition and perceptions of the campus racial climate on Latino college students' sense of belonging. *Sociology of Education, 70*(4), 324–345. https://doi.org/10.2307/2673270

Hurtado, S., Han, J., Sa'enz, V. B., Espinosa, L. L., Cabrera, N. L., & Cerna, O. (2007). Predicting transition and adjustment to college: Biomedical and behavioral science aspirants' and minority students' first year of college. *Research in Higher Education, 48*(7), 841–887. http://doi.org/10.1007/s11162-007-9051-x

Hussar, W. J., & Bailey, T. M. (2020). *Projections of education statistics to 2028.* National Center for Education Statistics, Institute of Education Sciences. https://nces.ed.gov/pubs2020/2020024.pdf

Jabbar, H., Epstein, E., Sánchez, J., & Hartman, C. (2021). Thinking through transfer: Examining how community college students make transfer decisions. *Community College Review, 49*(1), 3–29. https://doi.org/10.1177/0091552120964876

Joubert, S. (2021). *Career resilience: What is it and how to build it.* Northeastern University. https://www.northeastern.edu/graduate/blog/how-to-build-career-resilience/

Kajstura, A., & Keim, M. C. (1992). Reverse transfer students in Illinois community colleges. *Community College Review, 20*(2), 39–44.

Kelchen, R. (2018). *Higher education accountability.* Johns Hopkins University Press.

Kelchen, R. (2020). *Examining the feasibility of empirically predicting college closures.* Brookings. https://www.brookings.edu/research/examining-the-feasibility-of-empirically-predicting-college-closures/

Killeen, J., Sammons, P., & Watts, T. (1999). *Careers work and school effectiveness* (NICEC Brief). National Institute for Careers Education and Counseling & Department of Education and Employment, United Kingdom.

Laanan, F. S., Starobin, S. S., & Eggleston, L. E. (2010). Adjustment of community college students at a four-year university: Role and relevance of transfer student capital for student retention. *Journal of College Student Retention: Research, Theory & Practice, 12*(2), 175–209. https://doi.org/10.2190/CS.12.2.d

Lederman, D. (2017, April 28). *Clay Christensen, doubling down.* Inside Higher Ed. https://www.insidehighered.com/digital-learning/article/2017/04/28/clay-christensen-sticks-predictions-massive-college-closures

LeSane, C. B., II (2020). Enrollment. In The Chronicle of Higher Education (Eds.), *The post-pandemic college* (pp. 46–52).

Lester, J. (2006). Who will we serve in the future? The new student in transition. *New Directions for Student Services, 114,* 47–61.

Lester, J., Leonard, J. B., & Mathias, D. (2013). Transfer student engagement blurring of social and academic engagement. *Community College Review, 41*(3), 202–222. http://doi.org/10.1177/0091552113496141

Li, D. (2010). They need help: Transfer students from four-year to four-year institutions. *The Review of Higher Education, 33*(2), 207–238. https://doi.org/10.1353/rhe.0.0131

Lincoln, Y., & Guba, E. G. (1985). *Naturalistic inquiry.* Sage Publications. https://us.sagepub.com/en-us/nam/naturalistic-inquiry/book842

Lopez, C., & Jones, S. (2016). Examination of factors that predict academic adjustment and success of community college transfer students in STEM at 4-year institutions. *Community College Journal of Research and Practice, 43*(3), 168–182. http://doi.org/10.1080/10668926.2016.1168328

Lukszo, C. M., & Hayes, S. (2020). Facilitating transfer student success: Exploring sources of transfer student capital. *Community College Review, 48*(1), 31–54. https://doi.org/10.1177/0091552119876017

Lundy, K., El-Baz, M. (2022). *Six key financial and operational metrics pinpoint higher ed risk.* EY Parthenon. https://www.ey.com/en_us/education/strategy-consulting/six-key-financial-and-operational-metrics-pinpoint-higher-ed-risk

Ma, J., & Baum, S. (2016, April). *Trends in community colleges: Enrollment, prices, student debt, and completion* (Research Brief). College Board Research. http://trends.collegeboard.org/sites/default/files/trends-in-community-colleges-research-brief.pdf

Maestas, R., Vaquera, G. S., & Zehr, L. M. (2007). Factors impacting sense of belonging at a Hispanic-serving institution. *Journal of Hispanic Higher Education, 6*(3), 237–256. http://doi.org/10.1177/1538192707302801

Mandleco, B. L., & Peery, J. C. (2000). An organizational framework for conceptualizing resilience in children. *Journal of Child and Adolescent Psychiatric Nursing, 13*, 99–111. https://doi.org/10.1111/j.1744-6171.2000.tb00086.x

McIntosh, E. J., & Nelson, D. D. (2012). Transfer students: Thriving in a new institution. In L. A. Schreiner, M. C. Louis, & D. D. Nelson (Eds.), *Thriving in transitions: A research-based approach to college student success* (pp. 137–166). University of South Carolina, National Resource Center for The First-Year Experience and Students in Transition.

McMillan, D. W., & Chavis, D. M. (1986). Sense of community: A definition and theory. *Journal of Community Psychology, 14*, 6–23. https://doi.org/10.1002/1520-6629(198601)14:1%3C6::AID-JCOP2290140103%3E3.0.CO;2-I

Merriam, S. B., & Tisdell, E. J. (2015). *Qualitative research: A guide to design and implementation* (4th ed.). Jossey-Bass.

Moody's Investor Service. (2015). *Moody's small but notable rise expected in closures, mergers for smaller US colleges.*

Moody's Investor Service. (2018). 2019 *U.S. Higher education outlook.* Moody's Corporation. https://www.aascu.org/meetings/hegrc18/Shaffer.pdf

Moser, K. (2014). Exploring the impact of transfer capital on community college transfer students. *Journal of the First-Year Experience and Students in Transition, 25*(2), 53–57.

Munro, B. J., & Pooley, J. (2009). Differences in resilience and university adjustment between school leaver and mature entry university students. *The Australian Community Psychologist, 21*(1), 50–61. https://ro.ecu.edu.au/ecuworks/688

Nadworny, E. (2022, January 13). *More than 1 million fewer students are in college. Here's how that impacts the economy.* NPR. https://www.npr.org/2022/01/13/1072529477/more-than-1-million-fewer-students-are-in-college-the-lowest-enrollment-numbers-

Naz, A., Saeed, G., Khan, W., Khan, N. U., Sheikh, I., & Khan, N. (2014). Peer and friends and career decision making: A critical analysis. *Middle-East Journal of Scientific Research, 22*(8) 1193–1197. https://doi.org/10.5829/idosi.mejsr.2014.22.08.21993

O'Dwyer, L. M., & Bernauer, J. A. (2014). *Quantitative research for the qualitative researcher.* Sage Publications.

Parthenon EY Educational Practice. (2016). *Strength in numbers: Strategies for collaborating in a new era for higher education.* Ernst & Young LLP. https://cdn.ey.com/parthenon/pdf/perspectives/P-EY_Strength-in-Numbers-Collaboration-Strategies_Paper_Final_082016.pdf

Patton, M. Q. (2015). *Qualitative research & evaluation methods* (4th ed.). Sage Publications.

Peterson, S. L., & delMas, R. C. (2001). Effects of career decision-making self-efficacy and degree utility on student persistence: A path analytic study. *Journal of College Student Retention, 3*(3), 285–299. https://doi.org/10.2190%2F4D9V-DFW1-VDLX-K7GF

Phillips, S. D., Christopher-Sisk, E. K., & Gravino, K. L. (2001). Making career decisions in a relational context. *The Counseling Psychologist, 29*(2), 193–213. https://doi.org/10.1177/0011000001292002

Poisel, M. A., & Joseph, S. (Eds). (2011). *Transfer students in higher education: Building foundations for policies, programs, and services that foster student success.* National Resource Center for The First-Year Experience and Students in Transition.

Prince-Embury, S. (2006). *Resiliency scales for children and adolescents: A profile of personal strengths.* Harcourt Assessment, Inc.

Raphael, B. (1993). Adolescent resilience: The potential impact of personal development in schools. *Journal of Pediatrics and Child Health, 29,* S31–S36. https://doi.org/10.1111/j.1440-1754.1993.tb02258.x

Rubin, H. J., & Rubin, I. S. (2012). *Qualitative interviewing: The art of hearing data.* Sage Publications.

Saldaña, J. (2021). *The coding manual for qualitative researchers* (4th ed.). Sage Publications.

Sapiro, V. (2019). *The life course of higher education institutions: When the end comes* [Working paper]. Boston University.

Savickas, M. L. (1997). Career adaptability: An integrative construct for life-span, life-space theory. *The Career Development Quarterly, 45,* 247–259. https://psycnet.apa.org/doi/10.1002/j.2161-0045.1997.tb00469.x

Schlossberg, N. K. (1984). *Counseling adults in transition: Linking theory to practice.* Springer Publishing.

Schlossberg, N. K., Waters, E. B., & Goodman, J. (1995). *Counseling adults in transition: Linking practice with theory.* Springer Publishing.

Strada Education Network. (2021). *2021 Strada outcomes survey: Student outcomes beyond completion.* https://stradaeducation.org/wp-content/uploads/2022/01/2021-Strada-Outcomes-Survey-National-Report-121021.pdf

Strange, C. C., & Banning, J. (2001). *Educating by design: Creating educational environments that work.* Jossey-Bass.

Taylor, J. L., & Jain, D. (2017). The multiple dimensions of transfer: Examining the transfer function in American higher education. *Community College Review, 45,* 273–293. http://doi.org/10.1177/0091552117725177

Tinto, V. (1985). Dropping out and other forms of withdrawal from college. In U. Delworth & G. Hanson (Eds.), *Increasing student retention* (pp. 28–43). Jossey-Bass.

Tinto, V. (1993). *Leaving college: Rethinking the causes and cures of student attrition* (2nd ed.). The University of Chicago Press.

Tusaie, K., & Dyer, J. (2004), Resilience: A historical review of the construct. *Holistic Nursing Practice, 18*(1), 3–8.

van Manen, M. (1990). *Researching lived experience: Human science for an action sensitive pedagogy.* State University of New York Press.

van Manen, M. (2014). *Phenomenology of practice: Meaning-giving methods in phenomenological research and writing.* Left Coast Press.

Vasquez, M., & Bauman, D. (2019, April 4). *How America's college-closure crisis leaves families devastated.* The Chronicle of Higher Education.

Witt, R., & Coyne, K. P. (2019, September 22). *A merger won't save your college.* The Chronicle of Higher Education. https://www.chronicle.com/article/a-merger-wont-save-your-college/

CHAPTER ELEVEN

Students Who Transfer and Their Utilization of Career Services:
Using Big Data to Establish Connections to Student Success

Everett Weber and Philip D. Gardner

Our understanding of the transfer process is built upon extensive scholarly research and professional guidebooks (Gardner et al., 2021; Poisel & Joseph, 2018). The mechanics of transfer, academic adjustments, socialization, and attainment of expected outcomes anchor much of this literature. Researchers draw upon institutional data but are limited to the primary data source: student information systems. Few researchers who study the transfer transition incorporate information from other campus data sources, such as auxiliary support units and career services. Failure to consider such support services leads to a distorted picture of the factors that shape the transfer experience.

Richter and Weber's (2017) study on the outcomes of students who transferred to Michigan State University used traditional persistence and graduation (within six years) measures. The key explanatory variables were student characteristics (race/ethnicity, academic performance, and financial support). Unfortunately, the effort fell short of incorporating auxiliary data from support units that help students who transfer achieve these desired outcomes. The omission of auxiliary data was not intentional; the research team did not have access to data sets outside the central university information system.

Barefoot (2004) identified disconnected databases as a central problem with institutional data. Data held by departments are often inaccessible for broader use throughout campus. Concerns about data held by auxiliary units center upon the quality of the data, lack of experimental rigor, inconsistent definitions, or lack of motivation to prepare scholarly reports for publication. For example, many career offices track student attendance at events or appointments with career advisors. This information is aggregated for the office's annual activity report. However, the information seldom leverages the role career services plays in student success outcomes. Instead, institutional decision makers often obtain information on students' career resources and assistance through reports released by the Gallup Purdue Index or the *Career Services Benchmark Survey* from the National Association of Colleges and Employers. For students who experience transfer, few institutions capture data on their touchpoints with career services.

In this chapter, we attempt to achieve two important goals concerning students who transfer. To address the first goal, we employ advanced assessment methods using big-data analytics that connect student information (institutional) with career services information on student usage. This step documents the need for better analytical processes to determine student outcomes. We used high-level statistical methods that readers may not be familiar with; therefore, specific details on models are presented in footnotes to maintain clarity and understanding. The second goal is to determine if students who transfer and opt to use services provided by career services have different success outcomes (persistence and time to graduation) than students who transfer but choose not to participate in any career services programs or counseling. The findings provide insights into proactive ways career services connect with students who transfer.

Career Engagement and Student Success

Institutional data regarding students who transfer are available, specifically regarding their academic performance and persistence, but information on their engagement with career services and their preparation to transition into the workplace is visibly lacking. This lack of data leads to many assumptions about what constitutes successful career support to help students navigate the transfer experience. Not surprisingly, an institution's overall success strategies rarely include intentional and early interaction of students experiencing a transfer with career service professionals who can provide critical guidance for career decision-making, career planning, and employment goals. If such interactions happen, they are not well articulated or documented and are rarely shared campus-wide or with the broad academic community.

Tensions between major choice and career goals arise because of uncertainty about the value of college (Tinto, 1987). Hull-Blanks et al. (2005) found that students with strong job-related goals had higher persistence to graduation than students with poorly crafted career goals. Studies focused on students' career decision-making use instruments that measure career self-efficacy (Lent & Hackett, 1987), interests (Le et al., 2014), career maturity (Perry et al., 1999), and career thoughts (Kim et al., 2015) to understand student performance and commitment to college. Belser et al. (2017) contended that these studies failed to consider career readiness and did not address career planning interventions.

Career planning courses serve as a common intervention for researchers to investigate. For example, Belser et al. (2017, 2018) and Clayton et al. (2019) compared the persistence of students taking a career course to that of students who did not. In each study, the findings significantly indicated that taking a career course improved persistence from Year 1 to

Year 2, and Belser et al. (2018) found comparable results for persistence from Year 1 to Year 3. Unfortunately, we could locate no studies on career interventions for students who transferred.

Chapter 1 in this volume reviews research on the influence of career decision-making and career engagement on students who transfer. The limited research on support services, including career services, for students who transfer indicates the importance of career resources for student success. Furbeck (2011) completed an examination of orientation programs for students who transfer. He found that following transfer, students lacked information on logistical support, career counseling, and retention initiatives, among other campus services, compared to native students. Daddona and her colleagues (2019) investigated the campus services that students who transfer utilize to aid them in persisting. Daddona et al.'s sample of students used computer support services (approximately 74%), career services (43%), health services (38%), and tutoring services (32%) more frequently than other services. Students who transferred with an associate degree used career services slightly more than those without a two-year degree. The authors attributed this finding to transfers who enter with a completed degree being closer to needing assistance in preparing for their transition to the workplace. Their research, however, did not investigate the implications of this usage on persistence or time to graduation.

Chapter 1 and subsequent chapters in this volume identify a gap in the research on the role of career services in student success. Analyses presented in this chapter attempt to close this gap regarding students who transfer. The results highlight the role career services plays in boosting retention and reducing the time to graduation for a population critical to the workforce.

Profile of Michigan State University (MSU) Transfer Population

Richter and Weber (2017) examined the persistence and years to graduation of students who transferred, comparing their outcomes to those of students who enrolled directly into MSU (labeled "first time in any college" or FTIAC). The profile Richter and Weber discerned from their study serves as a backdrop and context for the work presented in this chapter. A brief review of their findings follows.

Students who transferred comprised approximately 20% of each new entering class, with 70% matriculating from two-year institutions (approximately 10% earned associate degrees) and 30% from four-year institutions. Based on their earned credits, approximately 25% entered as first-year students, 40% as sophomores, and 30% as juniors or third-year students. Slightly over half the students who transferred were men and 48% women; 78% were White and the majority were Michigan residents. Between 20% and 30% of the students who transferred switched from one of MSU's 13 colleges to another during their enrollment (i.e., changed their major).

Students who transferred to MSU performed well academically, with their GPAs improving from their first term on campus to graduation. Students who transferred had slightly higher persistence rates (84%) than FTIAC students (80%), and more students who transferred graduated within six years (83% for those entering from a two-year college and 82% from a four-year institution) than did FTIAC students (78%).

Richter and Weber (2017)'s analysis also showed that race/ethnicity did not influence success outcomes of students who transferred, although the small group of students who transferred from outside Michigan were 53% less likely to graduate than students who transferred from Michigan. A factor that affected graduation was the student's academic load for their first semester. Students who enrolled for 15 or fewer credits following transfer were less likely to graduate than students who enrolled for 16 or more credits. Transferring students who received a Pell grant graduated at a slightly higher rate than those who did not.

Parameters for the Study of Students Who Transfer

Study Population

Students who entered MSU between Fall term 2012 and Spring term 2016 comprised the study population: students who completed degrees in six colleges (Communication Arts & Sciences, Arts & Humanities, Social Science, Natural Science, Agriculture, and Nursing) and in James Madison College, the residential college for public affairs. Students who completed their degrees in the Colleges of Business and Engineering were excluded because information on student participation in career-related activities received a low priority and was collected inconsistently, except for career fair attendance, within these two colleges. We also excluded senior transfers because they took minimal courses to transfer to another university, completed additional courses for professional school admittance, or enrolled in a second bachelor's program. Finally, excluded from this study were international students. The study population contained 24,515 students, of which 5,926 were students who transferred—the focus of the work presented in this chapter.

Variables

Two university databases provide the measures included in our analyses. The student information system released student characteristics, including GPA, gender, ethnic affiliation, academic major, department, and college, first-generation attendee, and transfer status. Starting student level designated the year each student transferred into MSU and provided additional information on academic major changes, year-to-year persistence, and time to graduation. Family income information and Pell grant awards were not available for this study.

MSU does not offer required career courses or events for students. Any participation in career-related events and activities is at the student's discretion. After the 2008 recession, several colleges expanded activities and course offerings, including career and professional components. Advisors and faculty encourage students to engage in these opportunities, which have no mandated requirements. Career Services collects information, stored in the unit's data warehouse (i.e., the career engagement database), about students who utilize Career Services staff and programs. This database contains information about student contact with career advisors, career program attendance, and professional activity participation such as attendance at career fairs. Career Services attempts to capture all interactions but recognizes that some exchanges are not captured. Students who enroll in career courses offered by their academic colleges but taught or cotaught by Career Services receive designation as having participated in a career development engagement. We acknowledge that students can receive career support from other sources, including faculty, academic advisors, peers, parents, and other family members.

Career Services classifies student engagement into five categories: career advising (personal career counseling, aptitude assessments, career goal setting), career development (career exploration, career courses, career pathway sessions, meet and greet with professionals), professional advising (connection to work and internships, job search strategizing, connection to mentors), professional development (resume preparation, mock interviewing, etiquette and professional presence workshops, networking), and career fair attendance. After conducting basic analyses on the five categories, we simplified from five to three variables: career development (career advising + career development), professional development (professional advising + professional development), and career fair attendance. Career Services lacked reliable information concerning student participation in internships or other work-integrated activities. These activities fall under the purview of their academic colleges.

Analytical Approach

The large, linked databases presented challenges for us when selecting the best statistical procedure to evaluate the analytical models. First, the key dependent variables (participation, persistence, time to graduation) were categorical. Second, the substantial number of independent variables required an approach that allowed for comparisons within a variable (e.g., men and women) while holding other variables under consideration constant. Multinomial linear regression analysis (MLRA) proved the best technique for this study. MLRA requires a comparison group to be defined before running the model (Marill, 2004). For each model presented below, the comparison variables have been designated as men (gender), White (ethnicity), junior (class standing upon entry to MSU), and not first generation. GPA and the number of academic major changes were treated as continuous variables in each model.

Results

Participation in Career-Related Activities and Resources

This examination of student involvement in Career Services' programs and advising compared students who matriculated directly to MSU (denoted as FTIAC) with students who transferred to MSU. Sixty percent of FTIAC students and 48% of students who transferred had at least one interaction with Career Services during their years at the university (see Table 11.1). Between 25% and 30% of students in each group had one encounter; 32% of FTIAC students and 22% of students who transferred engaged in two or more activities. FTIAC students were significantly more likely to engage with Career Services than were students who transferred.

Table 11.1.

Percentage of Students Engaging with Career Services

Number of events attended	None	One	Two	Three	Four	Five
FTIAC	40	28	18	9	4	1
Transfers	52	26	14	6	2	.5

Students participated in the different activities offered by Career Services in about equal proportions. Approximately one third of FTIAC students selected activities from each of the three major groups, as shown in Table 11.2. Students who transferred participated at a much lower level, especially in career development (CD) activities (20%) and professional development (PD) events and career fairs (around 25%).

Table 11.2.

Percentage of Students Engaging in Career and Professional Development Activities

Career Service engagement	FTIAC	Transfers
Career development events	33	20
Professional development events	34	26
Career fairs	32	26
Attend any CD or PD advising or workshop	33	20
Unique users	60	48

Our results indicate that the timing of engagement with career services matters. Earlier participation in career services activities permits students to clarify career goals and plan accordingly. Later engagement signals interest in finding employment. Students' usage of Career Services resources shows a steady increase, as depicted in Table 11.3, based on their class standing. Approximately 19% of FTIAC first-year students sought Career Services resources, compared to 9% of students who transferred and entered as first-year students. Of the FTIAC students, 43% engaged with Career Services during their senior year, compared to 35% of the seniors who had transferred. Students who transferred did not seek assistance from Career Services during their first years on campus.

Table 11.3.
Percentage of Student Engagement with Career Services During Each Academic Year

Time of engagement	First year	Second year	Junior year	Senior year
FTIAC	19	19	28	43
Transfers	9	13	22	35

Both groups utilized career resources in a rush during their senior year. As illustrated in the accumulative engagement figures presented in Table 11.4, FTIAC students showed consistent growth in utilization of Career Services between their first year and their junior year. By the end of their second year, one third of FTIAC students had an engagement with Career Services, and by the end of their junior year, 47% had an engagement. By graduation, 65% of FTIAC students had taken advantage of resources offered by Career Services. In comparison, students who transferred were much slower in utilizing these services. By the end of their second year, only 15% had availed themselves of Career Services; the percentage increased to 28% by the end of junior year. By graduation, 48% of students who transferred had utilized Career Services.

Table 11.4.
Cumulative Percentage of Engagement with Career Services Across Four Years

Time of engagement	First year	Second year	Junior year	Senior year
FTIAC	19	32	47	65
Transfers	9	15	28	48

We dug deeper into the five individual categories of the five Career Services activities (career development workshops, professional development workshops, career advising, professional advising, and career fairs). Each model yielded significant results.[1]

The first-generation variable proved insignificant in all the models. In other words, usage of career services resources did not differ between first-generation attendees and students who were not first generation. In a key comparison, students who transferred were significantly less likely than FTIAC students to engage across all service categories. In other comparisons, men participated significantly less often in CD and PD services than women participated. However, men were significantly more likely than women to attend career fairs. Black students used all career resource categories more than other students did. Asian American and Hispanic/Latina students showed low participation in career and professional advising and workshops but attended career fairs at a high participation rate. Specific model details are presented in Appendix A.

Several critical observations surfaced from this stage of the analysis. First, FTIAC students increased their participation in Career Services activities more rapidly than students who transferred, especially in their second and third years on campus. This finding reinforces the idea that students who transfer plan to move through the university as quickly as possible, focusing on their academics. The students in this study engaged career resources in a rush during their last year at the university, cramming everything into a brief period. Black students, both FTIAC students and students who transferred, participated in all types of career activities, especially professional development during their fourth year. This last finding is contrary to what earlier researchers had reported (see Chapter 2). That men did not utilize Career Services was anticipated, given other literature showing avoidance of career resources by men (see Chapter 2).

Persistence

Table 11.5 presents the persistence calculation for students who transferred based on the year the student transferred into MSU. Transfer students who engaged early in any Career Services activity had extremely high persistence, losing less than 4% of their cohort from entry to graduation. Conversely, students who transferred and opted not to engage with Career Services witnessed the largest declines in persistence. The largest drop occurred between the first and second year for first-year students. The largest drop occurred between the second and third years for both sophomore and junior students who transferred.

---

[1] The overall *p* value was < .0001 for all models. The Hosmer and Lemeshow goodness of fit was acceptable for all models, except for the professional advising model.

Table 11.5.
Persistence Percentage of Students who Transferred, Organized by Starting Class and Engagement with Career Services

Starting Class		First year to second year	Second year to third year	Third year to fourth year
First year	Engaged in CS	99.3	97.7	96.7
	Did not engage	86.5	76.3	72.1
Second year	Engaged in CS	99.6	97.8	96.7
	Did not engage	93.8	82.0	77.1
Junior	Engaged in CS	99.6	97.7	96.6
	Did not engage	93.6	86.8	83.5

We modeled persistence at three specific times for students who transferred. Time Period 1 covered the year they entered MSU as students who transferred (designated Year 1) and returned for their second year (designated Year 2). Time Period 2 focused on students who transferred, enrolled in Year 2, and returned in Year 3. The final period covered students enrolled in Year 3 who returned in Year 4. Model parameters for goodness of fit can be found in the model statistics in the Appendix tables.[2]

The number of students who transferred who enrolled in Year 1 was 5,926, with 248 not returning in Year 2. Academic performance strongly influenced persistence in this period, with students earning higher grades persisting compared to those who earned low grades. The positive regression sign for GPA indicated that as GPA rose, students more likely persisted to the next year. Likewise, women persisted at a significantly higher rate than men who transferred. Students who transferred into MSU as first-year students persisted at a lower rate than students who arrived as sophomores and juniors, with sophomores reporting the highest persistence. Neither ethnic affiliation nor first-generation status contributed to the model. Our focus on engagement with Career Services revealed that students who transferred and participated in CD events, PD events, and career fairs showed significantly higher persistence levels from Year 1 to Year 2 than students who transferred but opted not to engage with Career Services.

The model for Time Period 2 (Year 2 to Year 3) started with 5,326 students, with 597 not returning for Year 3. As GPA rose, the likelihood of a student persisting increased. Students

---

[2] The parameters for persistence Year 1 to Year 2 (Model 1): The model's Hosmer and Lemeshow goodness of fit (.3330) was acceptable, with $R^2 = .1246$. The parameters for persistence Year 2 to Year 3 (Model 2): The model produced an acceptable Hosmer and Lemeshow goodness of fit (.3611), $R^2 = .1934$. The parameters for persistence Year 3 to Year 4 were not acceptable: Hosmer and Lemeshow goodness of fit (.0002), with $R^2 = .1988$.

who changed academic majors were more likely to persist than those who did not change majors. This action suggests that students who failed to identify an academic major or to be accepted into their preferred major left the university without considering another option at MSU. Students who enrolled as first-year students persisted at a significantly lower rate than those who entered as juniors. Gender, first-generation, and ethnic affiliation proved insignificant from second to third year among students who transferred. Participation in CD events, PD events, and career fairs by students who transferred contributed to significantly higher persistence than those students who transferred with no participation with career services.

The third period model (Year 3 to Year 4) produced poor results. The unfavorable model findings result from all students in the study reaching senior status or graduating. In addition, only two significant variables emerged from the model: the number of academic majors and career fair attendance. In summary, the persistence models over a three-year period revealed that participation by students who transferred in various Career Services activities persisted at a higher rate than those who did not participate. MLRA provides the odds ratio or the strength of the relationship between two events given a particular action (in this case, participating in a career activity or not). Figure 11.1 shows the likelihood that Career Services participation contributes to higher persistence. For example, students who transferred were 9% more likely to persist after participating in CD advising than were students who transferred but did not participate. PD workshops showed the highest odds of persisting at 15%. Please note that the odds ratios are not additive: Participating in CD workshops and PD workshops does not increase the odds of persisting by 26%.

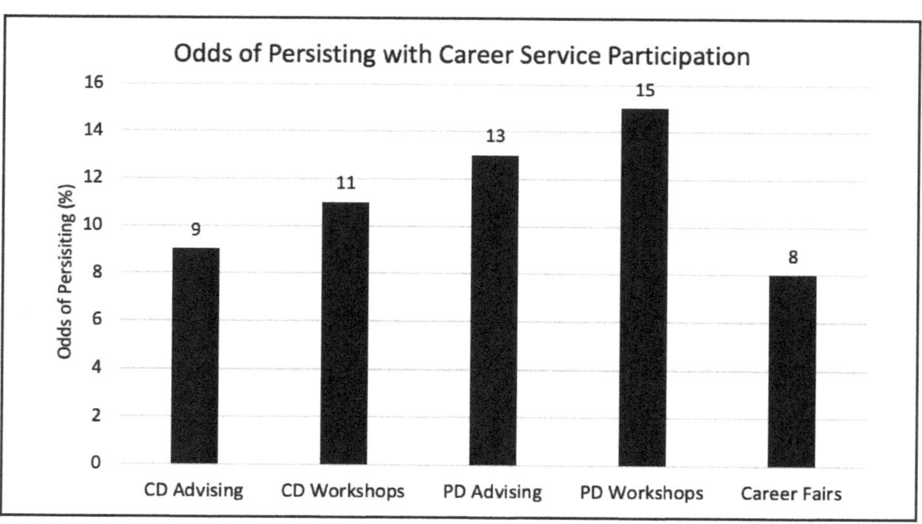

Figure 11.1.

Changing Majors

The persistence models indicated that if a student who transferred changed their academic major preference after enrolling, they were more likely to persist. A closer examination of the persistence patterns based on major changes seemed appropriate because this decision has career planning implications. In Table 11.6 persistence is compared for engagement with career services by the major changes they made with *only one major* (never changed major), *two majors* (one major change), and *three or more majors* (two or more major changes). Students who transfer and change major, regardless of the number of times, are likely to remain at the institution and persist to graduation. Students who elect to connect with career services persist at a higher rate than those not using career services. Using career service resources makes a difference in persistence, as those students who had only one major and chose not to utilize career services had a 73% retention after three years. Unengaged students with one or more major changes also reported declines in persistence. By comparison, those students who transferred and used career services persisted above 95%, regardless of number of majors. We cannot determine if utilizing career services causes higher persistence, but a correlation clearly exists that suggests an engagement with career services supports persistence. By connecting students who transfer to career services as early as possible, more students will likely remain in school and persist to graduation.

Table 11.6.

Percentage of Students who Transferred, Persisted, Organized by Major Change and Engagement with Career Services

		Persistence from		
		First year to second year	**Second year to third year**	**Third year to fourth year**
Engaged	1 major	99.1	96.1	95.0
	2 majors	99.9	99.1	97.9
	3 + majors	100.0	100.0	99.4
Did not engage	1 major	88.8	76.6	72.9
	2 majors	98.8	92.8	87.3
	3 + majors	100.0	97.4	92.9

Graduation Rate

Graduation rate reflects the proportion of students who transferred who then graduated within a specific period, based on the cohort they entered the university. Models were prepared for students who graduated in three years after enrolling with their cohort, in four years, and in five years (see Table C in the Appendix).[3]

Approximately 900 students completed their degrees within three years. GPA proved to be the only significant variable in the three-year model. The strongest academically prepared students moved quickly to graduation and seldom took advantage of their support resources.

Forty-two percent of the students who transferred graduated within four years. Higher GPAs contributed significantly to completing a degree within four years. Students who enrolled as juniors were more likely to graduate in four years than those enrolled as first-year students. Asian American students were more likely to graduate in four years than were students from other ethnic groups. Students who made fewer academic major changes were more likely to graduate in four years than those who made more changes. Students who participated in PD events and attended career fairs were more likely to graduate in four years than those who did not engage in these activities. However, participation in CD events did not contribute to the four-year model.

Sixty-nine percent of students who transfer graduated within five years. Students with higher GPAs were more likely to graduate in five years than those with lower GPAs. Those students who enrolled as sophomores graduated at a significantly higher rate than those who enrolled as juniors (very few juniors remained in school at this point). Asian American students graduated at a significantly higher rate in five years than did students from other ethnic groups. Making fewer academic major changes resulted in higher graduation rates in five years (i.e., changing major led to delays in graduating within five years). Students who participated in CD events and PD events and who attended career fairs had significantly higher five-year graduation rates than students who transferred but did not participate.

The findings from the five-year graduation model show that engagement with career services had a similar impact as that shown for persistence. As students approach graduation, the importance of professional development resources and activities increases by being used more. Students attending a PD workshop saw their odds of graduating in five years increase 15%; likewise, participation in a career fair resulted in a 16% increase, as shown in Figure 11.2. The effects may not be cumulative but rather work together to improve both the persistence and graduation of students who transferred. Unfortunately, we do not have

---

[3] The parameters for three-year graduation rate failed to produce an acceptable Hosmer and Lemeshow goodness of fit (.0273), with R^2 = .0996. The parameters for four-year graduation rate produced a barely acceptable Hosmer and Lemeshow goodness of fit (.0684), with R^2 = .0868. The parameter for five-year graduation rate revealed an acceptable Hosmer and Lemeshow goodness of fit (.1871), with R^2 = .1357.

other research or public data sets to compare and thus to establish the importance of career service engagement.

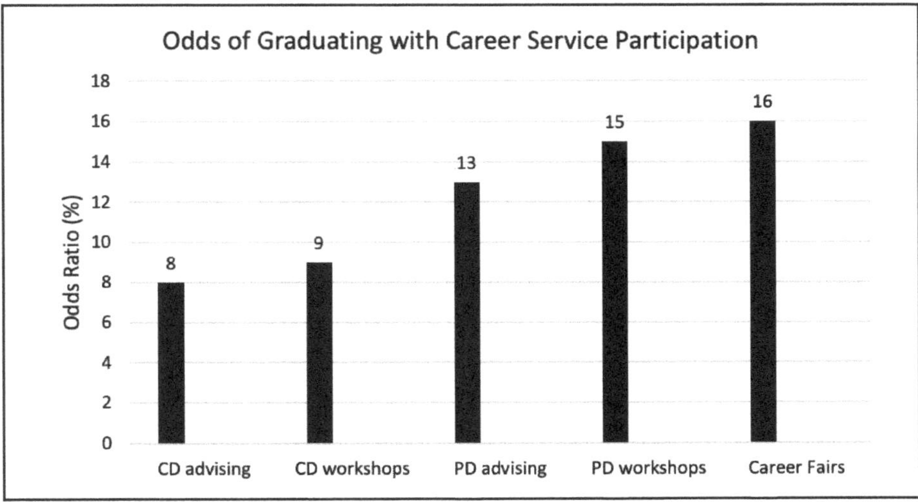

Figure 11.2.

Discussion

This study achieved a significant objective by demonstrating the ability to connect an auxiliary service database to the central student information system to predict student success. The process of connecting the database to the central student information system presented challenges that required programming the Career Services database for compatibility, specifying measurement parameters, and clarifying variable definitions. However, linking these databases allowed us to complete our other more noteworthy objective, establishing the importance of career service engagement for student success outcomes.

A student who transferred who connects to career services can find themselves being able to persistence and move quicker to graduation. One half of the students who transferred reached out to Career Services at some point during their residency at MSU. Career services is not an isolated unit passively awaiting students to enter their office; instead, engagement requires cooperation and collaboration across multiple services and between academic and career services to expand the introduction and enhance the use of career services. Although students who transfer believe they must move quickly through their new institution, adjusting the prevailing mindset allows them to take advantage of available career resources. A shift in thinking requires a broader community engaged in the transfer process than currently prevails. As a result, career services can play an integral role in student success to a greater extent than documented in administrative and scholarly studies.

Career services need a more prominent role with students who transferred. Few students who transfer engage in career services during their initial years at MSU and many other institutions. Most tend to cram their use of career resources and professional guidance from career services into the last year on campus. This pattern, which replicates previous research on how students who transfer use services, creates a natural pressure to "hit the ground running" and the challenge of fitting into the existing culture (Whang et al., 2017).

Another important finding is that Black students who transferred appeared more vested in utilizing career services at MSU than did other transfer groups. MSU has a rich tradition of advocating for underrepresented groups. For example, Career Services organized the first diversity career fair at a major university in the country, and the Black student community plays a key role in planning and hosting these events. The low participation by Hispanic/Latina students signals concerns on the best approaches for MSU to initiate campus-based interventions to invest in the students' career and professional development.

The lower rate of participation for men than for women is well established. Kantamneni and colleagues (2011) found that men shape their decisions to seek career counseling around societal attitudes. Men also wrap their identity closely to their careers and work and view career counseling as a weakness because their self-worth is so entwined with their career. Their participation in career service events, even advising, requires these actions to be clearly and directly connected to employment opportunities. Despite continued pressure on college campuses to provide critical career services, the underlying cross-current of the societal stigma attached to using such services dampens students' usage.

We always urge caution in generalizing from a single institution. MSU's transfer population does not necessarily reflect the characteristics of the transfer population across the United States (National Student Clearinghouse Research Center, 2018). Other institutions can replicate this study by using big data to discern the role of career services in student success. Career service offices can collaborate with the institutional research offices or the faculty in applied mathematics, engineering, or statistics to assist with big-data management. Results naturally may differ depending on the characteristics of an institution's transfer population.

In studies of student use of support services (see Chapter 1 in this volume), students who seek out career services may inherently differ in some respect(s) from students who do not seek out these services. The proclivity to engage may stem from noncognitive factors, parental influence, a proactive social network that supports career exploration, career maturity, or career self-efficacy. These measures were unavailable for our study but could be collected to augment future big-data studies. Understanding more about the student population allows career services to better target ways to engage current nonparticipants.

Conclusion

The use of big data provides a picture of the impact of auxiliary services such as career services, particularly those touchpoints that can aid students who transfer in persisting and graduating. Big databases exist throughout college campuses, but they are often unknown from the key stakeholders and or researchers who can use them effectively to review specific outcomes. Thus, their benefits are lost. Communities of practice around transfer experiences invite strong partnerships and highlight the need to allocate resources (including time) to collect, analyze, and interpret necessary information; build career interventions; and make decisions to improve student success effectively and efficiently. For career centers that do not have advanced data analysts on staff, this is the time to reach out to your institutional research group, applied mathematics or statistics departments, or other faculty working with large data sets to assist in gaining insights to improve student success.

References

Barefoot, B. O. (2004). Higher education's revolving door: Confronting the problem of student drop out in U.S. colleges and universities. *Open Learning: The Journal of Open, Distance and e-Learning, 19*(1), 9–18. https://doi.org/10.1080/0268051042000177818

Belser, C. T., Prescod, D. J., Daire, A. P., Dagley, M. A., & Young, C. Y. (2017). Predicting undergraduate student retention in STEM majors based on career development factors. *The Career Development Quarterly, 65*(1), 88–93. https://doi.org/10.1002/cdq.12082

Belser, C. T., Shillingford, M., Daire, A. P., Prescod, D. J., & Dagley, M. A. (2018). Factors influencing undergraduate student retention in STEM majors: Career development, math ability, and demographics. *Professional Counselor, 8*(3), 262–276. https://files.eric.ed.gov/fulltext/EJ1198867.pdf

Clayton, K., Wessel, R. D., McAtee, J., & Knight, W. E. (2019). KEY careers: Increasing retention and graduation rates with career interventions. *Journal of Career Development, 46*(4), 425–439. https://doi.org/10.1177/0894845318763972

Daddona, M. F., Mondie-Milner, C., & Goodson, J. (2021). Transfer student resources: Keeping students once they enroll. *Journal of College Student Retention: Research, Theory & Practice, 23*(3). 487–506. https://doi.org/10.1177/1521025119848754

Furbeck, O. F. (2011). Enrollment management of transfer students. In M. A. Poisel & S. Joseph (Eds.), *Transfer students in higher education: Building foundations for policies, programs, and services that foster student success* (pp. 13–28). National Resource Center for The First-Year Experience and Students in Transition.

Gardner, J. N., Rosenberg, M. J., & Koch, A. K. (Eds.). (2021). *The transfer experience: A handbook for creating a more equitable and successful postsecondary system*. Stylus Publishing.

Hull-Blanks, E., Kurpius, S. E. R., Befort, C., Sollenberger, S., Nicpon, M. F., & Huser, L. (2005). Career goals and retention-related factors among college freshmen. *Journal of Career Development, 32*(1), 16–30. https://doi.org/10.1177/0894845305277037

Kantamneni, N., Christianson, H. F., Smothers, M. K., & Wester, S. R. (2011). The exploration of role induction as a potential method for improving men's perceptions of career counseling. *The Career Development Quarterly, 59*(3), 219–231. https://doi.org/10.1002/j.2161-0045.2011.tb00065.x

Kim, B., Lee, B. H., Ha, G., Lee, H. K., & Lee, S. M. (2015). Examining longitudinal relationships between dysfunctional career thoughts and career decision-making self-efficacy in school-to-work transition. *Journal of Career Development, 42*(6), 511–523. https://doi.org/10.1177/0894845315578903

Le, H., Robbins, S. B., & Westrick, P. (2014). Predicting student enrollment and persistence in college STEM fields using an expanded PE fit framework: A large-scale multilevel study. *Journal of Applied Psychology, 99*(5), 915–947. https://doi.org/10.1037/a0035998

Lent, R. W., & Hackett, G. (1987). Career self-efficacy: Empirical status and future directions. *Journal of Vocational Behavior, 30*(3), 347–382. https://doi.org/10.1016/0001-8791(87)90010-8

Marill, K. A. (2004). Advanced statistics: Linear regression, part II: Multiple linear regression. *Academic Emergency Medicine, 11*(1), 94–102.

National Student Clearinghouse Research Center. (2018). *Signature report 15: Transfer and mobility: A national view of student movement in postsecondary institutions, Fall 2011 cohort.* https://nscresearchcenter.org/signaturereport15/

Perry, S. R., Cabrera, A. F., & Vogt, W. P. (1999). Career maturity and college student persistence. *Journal of College Student Retention: Research, Theory & Practice, 1*(1), 41–58. https://doi.org/10.2190/13EA-M98P-RCJX-EX8X

Poisel, M. A., & Joseph, S. (Eds). (2018). *Building transfer student pathways for college and career success*. National Resource Center for the First-Year Experience and Students in Transition.

Richter, S., & Weber, H. (2017, November 2). *Transfer students: An MSU success story*. Michigan AIR Conference.

Tinto, V. (1987). *Leaving college: Rethinking the causes and cures of student attrition*. University of Chicago Press.

Whang, L., Tawatao, C., Danneker, J., Belanger, J., Edward Weber, S., Garcia, L., & Klaus, A. (2017). Understanding the transfer student experience using design thinking. *Reference Services Review, 45*(2), 298–313. http://hdl.handle.net/1773/40336

Appendices

Statistical Tables for Models of Participation, Persistence and Time to Degree

A. Models for Five Career Services Activity Categories

Parameter		CD workshops		PD workshops		CD advising		PD advising		Career fair	
		Estimate	p	Estimate	p	Estimate	p	Estimate	p	Estimate	p
Intercept		−2.4376	**<.0001**	−2.4719	**<.0001**	−2.2737	**<.0001**	−2.4211	**<.0001**	−2.3325	**<.0001**
First year	First year	−0.5994	**<.0001**	−1.0373	**<.0001**	−0.7242	**<.0001**	−1.1959	**<.0001**	−1.6680	**<.0001**
Second year	Second year	−0.3027	**<.0001**	−0.3726	**<.0001**	−0.1719	**<.0001**	-0.3388	**<.0001**	−0.4907	**<.0001**
Junior	Junior	0.1704	**<.0001**	0.3628	**<.0001**	0.2477	**<.0001**	0.3876	**<.0001**	0.6111	**<.0001**
Transfer	No	0.6543	**<.0001**	0.3635	**<.0001**	0.2678	**<.0001**	0.2425	**<.0001**	0.2222	**<.0001**
Black	Yes	0.3728	**<.0001**	0.3874	**<.0001**	0.3857	**<.0001**	0.4164	**<.0001**	0.2257	**<.0001**
Asian American	Yes	−0.3257	**<.0001**	−0.0742	.1443	−0.2524	**<.0001**	−0.0545	.2762	0.1282	**.0071**
Hispanic/ Latina	Yes	0.1377	**.0023**	−0.0454	.3771	−0.0158	.7415	−0.0149	.7695	0.1579	**.0013**
Race not reported (RNR)	Yes	−0.0690	.4530	−0.0980	.3271	0.1040	.2515	−0.0459	.6396	−0.3843	**.0002**
Gender	F	0.1705	**<.0001**	0.0847	**<.0001**	0.1864	**<.0001**	0.1583	**<.0001**	−0.0978	**<.0001**
First generation	Yes	−0.00129	.9178	0.00392	.7752	0.0250	.0573	0.0185	.1811	−0.0555	**<.0001**

Note. Comparison groups: Class = Senior; Transfer =Transfer student; Ethnicity = White; Gender = Male; First generation = Not first generation

B. Model of Persistence

	First to second year persistence	Second to third year persistence	Third to fourth year persistence
Did not persist	248	597	755
Persisted	5678	5326	5171
Overall persistence rate	.958	.899	.873
H&L fit	.333	.3611	**.0002**
R^2	.1246	.1934	.1988
Max_rescaled R^2	.4245	.4031	.3726

Parameter		First to second year persistence		Second to third year persistence		Third to fourth year persistence	
		Estimate	*p*	Estimate	*p*	Estimate	*p*
Intercept		0.00509	.9944	−.8987	.0056	−0.0800	.1212
Cumulative GPA		1.1237	**<.0001**	1.0718	**<.0001**	−0.0103	.8481
Starting student level	First year	−.8525	**<.0001**	−.5527	**<.0001**	.1563	.3918
Starting student level	Second year	.3682	**.0004**	.0485	.4773	.3395	.1784
CD events	DNP	−.5556	**.0025**	−.3683	**<.0001**	−.1444	.5090
PD events	DNP	−1.2225	**<.0001**	−.9252	**<.0001**	.4717	.1751
Career fairs	DNP	−1.7896	**.0004**	−1.4007	**<.0001**	1.7322	**<.0001**
Gender	F	−.1669	**.0310**	−.0800	.1212	.0800	.1212
First generation	Yes	−.0525	.5066	−.0103	.8481	−0.0103	.8481
African American	Yes	.4317	.1199	−.1563	.3918	−.1563	.3918
Asian American	Yes	.2645	.4790	.3395	.1784	−.3395	.1784
Hispanic/Latina	Yes	−.0374	.9085	−.1444	.5090	−.1444	.5090
Race not reported (RNR)	Yes	−.6996	.1514	−.4717	.1751	−.4717	.1751
Number of academic majors (Majors)		2.7191	**<.0001**	1.7322	**<.0001**	1.7322	**<.0001**

Note. Comparison groups: Starting student level = Juniors; CD events, PD events & career fairs = participated; Gender = Male; First generation = No; Ethnicity = White

C. Model for Graduation Rate

	Graduate in 3 years	Graduate in 4 years	Graduate in 5 years
Enrolled	5027	3454	1839
Graduated	899	2472	4087
Graduation rate	.15	.42	.76
H&L fit	**.0273**	.0684	.1871
R^2	.0996	.0868	.1357
Max_rescaled R^2	.1737	.1168	.191

Parameter		Graduate in 3 years Estimate	p	Graduate in 4 years Estimate	p	Graduate in 5 years Estimate	p
Intercept		−5.2744	.8629	-1.3739	<.0001	-1.0806	<.0001
Cumulative GPA		.3928	**<.0001**	.4364	**<.0001**	.7595	**<.0001**
Starting student level	First year	2.7792	.9275	.3774	**.0137**	−.3113	.0701
Starting student level	Second year	2.9705	.9225	−.0463	.717	.3289	**.0168**
CD events	DNP	.0286	.558	−.0282	.4272	−.223	**<.0001**
PD events	DNP	−.0362	.4275	−.0685	**.0394**	−.1251	**.0012**
Career fairs	DNP	.0439	.3278	−.0721	**.0291**	−.1891	**<.0001**
Gender	F	.105	.0905	.0412	.162	.0806	**.0136**
First generation	Yes	−.0177	.7824	−.0412	.1912	−.0606	.0811
African American	Yes	2.1675	.9434	−.0883	.4399	−.1801	.1255
Asian American	Yes	−1.017	.9869	.3458	**.0098**	.2854	**.0536**
Hispanic/Latina	Yes	−1.4971	.9794	−.143	.3107	−.2563	.0765
Race not reported (RNR)	Yes	−2.1058	.9829	−.3085	.1944	−.0673	.7901
Number of majors (Majors)		−.3478	**.0074**	−.2175	**<.0001**	−.1481	**.0021**

Note. Comparison groups: Starting student level = Juniors; CD events, PD events, & career fairs = participated; Gender = Male; First generation = No; Ethnicity = White

CHAPTER TWELVE

Adult Learners:
Invisible Among Students Who Transfer

Philip D. Gardner, Heather N. Maietta,
and Niki Perkins

Adult learners, typically defined as students over the age of 25, comprise a significant portion of the undergraduate population (Hussar et al., 2020; Monje-Paulsen et al., 2019; Rose, 2012). Seldom do they follow a straight path toward securing their college degree, often transferring multiple times (Shapiro et al., 2018). They face challenges in securing a balance between their educational goals and family commitments, work demands, financial concerns, and other life priorities. Research on adult learner transfer success turns attention to minimizing loss of credits from one institution to another, capturing credits through life experiences, reducing financial concerns, and providing flexible learning opportunities (Gast, 2013; Wiggams, 2004). This attention addresses several adult learners' key concerns about affordability, flexible learning options, the streamlined application process, and shortened time to degree completion. Often left unaddressed are challenges that the transfer process presents to adult learners' career aspirations even though career-relevant education (raising earning potential, ability to change career pathways, and expanded employment opportunities) is a major goal for them (Bragg et al., 2019; Chiappone, 1992; Dukes, 2001). In this chapter, we attempt to shed light on adult learners' career perceptions and attitudes toward work to inform the transfer process by integrating career development into adult transfer programming and advising.

Hussar et al. (2020) disclosed that adult learners comprised 37% of undergraduate enrollment in 2017. Other observers have contended that adults' level of participation is higher (Monje-Paulsen et al., 2019; Rose, 2012), agreeing on a range from 35% to 40%. According to the National Center for Education Statistics report by McFarland et al. (2018), adult learners enrolled in full-time, four-year degree programs comprised 66% of all students at private for-profit institutions, with public and private nonprofit institutions reporting 9% and 13%, respectively. Adults comprised a higher proportion of enrollees attending part-time in pursuit of a four-year degree, with 40% at public, 59% at private nonprofit, and 82% at private nonprofit institutions. Looking at the Fall 2011 cohort (latest data available), researchers calculated that approximately 18% of adult learners transfer based on their enrollment at the time as compared to 45% for students 20 and younger (Shapiro et al., 2018). This figure neglects to capture adult movement in and out of institutions over time, with many adult learners attempting to earn college credit before their documented enrollment in 2011. While enrollment increases have occurred, adult learners experience low completion rates (Taniguchi & Kaufman, 2005). Colleges and universities often find themselves burdened by traditions and practices that prove ill suited for older students who are often invisible as a population when seeking support services (Coulter & Mandell, 2012; Flint, 2000).

Adult learners possess a range of traits, including self-motivation, curiosity about learning, extensive work and life experiences, critical thinking skills, aptitude to work in groups, and a solid ability to engage in reflection (Gianakos, 1996; Rahim & Finch, 2011). Traditional undergraduate pedagogy, dependent upon faculty-directed learning, is ill-matched for adult learners (Knowles, 1984), with adult traits essentially being neglected (Sissel et al., 2001). As Sissel et al. posited, "Whether it is policy, program, attitudes, classroom environment, or funding support, adult learners face institutional neglect, prejudice, and denial of opportunities" (p. 18). Campus services fail to "support the growth, development, and well-being of adults" (p. 21). Whether career service units fall under student services or academic affairs leadership, career development is student support performed campus-wide by career professionals, academic advisors, and faculty. These organizational arrangements impede the delivery of this service to assist adults (Sandler, 2000).

Adults often transfer with a lack of career clarity and knowledge of the processes to transition successfully into desired career paths. Support services within higher education should allocate need-specific resources that create equal spaces for this population to thrive. Instead, a gaping hole exists in resource allocation aligned with adult learner motivations. The inability of institutions to recognize the differing adult learner motivations and provide resources to meet their unique personalized needs is concerning. Creating an equal space means developing new understandings of adult learning roles, work roles, career roles, and their alignment during transfer and post-transfer. This chapter presents a profile of adult learners' work and career planning perceptions. This information identifies appropriate adult policies, procedures, and programs for transfer to minimize career disruptions and inform faculty, advisors, and professional support personnel who assist adult learners through the transfer process.

Literature Review

No single definition exists that fully embodies the adult learner. The Council for Adult and Experiential Learning (2000) identified adult learners as those who meet one or more of the following conditions: delayed entry into postsecondary education after high school, lack of a high school diploma, financial independence from parents, full-time work while enrolled part-time, and dependents other than a spouse or partner. A broader, more general definition of the adult learner is anyone 25 or older in postsecondary education (Voorhees & Lingenfelter, 2003). Since adults frequently "stop out" or withdraw from school to accommodate family responsibilities or unresolved academic issues (course scheduling difficulties, financial aid confusion), they acquire nontraditional, commuter, or re-entry labels. These labels marginalize adults as peripheral to higher education's primary task of educating 18- to 24-year-olds (Chen, 2017; Kasworm, 1993, 2010).

For this chapter, the definition of adult learner is an individual who is pursuing a postsecondary technical certificate, apprenticeship, two-year degree, or four-year degree and is age 25 and older. In addition, this definition includes individuals who attempted college earlier, earning credits but not a degree, and adults who have returned to upgrade their education through a formal degree program.

Adult Learner Motivations

Adult learners pursue higher education with varying motivations related to retirement, career change, loss of employment, or advancement within their field (DiSilvestro, 2013; Gardner et al., 2021). In addition, some adult learners seek to enhance their skills and abilities or enter higher education because they could not afford postsecondary education earlier in life (Bland, 2003). Soares (2017) highlighted five commonalities that nontraditional students share in the pursuit of higher education. They (a) are wage earners for themselves or their families, (b) combine work and learning at the same time or move between them frequently, (c) pursue knowledge, skills, and credentials that employers will recognize and compensate, (d) require developmental education to be successful in college-level courses, and (e) seek academic/career advising to navigate their complex path to a degree. Thomas (1980), Shamir and Arthur (1989), and Gardner et al. (2021) found adult learners to be more intrinsically motivated to seek postsecondary learning experiences when values are in play, while Scozzaro and Subich (1990) and Gardner et al. (2021) teased out extrinsic factors such as pay, security, and promotions, mainly as adults acquire more work experience. Some adult learners have strong extrinsic reasons stemming from uncertainty about the future of their jobs or having already been displaced. Others enroll for personal reasons to serve as role models for future generations or to attain long-held career aspirations. They have a precise idea (in some cases) of their talents, needs, and values (Schein, 1978) and explore these components within realistic time perspectives (Super & Hall, 1978).

We assume that the adult learners encountered in undergraduate programs still bear the characteristics Gianakos (1996) identified: more pragmatic, active, realistic, significant responsibilities outside of college; an advantage of richer life experiences; and more directed in educational/career decisions. Bean and Metzner (1985) suggested that environmental variables are more important than academic variables to nontraditional students. Although nontraditional students interact with their institutions, they also spend substantial time in the external environment (Bean & Metzner, 1985). Countryman (2006) pointed out that the external environment is composed of unique factors that can be challenging for many adult learners and that defining and addressing these challenges are critical. Environmental variables include finances, hours of employment, outside encouragement, family responsibilities, and opportunity to transfer (Metzner & Bean, 1987). Countryman (2006) supported these environmental variables but also included career services. However, adults experience confusion about career choices and lack knowledge of potential pathways in a disruptive workplace, and the higher education community must be aware and sensitive to these needs and respond accordingly.

Adults and Career Development

The assumption that adult learners are more directed than younger learners about their career decisions because their work and life experiences provide realistic perspectives has not gone unchallenged. Hoff's (1997) examination of the career development needs of adult students revealed four essential themes: (a) the need for self-awareness, (b) occupational knowledge requirements, (c) the need for decision-making strategies, and (d) challenges to career implementation. Hoff found that adults vary significantly in their levels of self-understanding, self-efficacy in their definitions of career, and the number and types of roles/responsibilities assumed. Also, she discovered that not all adults are necessarily knowledgeable about occupational requirements or environments. Some do not know where to find information, nor are they aware of their potential and occupational preferences and the skills required to make career decisions. These challenges to career implementation are as unique as individual adult learners.

Chen (2017) discussed the competing nature of life roles as a significant reason adult learners struggle with postsecondary education. Pursuing higher education positively affects short- and long-term career identity; however, taking on the student role also creates role strain (Goode, 1960). Conflict exists when adult learners experience the intersection of role strain and life stressors (Chen, 2017; Padulla, 1994). Role strain manifests in three ways. The first—role conflict—emerges when the needs of numerous roles conflict with one another. When there are too few resources to meet demand, role overload occurs. Finally, role contagion happens when a person is preoccupied with one role while doing another. As the adult learner assumes a student role, another variable is added to their experience of role strain (Chen, 2017). Isolation occurs when adult learners experience role strain in "what they feel is a youth-centric environment that does not understand them or attempt to accommodate them" (Chen, 2017, p. 4) as they struggle with thoughts of withdrawing (Markle, 2015).

Sandler (2000) and Lent and Brown (2002) examined adults' career decision-making self-efficacy (CDMSE), considering stress from their multiple roles. CDMSE "identifies the degree of confidence students express about their competency or ability (self-efficacy) to embark on informational, educational, and occupational goal planning activities" (Sandler, 2000, p. 538). In addition to academic integration, social integration, institutional commitment, and intent to persist, Sandler's research revealed two additional factors related to adult student persistence: (a) perceived stress or the stress experienced by adult students and (b) financial difficulty brought on by attending college. Sandler addressed several implications from his study:

- Academic and social systems of the undergraduate experience must be more attuned to adult learners' perceptions of confidence about their vocational needs.

- Support systems need to be structured to assist adult learners with critical development tasks of career decision-making planning that is at odds with current undergraduate practices of academic and social integration.

- Relevant curriculum related to adult lives needs to be developed to link curriculum directly to the world of work.

- Collaborative ties and experiences outside the university that reflect workplace realities and experiential learning need to be built.

- Education and experiential learning must instill confidence about the economic future in adult learners.

Monje-Paulsen et al. (2019) made an important distinction between job and career in their study of the vocational self-concept of adult learners. Adult learners tend to discuss jobs they have held or are currently in and fail at framing vocational experiences in a career context. In addition, the career preparation and campus resources—tailored to traditional-age students—fail to include prior work (Hamrick et al., 2002). Monje-Paulsen and colleagues contended that a lack of congruence between life/work roles and school inhibited career decision-making, requiring a shift in adult mindset related to jobs. Thus, there is a need for adult learners to work with professionals who appreciate and understand the adult career decision-making process. To summarize, Chiappone (1992) stated, "Adults who seek the services of career development professionals bring a variety of psychological issues that affect their career development. In addition, adults are continuously experiencing personal transitions that affect their career and career transitions that affect their personal life" (pp. 370–371).

Support Services for Adult Learners

Although adult learners make up a large and growing segment of the college population, enrollment varies widely across the country. The population of adult learners is high at some campuses while relatively low at others. Nevertheless, all campus staff can expect increased demand for support and services as birth rates decline, the country will see fewer traditional-aged students and more adult learners enroll in higher education. The need to continually reskill and refresh credentials to remain relevant in the workplace will be essential.

Student affairs research and practices have focused mainly on the traditional-aged college student (Iloh, 2017–2018). The track record for delivering full support services to adults has been mixed (Scott-Summers, 1992; Siarzynski-Ferrer & Pillar, 2021). Attention to academic support is prevalent due to adults' anxieties about returning to campus with rusty academic skills. Faculty in some schools recognize that academic services are inadequate for adult learners if access to advising, financial aid, tutoring, and enrollment/scheduling is difficult (Rangaswami, 1999). Lenhardt (1994) and Iloh (2017–2018) challenged student affairs administrators to design support services to meet adult learners' diverse needs and requirements. Byrne (1989) and Iloh (2017–2018) stressed the need for adult learner support beyond the campus environment to include families, employers, and supervisors.

A genuine concern exists that adult support services seem ineffective and haphazard, especially as compared to the services provided to traditional-aged students (Ackell, 1982; Pappas & Loring, 1985; Schlossberg et al., 1989). Kerka's (1989) concern was that adult learners are essentially segregated on campus, while Coulter and Mandell (2012) coined the lack of attention and support "invisibility" (p. 40). The Council for Adult and Experiential Learning [CAEL] (2005) addressed the problem by constructing a framework of eight principles to provide services to adult learners. While all eight principles are noteworthy, the principle of life and career planning—that the institution addresses adult learners' life and career goals before or at the onset of enrollment to assess and align its capacities to help learners reach their goals—pertains directly to career services support.

Compton et al. (2006) leveraged the CAEL principles to determine dimensions for adult support services: validate experiential learning, customize adult educational plans, support online learners, and deliver student support and services. They identified several initiatives that facilitate service delivery, including using the library as a focal point for resources and online connections, reducing barriers to connecting with support staff, and remaining flexible and creative in delivering unconventional approaches (as opposed to those designed for traditional-age students). These strategies require student affairs professionals to be aware of adult transitions on campus, acknowledge them, and assist in managing competing roles (family, work, and school). Two essential strategies are (a) finding creative ways to integrate adults into campus life and (b) proactive leadership in uncovering adult needs and concerns.

Method

Eight institutions, representing public, private, not-for-profit, and private for-profit institutions that serve adult learners, collaborated on this study. The survey captured adult work experience, career planning, learning motivation, and attitudes toward work. The study employed a purposive sampling technique described by Marshall and Rossman (2011) to collect approximately 7.200 complete responses.

Profile of Adult Learners

The study participants were primarily White (84%) and female (76%) students enrolled primarily in medical/health, business, education/human services, and technical/computer programs. After combining respondents who attained a postsecondary certificate/training with those who earned some college credit, we ran a chi-square test, which revealed that the current enrollment patterns were independent of level of education (χ^2 = 1941.43, p < .001). Individuals with high school degrees enrolled in technical certificate programs (9%) and associate degree programs (67%) more than expected, with lower enrollment in bachelor's programs (24%). Those with some college or postsecondary certificates have their enrollment preference centered on associate degrees (58%), with fewer than expected at the bachelor's level (35%). Associate degree holders' preference was for bachelor's degrees (78%), with only 20% pursuing a second associate-level degree. Table 12.1 provides a profile of the responding adult learners.

Table 12.1.

Profile Characteristics of Study Population (percentage)

Sample Profile	
Female	76
Male	24
Ethnicity	
White (non-Hispanic)	84
Black	9
Hispanic/Latina	2
Other	5
Age	38.5 average (range 25–78)
Education Attained	
High school diploma	38
Credential, apprenticeship post HS	8
Associate degree	23
College credit, no degree	32
First generation	70

table continues on page 228

table continued from page 227

Sample Profile		
Degree enrolled		
Technical certificate cred.	6	
Associate degree	53	
Bachelor's degree	41	
Program Pursuing	Associate Degree	Bachelor's Degree
Medical/Health	50	11
Business	23	40
Technical/Computer	14	13
Education/Human services	21	21

Motivation To Attend College

Adults are motivated to return to campus by many reasons. In the survey, respondents were provided five response options representing motivational reasons to enroll in college; they could select more than one response. Reasons included needing a degree to advance with current employer, seeking a career change, needing training because of downsizing or losing a job, achieving personal fulfillment, and serving as a role model for children. Some of these reasons were extrinsic (need a degree, need training, seek career change), and some were intrinsic (personal fulfillment, serving as a role model). Respondents were sorted into three groups, which were based on motivation as described by Gardner et al. (2021): Forty percent (40%) were classified as extrinsic, 43% as intrinsic, and 17% as balanced extrinsic and intrinsic. χ^2 tests indicated that the extrinsic respondents were more likely to be in technical certificate (9%) or associate degree programs (56%) than in a bachelor's degree program (35%; $\chi^2 = 135.35$, $p = .001$). Intrinsic and balanced respondents were more likely to be in bachelor's degree programs (45% in each group), with lower participation in associate degree programs (intrinsic 51% and balanced 49%) and technical certificates (balanced 6% and intrinsic 4%). Percentages are shown in Table 12.2.

Table 12.2.

Program Enrollment by Current Education and Motivation to Attend College (percentage)

Degree program enrolled	Overall	High school	Some college	Associate	Extrinsic	Intrinsic	Balanced
Technical certificate	6	9	6	2	9	4	6
Associate	53	67	58	20	56	51	49
Bachelor	41	24	35	78	35	45	45

Life Experiences

Life experiences including work history, current position, family responsibilities cause role conflict in a variety of ways.

Work History Profile

Respondents provided details on aspects of their work history, which allowed us to generate a work profile of these adult learners. Only 2% reported not holding any full-time positions, while 32% indicated they never worked a part-time job. Respondents averaged 15.7 years of full-time employment and nearly three years of part-time employment. On average, they worked for five organizations, held six jobs, received 2.5 promotions, and encountered two to three episodes of unemployment for three months or longer. The age range of participants (25 to 78) produced a wide variety among these measures. For example, 28% reported one episode of unemployment, 20% reported two, and 11% had three such episodes, while 8% reported that they were unemployed for three months or longer six or more times. Very few reported that these episodes were voluntary.

Table 12.3.

Work History Profile for Adult Learners

	Full-time (years)	Part-time (years)	Number of different organizations	Number of jobs	Number of promotions	Number of periods of unemployment
Average	15.7	2.5	5.3	6.1	2.5	2.4
Std. dev.	9.1	4.0	4.3	5.1	2.6	3.6
Range	1–40	1–57	1–50	1–70+	0–50	0–6+
% None	2	32			17	28

Current Position. Respondents provided information about their current position or the position they held before enrolling full-time in school and choosing not to work. Approximately 76% engaged in full-time employment and 19% had part-time employment, with 1% in volunteer or community service activities. The remaining 4% carried out family responsibilities and other activities. Most mentioned working multiple jobs, some in full-time and part-time positions and some in multiple part-times, with several reporting as many as six. Nearly 84% were directly employed by their organizations, with the remainder in fixed-term contracts, temporary positions, or self-employment. Their employers were primarily small companies, with nearly 65% at firms and establishments with fewer than 500 employees (40.5% with 100 or fewer and 24% with 101 to 500 employees). Only 17% worked at companies with more than 4,000 employees. For-profit establishments employed slightly more than 50% of the respondents;, health services employed 11%, government employed 5%, and nonprofits employed 6%, with 14% reporting industry categories not provided.

The average tenure in participants' current positions was 5.8 years, with 8% indicating that they had been in the position less than a year and 11% indicating they had been in the position for 11 years or more. Respondents reported a wide range of salaries, with 45% reporting less than $30,000, 21% reporting $30,000 to $40,000, 15% reporting $40,000 to $50,000, and 19% indicating salaries greater than $50,000. About one third reported receiving an annual bonus, and 14% received stock options. The most common benefits provided by their employers were vacation pay (61%) and healthcare (57%). Other reported benefits included sick leave (42%), flexible work schedule (23%), and childcare (2%).

Family Responsibilities. Fifty-four percent of the respondents indicated that they were married (including married but separated); 21% indicated they were single, 16% were divorced, and 9% said they lived with a partner. Their current living arrangements found 32% living with a partner and financially independent, 25% living with spouse or partner and financially dependent, 19% living independently with no financial support, 10% living independently with government stipend, 7% living at home with parents, and 2% living on own with support from parents. Very few reported homelessness at the time of the survey.

Nearly 60% of respondents held responsibilities for dependent children under 18, and 21% were responsible for dependent children over 18. However, about one fourth had responsibilities to assist dependent adults, and 8% were responsible for grandchildren. Juggling multiple roles can prove challenging while enrolled in courses. We used the Role Balance Scale (Marks & MacDermid, 1996) to capture the respondents' perceptions of handling multiple roles. Respondents agreed or disagreed with a set of eight items that included "I am pretty good at keeping the different parts of my life in balance" (68% agreed) and "Too often one of my life roles interferes with my desire to engage in another role" (47% agreed).

The eight items combined into one latent scale (coefficient alpha = .768), labeled Rolebalanceall, with an average of 2.98, which is slightly below the midpoint of neither agreeing nor disagreeing. A confirmatory factor analysis revealed two latent variables: Role Balance (coefficient alpha = .820) and Role Conflict (coefficient alpha = .650). Upon comparison of the means for these variables using ANOVA, the following significant differences appeared:

- Intrinsic motivators were significantly higher in agreement on Rolebalanceall and Role Balance than extrinsic and balanced motivators and significantly lower in agreement than extrinsic motivators on Role Conflict.

- Single respondents had significantly lower agreement on Rolebalanceall than respondents who were married, divorced, or living with partners. Single and divorced respondents were significantly lower than respondents in the other two groups on agreement for Role Balance. Married respondents significantly reported lower agreement than divorced and single respondents on Role Conflict.

- Respondents enrolled full-time reported higher agreement on Role Balance and Rolebalanceall than respondents enrolled part-time.

- Respondents working full-time while enrolled reported lower agreement on Role Balance and Rolebalanceall than respondents working part-time.

- Working part-time proved insignificant on all role balance measures; likewise, no group differences appeared on Role Conflict.

- For those learners not working while enrolled, their Rolebalanceall and Role Balance scores topped all groups that were compared.

In summary, intrinsically driven adults viewed themselves in better role balance than did extrinsic or balanced adults. Interestingly, single students and divorced students reported challenges with keeping their roles in balance and experienced more role conflicts than did married students/students with partners. Students enrolled full-time and students who were not working reported feeling in control of their multiple roles. However, work—whether full-time or part-time—caused role conflicts, making it hard to balance roles all the time.

Employment-Related Perceptions

Characteristics desired in a position, including workplace climate, structure, learning, value organizational image, and developmental support, and work identity, weight differently when considering workplace motivations and workplace balance.

Characteristics Desired in a Position

Twenty-two job/work characteristics, common in the literature on essential features that employees seek in a position, comprised the list presented to respondents, who were asked to rate the importance of each as if they were seeking a new job (rated from 1 = *little to no importance* to 5 = *extremely important*). Eight were rated highly important or higher (mean above 4.00, presented here from highest to lowest): job security, good benefits (health insurance), fair supervisors, opportunity to learn, opportunity for promotions, exciting and challenging work, feel needed and appreciated, and comfortable working conditions. Five characteristics rated little to some importance (average below 2.85): childcare support, assistance with aging parents, travel opportunities, limited overtime, and being at a prestigious company. Two were borderline very important: working with pleasant coworkers and receiving an annual vacation.

Factor analysis reduced the list to six key characteristic constructs:

- Workplace Climate: Working with pleasant coworkers, fair supervision, comfortable workplace, and feeling appreciated

- Workplace Structure: Limited overtime, regular hours, limited job stress, flexible hours, and an annual vacation

- Workplace Learning: Interesting and challenging assignments, working independently, and opportunities to learn new skills

- Workplace Value: Respectable income, promotion opportunities, job security, and benefits (health care)

- Organizational Image: Prestigious company, organization's image

- Dependent Support: childcare and adult care

Table 12.4 presents the mean ratings for each of these major work characteristic variables, organized by respondents' motivation to attend college. Overall, respondents rated Workplace Value associated with salary, health benefits, and promotion opportunities at the top, followed by Workplace Climate. Workplace Learning ranked third. The comparisons of ratings by motivation type showed no significant difference in mean ratings for Workplace Climate and Workplace Structure. Extrinsic individuals rated Workplace Learning significantly lower than intrinsic individuals did ($t = 5.702$, $p = .003$) but not lower than balanced individuals rated it. Intrinsic individuals rated Workplace Value significantly lower than the other groups did ($t = 9.021$, $p < .001$). Intrinsic individuals also rated Organizational Image and Dependent Support higher than the other groups did.

Table 12.4.

Desired Job/Work Characteristics, Organized by Respondents' Motivation to Attend College

Characteristics	Overall mean	Extrinsic (mean)	Intrinsic (mean)	Balanced (mean)
Workplace climate	4.04	4.02	4.05	4.07
Workplace structure	3.22	3.20	3.23	3.24
Workplace learning	3.92	3.89	3.93	3.96
Workplace value	4.15	4.17	4.02	4.20
Organizational image	3.07	3.05	3.11	3.04
Dependent support	2.08	2.00	2.19	1.99

In other comparisons (using ANOVA), the following significant differences appeared:

- Respondents enrolled full-time rated Workplace Structure and Workplace Learning lower than respondents not enrolled full-time rated those work characteristics.

- Respondents enrolled part-time rated Workplace Climate, Workplace Structure, and Workplace Learning higher than respondents not enrolled part-time.

- Respondents working full-time rated Workplace Structure, Workplace Learning, and Workplace Value higher than respondents not working full-time and rated Dependent Support lower.

- Respondents working part-time rated Workplace Learning and Workplace Value lower and Dependent Support higher than respondents not working part-time.

- Respondents who were not working while enrolled rated Workplace Structure, Workplace Learning, and Workplace Value lower while rating Dependent Support higher than respondents who were working.

Work Identity

Kanungo (1982) considered work involvement to be the extent to which a person is interested in, identifies with, and immerses themselves in work compared to other aspects of their life. Using Kanungo's (1982) modified scale, respondents rated their attachment to work using the six-item Work Involvement Scale. The combined items formed one variable, Work Identity, with a solid coefficient alpha (.755) and mean of 2.61.

Regardless of motivation to enroll, respondents were equally involved with work. However, respondents with high school diplomas reported significantly higher Work Identity than did individuals with some college and individuals with associate degrees. Age comparisons showed that respondents over the age of 46 reported significantly higher attachment to work than younger respondents did. The adult learners in this study had relatively low Work Identities, and the data were similar to those from other young adults measured on the same scale (Chao & Gardner, 2007).

Career Planning, Involvement, and Concerns

Respondents were asked additional questions on their career planning, career involvement or career uncertainty, concerns about their future work and ability to obtain occupational information.

Career Planning

Three items from Gould's career planning scale (1979) formed this construct (for example, "I have a plan for my career" and "I have a strategy for achieving my career goals"). The coefficient alpha was .846 with a mean score of 3.89. Slightly more than 70% agreed that they had a career plan, with only 11% indicating otherwise. In other words, respondents agreed that they had a career plan upon enrolling in school and possessed the strategies necessary to achieve their goals.

Career Uncertainty

Six items from Gould's career planning and involvement scale comprised this construct (for example, "My career objectives are not clear" and "Sometimes I wish I had chosen a different career field"). The coefficient alpha was .827 with a mean of 2.21. Only 15% of the respondents indicated they faced uncertainty about their careers or chosen line of work. Most respondents believed they were involved in an appropriate career fields or line of employment.

Concern About Future Work

Based on work by Westbrook, et al. (1985) respondents were asked to express their concerns about finding a job, getting started in a new career field, or advancing new career goals after completing their degrees. Six items comprised this construct (for example "Finding a line of work that I am best suited for" and "Settling down in a job I can live with"). The coefficient alpha was .909 and the construct had a mean of 4.07. Respondents expressed concerns about obtaining suitable work or establishing themselves in the field of work that would match their degree qualifications. Comparison based on the current education level revealed that respondents with associate degrees rated their concerns significantly lower than respondents with some college or with high school degrees. Also, while all motivation groups reported means over 4.0, intrinsic individuals reported lower concerns than did extrinsic and balanced groups. Finally, respondents who reported higher role conflict levels showed deeper concerns over finding work or establishing their career.

Occupational Information

Because of concern about finding appropriate future work, the occupational information subscale from the Career Decision-Making Self-Efficacy (CDMS) scale provided insight on participants' confidence with finding information about employers, employment trends, and key people needed to advance their job search and career plans. The mean of the occupation information scale was 3.79, indicating that most respondents were confident they could acquire the information they needed. However, 20% expressed very little or no confidence in their ability to find information needed to advance their job search and career plans.

These findings suggest that most adults come to campus with assurance about their career plans and strategies to reach their next steps. However, it appeared that between 20% and 35% of the respondents, depending on how the variables are aligned, lack confidence in their job search plans, are unfamiliar with sources of information necessary to make educated career decisions, and remain uncertain about the direction they should take with their academic and career plans. Extrinsic individuals, defined as those pursuing education to remain employed or to be qualified for available positions, displayed more role imbalance and less certainty about their careers than intrinsic individuals. Single and divorced individuals expressed more concern about role imbalance, particularly those responsible for dependents than individuals who were married or living with a partner. Working, either full- or part-time, triggered role imbalances and career uncertainty.

On the other hand, students who were enrolled full-time, married or living with one's partner, and holding responsibility for dependent children showed little sign of role conflict nor expressed career concerns. Thus, about one third of this sample would directly benefit from engagement with career service professionals. The remainder required information and resources framed to meet their expectations and experiences.

Implications for Working with Adult Learners Who Transfer

Career services and auxiliary support services dedicated to working with adults who transfer will benefit from an increased understanding of the differences between adult learners and traditional-aged students who transfer. Gianakos (1996) and Seltz and Collier (1977) posited that adult learners are pragmatic in their academic and career decision-making, are self-directed in their learning, and seek meaningful opportunities that are more values driven. The authors also noted that adult learners seek problem-centered education and have immediate experiential application. These findings are consistent with the data presented in this chapter and by Gardner et al. (2021). Understanding what motivates adults to pursue education, factors that affect their decision to transfer (when and where), and what supports are best suited to help adults navigate transfer transitions will increase priority as more and more adults seek workforce advancement. Career services and auxiliary support staff may want to consider using self-directed, pragmatic, and experiential methods in addressing adults' transition-related needs and concerns, precisely the nature of adult transitions and the events that trigger adults to stop in and out of college. Staff who support adults who transfer will need to find a way to associate the pursuit of education with working and family responsibilities and create an even broader and deeper supportive environment than for the traditional transfer student—if there is such a label to be given. This support, for instance, may come in the form of connecting extracurricular service organizations to college credit to offer adults in transition the personal fulfillment needed to cross the finish line.

Transitioning In and Out

Transitions have relativity, context, and impact, influencing how they are experienced. Adult perceptions of the shift drive them to feel whether and how much they perceive a transition is occurring and as a result, their awareness affects its relativity (Schlossberg et al., 1995). Schlossberg's theory (see the Introduction to this volume) directly applies to adults experiencing transfer. How much the change will affect life circumstances designates its impact.

The most important consideration in understanding a situation is the expanse between life before and after the event (Schlossberg et al., 1995). Many adults who transfer "stop out" in the transfer process. Their transfer time is not fluid from sending to receiving institutions; instead, there are time gaps between exit and re-entry. This "stop out" further complicates the transfer for adult learners and institutions responsible for their support. Schlossberg et al. delved into the importance of time. A significant transition prompts a continuum for an individual's lifespan; reactions to and associations with the change may vary as time goes by. These feelings and associations may be integrated within a structure that recognizes adults move into them, out of them, and through them. As adults process the transfer on this continuum, their assets or liabilities may fluctuate. Adult movement into, through, and out of institutions—this repetitive process—is a form of transfer. The educational models we offer students who transfer must fit their life stages and needs. We cannot overlook or disregard these transitions. Adult learners are most inclined to ignore frequent, conforming, and prefabricated curricular mapping and degree-earning paths because they are difficult. Colleges can do a better job building on the existing traditional (youth-centric) model of services and tailoring these services to meet the needs of adult learners. More specific career-related services that focus on adult learners, such as mid-career transitions, displaced employment searches, and alternative careers post-retirement, are just a few options.

Mattering

Sissel et al. (2001) posited that "to create a privileged space for adult learners, we need institutions that promote leadership for all learners" (p. 25). Informed by the early work on adults experiencing transition (Astin, 1977; Schlossberg, 1984), Schlossberg (1989) introduced the constructs of marginality and mattering. In short, Schlossberg grew to believe that "people in transition often feel marginal and that they do not matter" (para 6). As a result, adult students may experience feelings of isolation (marginality) and belonging and significance to another (mattering). Transitioning into higher education, for example, could prompt adults to feel marginalized. Even though many universities and programs espouse egalitarian goals and propose open access and support for all students, few institutions provide an equal playing field, let alone a nurturing environment for all students. "Whether it is policy, program, attitudes, classroom environment, or funding support, adult learners face institutional neglect, prejudice, and denial of opportunities" (Sissel et al., 2001, p. 18). Academic and social systems that cater to the undergraduate experience must be more attuned to adult student perceptions of confidence about their vocational needs.

Mattering directly affects self-efficacy, which has a direct correlation to career decision-making. Self-efficacy represents an individual's perception and judgment and their ability and competencies to organize and execute causes of action required to fulfill specific types of behaviors or performance (Bandura, 1997). Adult students' professional decision-making self-efficacy influenced their views about being a part of college academic and social life adversely but positively influenced their interests and attitudes in re-enrolling at the institution for a future term of study, according to Sandler (2000). Engagement increases one's career self-efficacy, that is, their confidence in their ability to complete the necessary tasks associated with successfully making career decisions (Betz et al., 2005; Bandura, 1977, 1997; Taylor & Betz, 1983). In short, adult learners need support to achieve their goals in an environment where they feel they matter. The curriculum must be linked to the world in which adult learners work and live—an environment where adult learners' needs are considered in the context of their learning and career development. Higher education must find ways to increase confidence about the economic future of adult learners and to understand how their career decision-making self-efficacy affects their decision to re-enroll at an institution and persist to graduation. Only when this happens will adult students who transfer genuinely feel like they belong.

Concluding Thoughts

Adult learners pursue credentials and degrees for a variety of reasons. Survey respondents who were intrinsically motivated and were encountering minimal role conflicts expressed confidence in their career planning and achieving their career goals. For these learners, access to career and professional resources may not be a high priority. Extrinsically motivated adult learners and learners faced with conflicting roles may need timely, applicable information on career pathway confirmation, job outlooks, and job search strategies. This need is exacerbated by multiple instances of transfer between institutions and stepping out of school for periods of time before re-enrolling. Thus, matching the delivery of career and professional development resources to this group becomes problematic, thereby justifying the continuation of approaches more in line with traditional-age student resource delivery. The challenge is to develop approaches that sync with adult learning styles (convenience), timing, and relevance to adult aspirations. The transfer process for adults needs to be augmented with appropriate, accessible resources that convey easily over multiple transfer episodes.

"Adults in America today—and even more so in the future—cannot stop learning. They will be back, over and over, through their lifetime" (Aslanian, 2001, p. 58). Moreover, consequences of COVID-19 triggered new learning expectations and a repeated need for higher education institutions to engage in learning. Thus, we can expect adult learners to repeatedly experience transitions into and out of higher education. "Given the primary role of work in adult learners' decision to engage with postsecondary education, more robust career services designed for students in higher job positions would be especially welcomed, as well as services focused on more adult-centric career themes such as career transitions or second career seekers" (Chen, 2017, p. 9). Creating an equal space for adult learners first requires recognizing the differing adult learner motivations, and providing resources to meet their unique personalized guidance needs is a step in the right direction.

References

Ackell, E. F. (1982). Adapting the university to adult students: A developmental perspective. *Continuum. 46*(2), 30-35. https://eric.ed.gov/?id=EJ259002

Aslanian, C. (2001). You're never too old. *Community College Journal, 71*(5), 56–58. https://eric.ed.gov/?id=EJ625298

Astin, A. W. (1977). *Four critical years.* Jossey-Bass.

Bandura, A. (1977). Self-efficacy: Toward a unifying theory of behavioral change. *Psychological Review, 84*, 191-215. https://doi.org/10.1037/0033-295X.84.2.191

Bandura, A. (1997). *Self-efficacy: The exercise of control.* Freeman.

Bean, J., & Metzner, B. (1985). A conceptual model of nontraditional under-graduate student attrition. *Review of Educational Research, 55*(4), 485-540. https://doi.org/10.3102/00346543055004485

Betz, N. E., Hammond, M. S., & Multon, K. D. (2005). Reliability and validity of five-level response continua for the Career Decision Self-Efficacy Scale. *Journal of Career Assessment, 13*, 131-149. http://doi.org/10.1177/1069072704273123

Bland, S. M. (2003). Advising adults: Telling or coaching? *Adult Learning, 14*(2), 6-9. https://doi.org/10.1177%2F104515950401400202

Bragg, D. D., Endel, B., Anderson, N., Soricone, L. & Acevedo, E. (2019). *What works for adult learners: Lessons from career pathway evaluations.* Jobs for the Future.

Byrne, A. (1989). The process of adult socialization in higher education. *Equity and Excellence, 24*(3), 9-10. https://doi.org/10.1080/1066568880240303

Chao, G. and Gardner, P. (2007). *How central is work to young adults?* MonsterTrak and CERI https://ceri.msu.edu/_assets/pdfs/young-pro-pdfs/work_young_adults.pdf

Chen, J. C. (2017). Nontraditional adult learners: The neglected diversity in postsecondary education. *SAGE Open.* https://doi.org/10.1177/2158244017697161

Chiappone, J.M. (1992). The career development professional of the 1990s: A training model. In H. D. Lea & Z. B. Leibowitz (Eds.). *Adult career development: Concepts, issues, and practice.* (2nd ed). 364-379. National Career Development Association.

Compton, J. I., Cox, E., & Laanan, F. S. (2006). Adult learners in transition. *New directions for student services, 114*, 73-80. https://doi.org/10.1002/ss.208

Coulter, X. & Mandell, A. (2012). Adult higher education: Are we moving in the wrong direction? *The Journal of Continuing Higher Education, 60*(1), 40-42. http://doi.org/10.1080/07377363.2012.649133

Council for Adult and Experiential Learning. (2005). Introduction to the Adult Learning Focused Institution Initiative (ALFI).

Countryman, K. C. (2006). *A comparison of adult learners' academic, social, and environmental needs as perceived by adult learners and faculty* (Publication No. 3215699) [Doctoral dissertation, Auburn University]. ProQuest Dissertations and Theses Global.

DiSilvestro, F. R. (2013). Continuing higher education and older adults: A growing challenge and golden opportunity. *New Directions for Adult and Continuing Education, 140*, 79-87. https://doi.org/10.1002/ace.20076

Dukes, D. L. (2001). *A multiple case study of how college career centers are responding to the needs of adult students.* University of Georgia.

Flint, T. A.. (2000). *Best Practices in Adult Learning: A CAEL/APQC Benchmarking Study.* Council for Adult Experiential Learning.

Gardner, A. C., Maietta, H. N., Gardner, P. D., Perkins, N. (2021). Postsecondary adult learner motivation: An analysis of credentialing patterns and decision-making within higher education programs. *Adult Learning.* https://doi.org/10.1177/1045159520988361

Gast, A. (2013). Current trends in adult degree programs: How public universities respond to the needs of adult learners. *New Directions for Adult and Continuing Education, 2013*(140), 17-25. https://doi.org/10.1002/ace.20070

Gianakos, I. (1996). Career development differences between adult and traditional-aged learners. *Journal of Career Development, 22*(3), 211-223. https://doi.org/10.1177/2F089484539602200304

Goode, W. J. (1960). A theory of role strain. *American Sociological Review, 25,* 483-496. https://doi.org/10.2307/2092933

Gould, S. (1979). Characteristics of career planners in upwardly mobile occupations. *Academy of Management Journal, 22,* 539 –550. https://doi.org/10.2307/255743

Hamrick, F.A., Evans, N.J., & Schuh, J. (2002). *Foundations of Student Affairs Practice: How Philosophy, Theory, and Research Strengthen Educational Outcomes.* Jossey-Bass.

Hoff, K. S. (1997). *Emerging career development needs as reported by adult students at four Ohio institutions of higher education: A qualitative study* (Publication No. 9804303) [Doctoral dissertation, Bowling Green State University]. ProQuest Dissertation and Thesis Global.

Hussar, B., Zhang, J., Hein, S., Wang, K., Roberts, A., Cui, J., Smith, M., Bullock Mann, F., Barmer, A., & Dilig, R. (2020). *The Condition of Education 2020* (NCES 2020-144). U.S. Department of Education: National Center for Education Statistics.

IIoh, C. (2017-2018). Toward a New Model of College "choice" For a Twenty-first-century Context. *Harvard Educational Review* 1 June 2018; 88 (2): 227–244. doi: https://doi.org/10.17763/1943-5045-88.2.227.

Kanungo, R. N. (1982). Measurement of job and work involvement. *Journal of Applied Psychology, 67*(3), 341–349. https://doi.org/10.1037/0021-9010.67.3.341

Kasworm, C. (1993). An Alternative Perspective on Empowerment of Adult Undergraduates. *Contemporary Education, 64,* (3), 162–165.

Kasworm C. (2010). Adult learners in a research university: Negotiating undergraduate student identity. *Adult Education Quarterly, 60*(2), 143-160. https://doi.org/10.1177/0741713609336110

Kerka, S. (1989). Retaining adult students in higher education. *ERIC Digest, 88.* https://eric.ed.gov/?id=ED308401

Knowles, M. (1984). *The adult learner: A neglected species* (3rd ed.). Gulf Publishing.

Lenhardt, A.M.C. (1994). Support services for re-entry students: Dislocated workers educational training. *NASPA Journal, 32*(1), 55-66. https://doi.org/10.1080/002209 73.1994.11072379

Lent, R. W., & Brown, S. D. (2002). Social cognitive career theory and adult career development. In S. G. Niles (Ed.), *Adult career development: Concepts, issues and practices* (pp. 76–97). National Career Development Association

Markle, G. (2015). Factors influencing persistence among nontraditional university students. *Adult Education Quarterly, 65,* 267-285.

Marks, S. R., & MacDermid, S. M. (1996). Multiple roles and the self: A theory of role balance. *Journal of Marriage and the Family,* 417-432.

Marshall, C., & Rossman. G. (2011). *Designing qualitative research* (5th ed.). SAGE Publications.

McFarland, J., Hussar, B., Wang, X., Zhang, J., Wang, K., Rathbun, A., Barmer, A., Forrest Cataldi, E., and Bullock Mann, F. (2018). *The Condition of Education 2018* (NCES 2018-144). U.S. Department of Education & National Center for Education Statistics. https://nces.ed.gov/pubs2018/2018144.pdf

Metzner, B., & Bean, J. (1987). The estimation of a conceptual model of nontraditional undergraduate student attrition. *Research in Higher Education, 27*(1), 15-38. https://doi.org/10.1007/BF00992303

Monje-Paulson, L. N, Olson, A. B., Pizzolato, J. E., Sullivan, K. A. (2019). Adult learner career trajectories: Vocational self-concept development in CalWORKs Community College students. *College Student Affairs Journal, 37*(1). 68-82. https://doi.org/10.1353/ csj.2019.0005

Padulla, M. A. (1994). Reentry women: A literature review with recommendations for counseling and research. *Journal of Counseling and Development, 73,* 10-16. https://doi.org/10.1002/J.1556-6676.1994.TB01703.X

Pappas, J. P., & Loring, R. K. (1985). Returning learners In L. Noel, R. Levitz, and D. Saluri *Increasing student retention.* Jossey-Bass.

Rahim, E., & Finch, A. (2011). Adult learning styles and technology-driven learning for online students. *Academic Leadership, 9*(2), 39–53.

Rangaswami, A. K. (1999). *Nontraditional student support services: The challenge to higher education.* Unpublished doctoral dissertation. Widener University, Chester, PA.

Rose, M. (2012). *Back to school: Why everyone deserves a second chance at education.* The New Press.

Sandler, M. (2000). Career decision-making self-efficacy, perceived stress, and an integrated model of student persistence: A structural model of finances, attitudes, behavior, and career development. *Research in Higher Education, 41*(5), 537-580. https://doi.org/10.1023/A:1007032525530

Schein, E. H. (1978). *Career dynamics: Matching individual and organizational needs.* Addison-Wesley.

Schlossberg, N. K. (1984). *Counseling adults in transition.* Springer.

Schlossberg, N. K. (1989). Marginality and mattering: Key issues in building community. *New Directions for Student Services, 48,* 5–15. https://doi.org/10.1002/ss.37119894803

Schlossberg, N. K., Lynch, A. Q., & Chickering, A. W. (1989). *Improving higher education environments for adults.* Jossey-Bass.

Schlossberg, N. K., Waters, E. B., & Goodman, J. (1995). *Counseling adults in transition: Linking practice with theory* (2nd ed.). 1-17. Springer.

Scott-Summers, D. G. (1992). *Assessing student service needs of evening community college students* [Unpublished doctoral dissertation]. University of San Francisco.

Scozzaro, P. P., & Subich, L. M. (1990). Gender and occupational sex-type differences in job outcome factor perceptions. *Journal of Vocational Behavior, 36,* 109–119. https://doi.org/10.1016/0001-8791(90)90018-W

Seltz, N. C., & Collier, H. V. (Eds.) (1977). *Meeting the educational and occupational planning needs of adults.* Indiana University, School of Continuing Education.

Shamir, B., & Arthur, M. B. (1989). An exploratory study of perceived career change and job attitudes among job changers. *Journal of Applied Social Psychology, 19,* 701–716. http://doi.org/10.1111/j.1559-1816.1989.tb01253.x

Shapiro, D., Dundar, A., Huie, F., Wakhungu, P. K., Bhimdiwala, A., Nathan, A., & Hwang, Y. (2018). *Transfer and mobility: A national view of student movement in postsecondary institutions, fall 2011 cohort.* Signature Report 15. National Student Clearinghouse Research Center.

Siarzynski-Ferrer, K., & Pillar, G.D. (2021). The Importance of Student Services for Adult Learners. In C. L. B. Jennings (Ed.) *Ensuring adult and non-traditional learners' success with technology, design and structure.* IGI Global. http://doi.org/10.4018/978-1-7998-6762-3.ch010

Sissel, P. A., Hansman, C. A., & Kasworm, C. E. (2001). The politics of neglect: Adult learners in higher education. *New Directions for Adult and Continuing Education, 91,* 17-27. http://doi.org/10.1002/ace.27

Soares, L. (2017, January). *Post-traditional learners and the transformation of postsecondary education: A manifesto for college leaders.* American Council on Education. https://www. acenet.edu/Documents/The-Post-Traditional-Learners-Manifesto-Revisited.pdf

Super, D. E., & Hall, D. T. (1978). Career development: Exploration and planning. *Annual Review of Psychology, 29,* 333–372. https://doi.org/10.1146/annurev. ps.29.020178.002001

Taniguchi, H. & Kaufman, G. (2005). Degree completion among nontraditional students. *Social Science Quarterly, 86,* 913-927. https://www.jstor.org/stable/42956102

Taylor, K. M., & Betz, N. E. (1983). Applications of self-efficacy theory to the understanding and treatment of career indecision. *Journal of Vocational Behavior, 22,* 63-81. https://psycnet.apa.org/doi/10.1016/0001-8791(83)90006-4

Thomas, L. E. (1980). A typology of mid-life career changers. *Journal of Vocational Behavior, 16,* 173-182. https://doi.org/10.1016/0001-8791(80)90048-2

Voorhees, R. A., & Lingenfelter, P. E. (2003). *Adult learners and state policy.* State Higher Education Executive Officers & Council for Adult and Experiential Learning.

Westbrook, B. W., Sanford, B. W., O'Neal, P., Horne, D. F., Fleenor, J., & Garren, R. (1985). Predictive and construct validity of six experimental measures of career maturity. *Journal of Vocational Behavior, 27*(3), 338-355. https://doi.org/10.1016/0001-8791(85)90041-7.

Wiggam, M. K. (2004). *Predicting adult learner academic persistence: Strength of relationship between age, gender, ethnicity, financial aid, transfer credits, and delivery methods* (Publication No. 3141725) [Doctoral dissertation, The Ohio State University]. ProQuest Dissertation and Thesis Global.

CONCLUDING THOUGHTS

Strengthening the Transfer Process by Scaling Better Practices: Collaborate on Data Collection, Co-Create With Career Services, and Drive Professional Readiness

Heather N. Maietta and Philip D. Gardner

The incentive for undertaking this book project centers on broadening the voices participating in the transfer process. This broadening includes career professionals who strive to advance successful outcomes for all students, particularly those engaged in the transfer process. In the current transfer literature, we expose the absence of career development in all its forms: career resources, career advising, career coaching/counseling, professional readiness, and job search strategizing. Despite this deficiency, attaining meaningful work and post-graduation success are clearly stated goals of an exemplary transfer experience. Adams (see Chapter 2) underscores this absence in her synthesis of news feeds and forum discussions on the Transfer Nation social media platforms, which engages thousands of higher education professionals supporting students who transfer.

This publication presents antecdotal and data-driven evidence of career development and professional readiness being infused at various universities to offset the imperceptible career voice in current transfer literature. Students' personal testimonials highlighting the value of career-related interventions and evidence from a big-data exercise illustrate the important contribution that career engagement makes during the assimilation of transfers to, into, and through their receiving institution. Heeding Grant's warning (2021), we provide these experiments as "better" practices. Grant argued that the label "best practices" freezes thinking, preaches to their virtues, and impedes learning, which presents long-term growth and rethinking obstacles. Instead, according to Grant, "better practices" serves as a more appropriate descriptor, as it implies continued rethinking to keep improving—in this case, the transfer process. While the outcomes commonly measured when considering the transfer process are critical for every student's success (e.g., academic performance, persistence through college, and time to degree), outcome accountability requires balance for process accountability. Process accountability allows different voices to enter the discussions, sharing opinions and insights on transfer decisions. The research in this volume illustrates the importance of process accountability with new voices rethinking the program plans and initiatives. In this light, we consider the contributions of this book as better practices, as we continually consider new processes to enhance success for students who transfer while expanding the measurable outcomes documenting transfer.

Through the insights and evidence presented by the chapter authors, several career-related themes emerged—many supporting the predictions in Chapter 1—tying this body of work together. These themes are discussed, in turn, in the following sections.

Academic Major to a Job Is a Myth

Butler and Hunsaker (see Chapter 4) underscore the fallacy of the widely held belief that students who emerge from the transfer process with a declared academic major understand how this major translates into a career post-graduation. The transfer literature focuses narrowly on early academic success and disciplinary adjustments, implying the culminating outcome will be career success (Poisel & Joseph, 2011).

Atkinson and Allen (see Chapter 6) share that academic performance was a critical determinant of acceptance into the University of Oregon journalism program but needed to be balanced with a grounded understanding of career pathways emanating from the curricular offerings within the college. Career pathways have multiple directions. Starting at a common point, an academic major can open paths to many different ends (i.e., multifinality). A student with a desire for a specific job or career endpoint may find that multiple academic paths exist (i.e., equifinality). Students who transfer require timely information about changing conditions in the workplace, demands of employers, and clarification of potential pathways into and through their early careers.

As Weber and Gardner (see Chapter 11) point out, many students who transfer postpone their career engagement or seek career assistance in their final academic term before graduating. If students are taught how to develop behavioral and adaptive components of exploration and planning prior to the transfer process, they can learn to use these skills in the short term (i.e., prior to choosing a major) and the long term (i.e., prior to and as they are choosing a career path) to promote their academic career success (Fouad et al., 2015). For this to happen and be most effective, career and workplace information and engagement activities must be integrated prior to and throughout the transfer process.

Adult Learners Experience Career Confusion

Stories shared by adult learners in this volume and research addressing adult learners indicate their need for career decision-making and support for exploratory career behaviors. Adults, many of whom are working while enrolled, may possess a sound career plan but feel more certain about their choices than traditional college students under the age of 25. They express concern over gaining access to the types of employment and expected career paths upon completion of their studies. They have limited information about opportunities open to them through their new credentials, employers to engage with, and the processes with which they are involved. Without that foundation, an individual can undoubtedly drift through the workplace after graduation, as illustrated by the George Mason student discussed in Chapter 5.

Adult students seek assistance; however, they need advisors who are knowledgeable about adult transitions and the multiple work, family, and life roles that shape how each student approaches learning, the job search, and future-centered career planning. Their needs and the type of assistance they require are at odds with planning offered to traditional students, including traditional-age students who transfer.

Telling One's Story Increases the Likelihood of Connecting to Deeper Supports and More Abundant Strategies

As discussed in multiple chapters, students who transfer face more hurdles than nontransfer or native students, and these hurdles are evident when students are asked to explain their transfer experience during the job search or other career-advancement situations (e.g., graduate school applications). Maietta (see Chapter 10) highlights an emerging hurdle, the forced transfer— we have yet to realize the impacts and supports needed to fully address this transfer experience. Forced transfer is one of the nine strands of transfer requiring varying strategies for diverse student bodies.

Butler and Hunsaker (see Chapter 4) developed a life design course that requires students to build cultural and social capital through robust engagement with their new campuses. Innovative courses or programs, such as life design, help students through the transfer transition by encouraging career exploration, career agency, and career preparation both short and long term. Cerezo (see Chapter 9) shares evidence that early and often mentorship positively affects students following transfer, and Vallejo (see Chapter 3) shares her intimate journey as a student who transferred and then became a career service professional who has dedicated her career to ensuring that students who transfer receive the needed career support by "living her transfer story." Career advisors must acknowledge that the transfer experience and students who transfer are indeed different from traditional nontransfer or native students; therefore, they require and must be provided services attuned to their vocational needs.

Re-Evaluate and Refocus on Processes

The entire span of transfer support (from entry to exit) needs to be rethought—especially following the COVID-19 pandemic and in supporting transfer due to college closure—to determine where career development and professional readiness strategies weave within existing and newly created support processes. Transfer resulting from college closure produces a demand for resources and supports that simply do not yet exist. COVID-19 disrupted some programs already in motion to assist students who transfer, sometimes stopping the programs or support initiatives altogether. However, COVID-19 also forced virtual options, introduced a new lens to evaluate transfer programming (see Chapter 5), and provided the opportunity to rethink the entire transfer process whereby resources can be realigned with the developing changes in the higher education workplace. Emerging research on the transition needs of students experiencing transfer resulting from college closure (see Chapter 10) offers a baseline on needs and options to bridge the transition between sending and receiving institutions. Re-evaluation and focus on processes for students who transfer must continue post-COVID, as the higher education market realizes the impacts of the pandemic on the industry and re-envisions a new strategic future.

Scaling the Solutions

Providing career support is an all-campus responsibility; it should not to be left to the student to find their way to the career center for assurance of receiving services. Multiple chapters in this book highlight examples of successful, scalable career support initiatives, each designed to meet the needs of the populations served. Successful transfer-friendly programs that value sound decision-making should embody daily practice across all campus units, and these units should be trained and well versed in the value of entry to existing career support.

Still, scaling solutions that introduce career engagement in the transfer process are fraught with challenges, as illustrated by several authors. To overcome scaling issues requires better collaboration across campus, leveraging digital technologies, and sufficient administrative support. Weber and Gardner (see Chapter 11) highlight a strong, positive link between student engagement in career and professional development activities and student outcomes. Scaling is worth the effort!

Collaboration

Supporting students who transfer takes multiple communities of practice to come together to ensure scalable services are possible and sustainable. The delivery of timely and meaningful programs and resources to students who transfer involves collaboration across academic and support service units. Presently academic and programmatic silos dominate college campuses, a situation that imperils the potential for optimum delivery of expertise and the circulation of information and resources (Tett, 2016). Students thrive, both academically and professionally, when everyone can become partners and agents to drive success (see Chapters 4, 5, 7, and 8). Breaking down institutional silos requires recognizing the limits of one's expertise and the willingness to invite other knowledge partners to join in advancing a common cause; it requires sharing resources rather than duplicating them, and it requires collaborators to add new dimensions to their roles while giving up some longstanding responsibilities.

Some institutions are increasing partnerships using uncomplicated and necessary first steps like integrating career and academic advising conversations into "course registration." These discussions help students realize the academic-to-career connection early in the transfer process. Learning Management System and Career Resource Management platforms are seen as cohesive choices for student support and database management to assist in cross-campus communication and collaboration efforts (Dinse, 2021). With shared programs such as Starfish, LiveText, and Handshake, faculty and various campus departments can engage students in their progress, remove obstacles, and assess the effectiveness of an institution's efforts to help students succeed.

Students who transfer need not participate only in orientation-based career advising but also need continued career advising structured to nudge students toward each developmental stage as an undergraduate. Ironically, the foundation for student success, whether academic success or professional preparation, rests on the same driving forces—knowing how academic decisions affect career trajectory, gaining confidence in the college environment overall, and establishing a purpose for successful undergraduate completion.

Recalibrating the Transfer Process

Career services appear to be on the outside looking in when it comes to delivering support to students who transfer, but it does not have to be that way. Those executing the transfer process must rethink and recalibrate to include new voices. Career professionals' voices bring understanding of the needs of undergraduates and of adult learners and first-generation college students in particular—two groups that make up a sizable percentage of students who transfer (see Chapters 9 and 12).

In the following sections, we identify several areas in which career professionals can enhance the climate for students who transfer, making educated suggestions about better practices for these target populations. While the list is not exhaustive, these areas pose exciting opportunities for increasing the connection between career services and students who transfer.

Mindset

Campus mindset regarding the value of career education and what campus career services offer needs to change. Not only does the mindset of students' perceptions and acceptance of career engagement need to reset; the mindset (or the established set of attitudes) of faculty and transfer administrators/advisors toward career engagement as an auxiliary service needs to shift from a fixed (static) outlook to a growth-oriented one. No longer can career services be "something a student seeks if they think they need to;

otherwise, they carry the emotional and technical aspects related to transferring." Instead, the transfer process receives continual re-evaluation through assessments of the existing fixed practices that are tweaked for better efficiency but remain measured against equally fixed standards (GPA, persistence, and time to degree). A growth-oriented mindset thrives on the expansive challenges for student success, embracing broader effort, willingness to try different strategies, learning from past experiments, and pushing for new initiatives while taking into consideration realigning success indicators in the workplace.

The mindset related to the role of career services in the advancement of success for all students, whether transfer or nontransfer, needs to be one of acceptance and support. From the available evidence, faculty and academic advisors currently view career development as a supplementary service only to be sought if needed. Confusion and limited knowledge of the career development and work readiness process stymie the access to and use of the wide variety of resources, tools, and coaching available. It is unacceptable that barely half of the student population on a campus seeks assistance from career services, often late in their college career. Academic players, especially academic advisors and faculty, embrace career and professional development and recognize that intellectual and professional growth are critical elements of learning. On many campuses, career service units are being repositioned, realigned, or elevated through title changes for career service leadership and in some instances shifting oversight of program services to chief academic officers. These are undoubtedly critical first steps, but they do not ensure that career service professionals are engaged in curricular and advising support conversations with academic counterparts when decisions are being made and programs are being planned. To advance another step requires deep and trusting collaboration. Collaboration presents itself in many forms, as evidenced throughout this publication. Career pathways and professional readiness are two distinct areas in which collaboration can and should improve for more significant support of students who transfer.

Career Pathways

Several programs presented in this volume integrated academic and professional development to leverage job opportunities and career progression (see Chapters 5 and 7). As Bragg and colleagues (2019) contended, "Creating effective pathways to and through postsecondary education is a foundational strategy for transforming the delivery of education and workforce training in this country" (p. 6). Career pathways target neglected populations, including English language learners, re-entry students, and new populations seeking access to postsecondary credentials (Bragg et al., 2017). These groups comprise a high percentage of students who transfer and are being prepared through pathway programs. In addition, Bragg and others (2019) presented evidence that well-designed career pathways positively affect academic and employment outcomes for adults and traditional-aged students.

Increasingly students who transfer are likely to have experience with career pathways. Four-year institutions mimic career pathways in different ways. Some, like Lake Forest College, build pathways around career communities (e.g., business and finance, science and health, build your own). The University of Vermont focuses on career interest groups, National Career Development Association advocates professional pathways (Chudasama, 2021), and Rutgers advances industry-centric cluster model (Jones & Broyles, 2018). Students who transfer can expect to adjust to different terminology and program practices at four-year schools, yet the core elements of career pathways, curriculum and instruction, work-integrated learning opportunities, industry-recognized credentials, proactive student support, career guidance, and job placement need to be more accessible at their new campuses, and students who transfer need to be made aware of these resources (Bragg et al., 2019).

Career progression is a key focus that students who transfer will bring with them upon their transfer. They seek to advance beyond the entry-level work that many have already experienced. These learners emphasize their desire to pursue occupationally and technically supported curricula and postsecondary education necessary to position them for strong job entry and career advancement. The challenge for career professionals rests on adjusting traditional programs to address these expectations with populations with which some are not familiar.

Professional Readiness

The attitude regarding the transfer process and students who transfer must be redefined. Before institutions can develop a transfer-receptive culture, higher education needs to view students who transfer as individuals who have experienced a transitional event during their undergraduate career, not as a group with "transfer" as a label. Our literature review raised red flags regarding potential transfer barriers faced by students that could derail their career aspirations and job prospects. Minimizing these barriers could support students who transfer, seeking out and utilizing the career resources and professional staff available. To transition smoothly and successfully—that is, to navigate the community college experience; to take the appropriate coursework; to apply, enroll, and successfully earn a baccalaureate degree in a timely manner—students who transfer need to be supported as unique students who need individual reinforcements (often diverse even from one another) to persist before, during, and after experiencing transfer. This support is quite different from offering orientation services to a group of students who transfer. Instead, the result should be diverse strategies for championing students toward the finish line.

Call for Additional Data

Investigations of the career development needs of students who experience transfer and the impact on career-related interventions are desperately needed to fill a large gap in the literature. There are many ways to accomplish this investigation. For instance, statewide and institutional data are used to identify and evaluate transfer needs, patterns, and performance measures at key points during the transfer process. Documentation of the successes for students who transfer is necessary to determine how and what support strategies are needed and delivered at necessary intervals. As Poisel and Joseph (2011) postulated, "Institutions must develop a model of review, research, and reflection to determine whether they are providing the best pathway for transfer students' retention, progression, and graduation" (p. 116).

Drawing on the recommendations of Marling and Jacobs (2011), we recommend the following process for capturing and using institutional data to develop a clear sense of the unique needs of transfers for more informed decision-making and subsequent support:

1. Develop a clear sense of the questions to be answered and data to be collected.

2. Align institutional data and question sets with the individual's goals.

3. Work with departments of institutional research to interpret data in a timely manner.

4. Understand the urgency of data release while allowing for reliable and valid reports.

Once the data and question responses are collected, analyzed, and released, we recommend assembling a task force of advocates, from senior leadership to grassroots advising and including career services, to ensure the creation and implementation of support strategies.

Initial Steps for Advancing the Process of Transfer

Several steps can be taken to begin to recalibrate the transfer process. Some can be easily undertaken, and others will require work. Which steps to select depends on where your institution is currently addressing process accountability. Our best advice is to start with small steps and keep moving forward.

- Initiate dialogue among transfer administrators, academic advising, and career services to transform transfer practices and policies, inviting new voices from all areas of campus and the community.

- Recognize career service professionals as facilitators and trainers for students, faculty, and staff engaged in the transfer process. Begin with some basic professional development workshops.

- Advance work-integrated learning, and leverage the work/life experiences of students who transfer.

- Keep abreast of real-time labor market changes, the influence of digital technologies, and the rapidly evolving workplace expectations.

- Provide proactive support to students who transfer, including continued career guidance.

- Undertake rigorous program evaluation and continuous improvement with all the voices who participate in and contribute to the transfer process.

- Engage faculty, staff, employers, workforce, and community partners in programs and professional development activities that involve students who transfer.

- Experiment with demonstration projects for different groups within the transfer population on campus.

- Develop a language and knowledge base shared among higher education offices and partners.

- Adapt career resources and their delivery to the life roles of the transfer population, recognizing that many have work and family responsibilities.

- Strengthen the relationship between faculty and career services, noting that approximately 50% of current students report speaking with faculty about future careers (Strada Education Network & Gallop, 2017).

Final Thoughts

Challenges will derail students, preventing a successful transition from sending to receiving institution. Closing the gap in research on the impact of career interventions on increasing career preparedness and postgraduate transition success, which is explicitly what career services are charged with providing, can help mitigate some of these challenges. Students who have experienced transfer and who successfully enter the labor market and obtain meaningful work would be the proof. A seamless transfer involves collaboration and input from multiple campus and off-campus constituencies, and students who transfer successfully become graduates who transition successfully. Helping students who transfer to develop a career purpose at the beginning of their educational journeys and then working throughout the complete experience to navigate intentional decision-making rooted in educational experiences that feed into and support long-term career goals is the charge. We echo Potter's (2022) challenge that the transfer community needs innovative approaches, perspectives, and voices. It is time—let us make it happen!

References

Bragg, D. D., Endel, B., Anderson, N., Soricone, L., & Acevedo, E. (2017, December). *What works for adult learners.* Jobs for the Future (JFF), New America, Washington, DC. https://www.allies4innovation.org/wp-content/uploads/2017/12/AECF-Findings-Brief_120717FINAL.pdf

Bragg, D. D., Endel, B., Anderson, N., Soricone, L., & Acevedo, E. (2019). *What works for adult learners: Lessons from career pathway evaluations.* Jobs for the Future. https://files.eric.ed.gov/fulltext/ED598339.pdf

Chudasama, S. Y. (2021). *Power of peer connections and learning through cohort-based career professional development groups.* Career Convergence, National Career Development Association.

Dinse, E. (2021). Crossing the boundaries: Referral of services. In H. N. Maietta (Ed.), Cases in career services: A working guide for practitioners, 317-324. National Association of Colleges and Employers.

Fouad, N. A., Ghosh, A., Chang, W., Figueiredo, C., & Bachhuber, T. (2015). Career exploration among college students. *Journal of College Student Development, 57*(4), 460–464. https://doi.org/10.1353/csd.2016.0047

Grant, A. (2021). *Think again: The power of knowing what you don't know.* Viking.

Jones, W., & Broyles, J. (2018). *#Rutgersworks: An update on the industry-centric cluster model.* National Association of Colleges and Employers. https://www.naceweb.org/career-development/organizational-structure/rutgersworks-an-update-on-the-industry-centric-career-cluster-model/

Marling, J. L. & Jacobs, B. C. (2011). Establishing pathways for transfer student success through orientation. In M. A. Poisel, & S. Joseph (Eds.). *Transfer Students in Higher Education: Building Foundations for Policies, Programs, and Services that Foster Student Success.* (pp. 71–88). National Resource Center for The First-Year Experience and Students in Transition, University of South Carolina.

Poisel, M. A., & Joseph, S. (Eds). (2011). *Transfer students in higher education, Building foundations for policies, programs, and services that foster student success.* National Resource Center for The First-Year Experience and Students in Transition.

Potter, C. (2022). Predictors of transfer behaviours in adult university students. *Journal of Adult and Continuing Education, 28*(1), 119-150. https://doi.org/10.1177/14779714211992786

Strada Education Network & Gallup. (2017). *Crisis of confidence: Current college students do not feel prepared for the workforce: 2017 college student survey.* https://cci.stradaeducation. org/report/crisis-of-confidence-current-college-students-do-not-feel-prepared-for-the-workforce/

Tett, G. (2016). *The silo effect: The peril of expertise and the promise of breaking down barriers.* Simon & Schuster Paperbacks.

ABOUT THE AUTHORS

Heather Adams is the senior manager at The Aspen Institute College Excellence Program, leading the development of transfer engagement initiatives. Before joining Aspen, Heather served as director of the UCLA Transfer Student Center and director of UCLA College Learning Communities. She is also the founder and CEO of Transfer Nation, a community for collaboration, conversation, and connection on transfer globally. The core focus of Heather's work has centered on generating institutionalized receptivity, support, and policy restructuring for historically marginalized student communities through strategic partnership and practice. She advocated for establishing the UCLA Transfer Student Center and transformed a program serving 300 students annually into a thriving and collaborative campus center that provides numerous resources and support to more than 27,000 transfer students each year. A proud community college transfer student, Heather earned an AA in psychology from Santa Monica College and transferred to UCLA, where she obtained a BA in psychology and an EdD in educational leadership.

Rachel Allen serves as the associate director of student services within the School of Journalism and Communication at the University of Oregon. Throughout the last 10 years, Rachel has championed the integration of career and academic advising within her department and the field of career services. She earned a BA in sociology from the University of Oregon and an MEd in college student services administration from Oregon State University. Since the start of her advising tenure, Rachel has been actively involved in The Global Community for Academic Advising (NACADA) and her campus community. In addition, Rachel is passionate about creating comprehensive and holistic advisor training programs, supporting first-generation students, and career coaching. Raised in Oregon, Rachel enjoys experiencing all the seasons while walking her dog, perfecting vegetarian recipes, and finding alternative solutions for sustainable living.

Miranda Atkinson serves as the executive director of #instaballet, a local nonprofit dance company that facilitates community-generated choreography to impact equitable access to dance in the community. She has worked in advising for 13 years, 12 of them at the University of Oregon. She has held multiple leadership roles in advising units, most recently as the director in Tykeson College and Career Advising. In her prior role within the School of Journalism and Communication, she focused on integrating academic and career advising within her unit and contributions to the field. After earning her BS in psychology with minors in biology and English, Miranda completed an MEd in counseling psychology, with a sport psychology emphasis, from the University of Missouri. She is passionate about integrating career and academic advising, student mental health, and supporting equitable student access to advising, resources, and opportunities. In her role as an arts administrator, Miranda focuses on increasing equitable access to dance and equity within the dance community. You can find Miranda dancing, enjoying being outside in Oregon, and spending time with her family in her free time.

Heather Butler is an associate professor in the Psychology Department at California State University, Dominguez Hills. She has many research interests grounded in human cognition (critical thinking, advanced learning technologies, student success programs). Heather's most productive area of research explores the ways one's ability to think critically affects everyday life. She is the director of Transfer Student Experience and Career Readiness at CSUDH. As part of that role, she coordinates the Design Your Life program and assesses the program's impact on students.

Tasia Cerezo is the co-founder and CEO of Meryl's Safe Haven, which works to provide shelter and supporting services to families and youth who have aged out and is in the process of transitioning out of foster care. A pre-adoptive parent herself, Tasia's most recent project, a children's book titled "Fostered Love", follows a family's journey through fostering. With a passion for working with families and youth of low-economic backgrounds and experience as a academic advisor, transfer counselor, and experience in youth workforce development, Tasia recognizes the challenges that marginalized students face along their journey to degree completion which emboldened her to continue her research addressing first-generation students and students at community colleges barriers to success. Originally from Miami, FL, Tasia resides in central Massachusetts with her family.

Aimée Eubanks Davis is the founder and CEO of Braven, which works to ensure that underrepresented college students develop the skills, confidence, experiences, and networks to get strong first jobs after graduation. She founded Braven based on her deep belief that our next generation of leaders will emerge from everywhere, and it was named one of America's Best Startup Employers in 2022 by Forbes. Aimée spent the majority of her career at Teach For America, where she held various senior leadership roles, including leading the organization's groundbreaking work related to human capital and diversity efforts. In addition, Aimée taught sixth grade earlier in her career, led the Breakthrough/Summerbridge New Orleans site, and worked for the national organization. She is a recipient of The 1954 Project's 2021 Luminary Award, a 2020 Leadership Greater Chicago Fellow, 2019 Obama Foundation Fellow, Pahara-Aspen fellow, a member of the Aspen Global Leadership Network, a Braddock Scholar, a Draper Richards Foundation Entrepreneur, and a Camelback Ventures Fellow. A graduate of Mt. Holyoke College, Aimée resides in Chicago with her husband and three children.

Alejandra De Alba graduated from the University of California, Los Angeles with a bachelor of arts in psychology. Like many recent college graduates, she was unsure about her next steps in life and career. However, through intentional career exploration, self-reflection, and mentorship, she discovered that a career in counseling and development would be a true match based on her interests, values, and skills. She completed a master of arts in guidance and counseling at Loyola Marymount University and is dedicated to supporting college students and career professionals as they seek to discover and enhance their careers across diverse industries. With eight years of experience in student affairs, she collaboratively identified innovative ways to engage nontraditional college students and ensure persistence to and through college. Alejandra continues to seek new opportunities to reach students. She attributes her personal and career success to adopting her mother's growth mindset and creating a morning routine filled with movement, energy, and positivity.

Philip Gardner served as executive director of career services at Michigan State University and director of the Collegiate Employment Research Institute, where he actively researched issues related to college and work. For 35 years, he has pursued research focused on the transition from college to work, early socialization in the workplace, national labor market trends for new college graduates, and work-integrated learning (internships, cooperative education, and experiential learning). His work includes investigating and advocating the T- professional model as a means to reimagine undergraduate education. Philip served as a Fulbright specialist to New Zealand in work-integrated learning, recognized by the Cooperative Education Internship Association and the World Association of Cooperative Education in understanding and advancing work-integrated learning. He was recently elected to the Academy of Fellows of the National Association of Colleges and Employers.

Kerin Hilker-Balkissoon brings more than 20 years of experience engaging PK–12, community college, university, nonprofit, and workforce sectors to address systemic inequities and barriers to college access, success, and career attainment. Kerin's innovative efforts are grounded in justice, equity, diversity, and inclusion (JEDI), integrating career pathways, high-impact educational practices, asset-based approaches, and developmental, holistic student supports. A NISTS Transfer Champion-Catalyst award winner, Kerin has a proven track record in designing data-driven interventions that enhance postsecondary inclusive excellence for underserved and minoritized groups. She specializes in supporting community college transfer students and intersecting populations, including student parents, first-generation and differently abled students, foster youth, and immigrant and post-traditional (adult) students. At George Mason University, Kerin oversees College of Science pathways that enhance STEM equity and success and teaches in the Scientific Leadership and Practice program. In addition, she actively engages in university-wide inclusive excellence efforts, including leadership roles in first-generation, transfer, and student-parent efforts. Kerin completed her Bachelor of Science in psychology at the University of Massachusetts at Amherst, her master's degree in counseling at Johns Hopkins University, and her counseling licensure requirements at the George Washington University. She is pursuing coursework toward her doctoral degree in peace and conflict studies, collaborative community action at George Mason University. A first-generation Latina college graduate, Kerin advocates and supports the Hispanic and Autistic communities; she holds a leadership role with the nonprofit Friends in Need Virginia and is a Board Member for the Virginia Latino Higher Education Network (VALHEN).

Marc Hunsaker has been helping students learn to navigate college and figure out their futures for more than 18 years. Marc's vocational journey has unfolded across a wide range of roles, including stints as a campus minister at Washington University, director of college & vocation at Central Presbyterian Church, and as Michigan State University's purpose & career design consultant. Since 2019, he has served as dean of personal & professional development at Berry College, where he leads the Center for Personal & Professional Development, which includes Berry's Career Development Network and signature LifeWorks (i.e., student employment) program. He also serves as facilitator and board member for Stanford University's Life Design Lab. He is honored to regularly write, train, and consult with other higher education leaders on how to weave life design, purpose development, and career exploration into their course curricula and campus programs. Marc earned his PhD in higher, adult, & lifelong education from Michigan State University, where his doctoral research focused on his long-term passion for vocational formation (i.e., the integration of faith and work) amongst Christian young adults.

Heather Maietta is a professor in the Doctorate of Higher Education Leadership program at Regis College. Her research examines the impacts of college closure, first-generation doctoral students, and the success of adult learners. Her most recent publications include journal articles on adult learners, a monograph entitled *Career Coaching: Fundamentals, Applications, and Future Directions*, a coedited book entitled *The T-professional Model and Undergraduate Education: Advancing Talent Development*, and a book chapter entitled *When First-Generation College Students Become Doctoral Candidates*. She sits on the editorial board for the *Journal of the First-Year Experience and Students in Transition*, is a board certified coach, a National Association of Colleges and Employers coaching faculty member, and a Facilitating Career Developments national trainer. Her full bio can be found at heathernmaietta.com. She lives in the Greater Boston area.

Janet Marling is the executive director of the National Institute for the Study of Transfer Students (NISTS), where she leads a team committed to ensuring today's diverse and mobile learners have equitable and inclusive access to educational opportunities and the ongoing resources needed to achieve their academic goals. An associate professor of education at the University of North Georgia, Janet coordinates the post-master's certificate in transfer leadership and practice. Her portfolio includes executive and practitioner roles in student affairs and enrollment management, orientation and transition programs, personal and career counseling, peer mentoring, leadership, and learning support. In addition to her speaking, writing, and consulting activities, Janet currently serves on the Council for Standards in Higher Education (CAS), College Board's Counseling and Admission Assembly Committee, and the advisory board of the National Resource Center for The First-Year Experience and Students in Transition (NRC); she is a past appointed board member for the National Association for College Counseling (NACAC). Janet holds a Ph.D. in higher education administration from the University of North Texas, a M.S. in counseling psychology from the University of Southern Mississippi, and a B.S. in psychology from Texas Christian University—Go Frogs! Her proudest accomplishment is parenting three amazing children—Jackson, Cooper, and Andersen—alongside her favorite human, David.

Niki Perkins is a faculty member in the College of Business at Western Governors University. Previously she was a faculty member in the College of Business at Baker College, where she teaches undergraduate change management and training and development courses. She has worked in higher education for almost 20 years. In addition to teaching, Niki is a senior instructional designer at Six Red Marbles. In this role, she leads higher education and corporate training program design projects that lead to engaging learning experiences for students and trainees. Niki received a BFA in fine arts from Michigan State University and an MBA in leadership studies from Baker College Center for Graduate Studies. She became interested in adult learners working in career services, and her research on this population has been published in Sage Journals. Niki was awarded the Midwest ACE Presidents Award, which recognized her leadership in career services. As a faculty member, Niki uses student-centered teaching and empathetic learning theory to help students succeed in their education and career goals. Creating transparent and inclusive classrooms for all learners is her goal as a faculty member and instructional designer. She also incorporates gamification techniques into her instruction and course development when appropriate. Niki continues her passion for career services by assisting students with their career journeys through her training as a certified professional resume writer (CPRW). Her current research interests include empathetic learning, career development, the transition from college to work, and gamification techniques that lead to understanding.

Padmanabhan Seshaiyer is a tenured professor of mathematical sciences at George Mason University (GMU) and has served in multiple leadership positions, including the associate dean for academic affairs, director of STEM Accelerator Program, and director of COMPLETE (Center for Outreach in Mathematics Professional Learning and Educational Technology) at GMU. Padmanabhan has also served as a program director at the National Science Foundation. His research interests are in the broad areas of computational mathematics and STEM education. During the last decade, Padmanabhan initiated and directed various

STEM educational programs, including graduate, undergraduate, community college student research, K–12 outreach, teacher professional development, and enrichment programs to foster students' and teachers' interest in STEM at all levels. He has also worked on understanding structural barriers and challenges in student educational experiences at various levels, including K–12, two and four-year institutions, and has helped to develop novel pathways and programs that have helped to build institutional and STEM-specific articulations with an equity-minded lens, culturally responsive advising and teaching, and equitable access to transferable courses as well as career explorations in the STEM workforce. Padmanabhan was selected as one of the 2019 "Figures that Matter" and was awarded an honorary doctorate from Vrije Universiteit Brussel for being a committed scientist who transcends the boundaries of their own discipline and is at the frontier of societal change. In 2021, he was also appointed to the new STEM Advisory board to the Governor of Virginia.

Priscilla Vallejo is part of the career counseling team at UC Berkeley's Career Center and has served in interin roles on the employer relations team. She helps students navigate the career planning process by providing the necessary tools to help them become career ready during their time at Cal and beyond. She also develops career programs to engage students in career exploration and networking opportunities with alumni. Priscilla has worked in various roles within career services, including career counseling, employer relations, event planning, program management, and DEI at community colleges as well as private and public institutions. As a former transfer student and practitioner in career services, she has experience serving transfer students throughout their academic and professional journeys. She is passionate about working with students from all walks of life and helping them unveil their career aspirations, interests, and skills. She is driven by creating space in which students feel welcomed, empowered, and brave. She is an active member and volunteer with the Mountain Pacific Association of College and Employers and currently serves as the regional director for the Pacific Central region. Priscilla is a first-generation Latina student and holds a master's degree in college counseling and student development from Azusa Pacific University, a bachelor's degree in human services from CSU Fullerton, and an associate degree from Rio Hondo College

Everett "Rett" Weber is an ecologist by training, now a data scientist working for Dartmouth University. Previously he served as a data scientist with Career Services at Michigan State University and was faculty in the Department of Biology at Murray State University. Rett is certified in Qualtrics and is sought as an expert in survey integration and survey design. In his free time, Rett researches insect bioinformatics and consults with researchers on statistical analyses. In addition, he builds platforms that facilitate reporting and analysis, integrating data collected and curated by career services with institutional data at Michigan State University and Dartmouth University.

INDEX

NOTE: Page references followed by *f* indicate figures; those followed by *t* indicate tables.

A

academic development, 14. *See also* career development

academic expectations, 57, 189. *See also* resilience

academic integration. *See also* social integration

    institutional commitment and, 183–4

academic load, success outcomes of MSU transfer students and, 204

academic major to job, as myth, 246

academic services

    adult learners and, 226

    forced transfers and, 190

Accelerated Transfer Academy, University of Houston, Downtown (UHD), 39

Accelerator Course, Braven's, 123, 124, 125, 127–30

acceptance, design thinking and, 71–3, 72*f*

action-planning strategies, 41

active listening

    empathy step in design thinking and, 73

    sense of belonging and, 81

Adams, H., 6, 8, 245

adaptability, resilience, forced transfers and, 188–9

adult learners. *See also* mature achievers; nontraditional students; older students; part-time students

    career confusion, 246–247

    career development and, 224–225

    career planning, involvement, and concerns, 234–235

    current work position and, 230

    definition, 222–223

    employment-related perceptions, 231–233

    family responsibilities, 230–231

    life experiences and, 229–231

    literature review, 222–226

    mattering, 237

    motivations, 223–224, 228, 229*t*

    profile, 227, 227–228*t*

    study method, 226–235

    support services for, 9, 225–226, 237–238

    as transfer students, 221–222

    transitioning in and out, 236

    work history profile, 229, 229*t*

    working with, 235–237

advising, academic. *See also* developmental advising

    adult learners and, 223, 226

    career decision-making and, 17–19

    career development and, 8

    Educational Opportunity Program at CSUMB and, 58

    first-generation college students seeking, 161

    forced transfers and, 190

    integrating career advising and, 18–19, 109–10, 117, 121, 248–249

    literature review, 6

    Offices of Career Services and, 15

    sending-to-receiving, 26

    transfer students and, 27, 68, 91, 164

    21st century STEM career pathways knowledge and, 90

    at UO's School of Journalism and Communication, 108–9

advising, career. *See also* career services

    adult learners and, 223, 247

E

Early Career Engagement Certification Program (ECECP), UCLA's. *See also* Career Ready Bootcamp (CRB), at UCLA
    launch of, 144, 148
    lessons learned and recommendations, 152–4
    outcomes, 148–52, 150f
    overview, 141–2
    supporting transfer students to, 142–3
    synopsis, 8
early intervention, 167. *See also* graduation rates
East Coast Holistic Review Institute, 99
economic mobility
    bachelor's degrees and, 125
    Braven Foundation and, 8
educational attainment, 227, 227–228t
Educational Opportunity Program (EOP), at California State University, Monterey Bay, 7, 56–9, 61–2
Eismann, L., 162, 163
electives, credit-bearing career development as, 25
emerging adulthood, 67
emotional states, building self-efficacy with, 71
empathy, 71, 72f, 73, 92–4
employers, adult learners and, 223
employment readiness services, 15, 145
#EndCCStigma, 44
engagement. *See* social integration
enrollment
    dual credit, 14, 176
    financial challenges and, 173–4
    pandemic and, 191
    statistics, community colleges, 52–3
entrepreneurship, STEM identity and

professional development at GMU and, 100
ethical obligations, to support transfer students, 70
ethnicity. *See also* Asian students; color, students of; diversity, equity, and inclusion (DEI), at GMU; minority student populations
    of adult learners, 227
    engaging in career services at MSU and, 208
    in MSU transfer student study, 205
    success outcomes of MSU transfer students and, 204
experiential learning
    adult learners and, 226
    Braven Foundation and, 132
    financial challenges and, 23
    at GMU's College of Science, 99, 101
    Journalism Transfer Seminar at OU and, 112, 119–20, 119t
    transfer students and, 26–7

F

Facebook. *See also* Transfer Nation
    joining TN discussion on, 45
faculty
    Braven Foundation and, 123
    career advising at SOJC and, 118–9, 118t
    career goals and, 176
    decision-making and support from, 185
    disconnect, forced transfers and, 185, 186
    expectations, transfer students and, 57
    forced transfers and, 190
    Journalism Transfer Seminar at OU and, 111

G

H